A
Joyful
Noise

A JOYFUL NOISE

Some authors, their times and their hymns

CHARLES MOSELEY

DARTON·LONGMAN+TODD

First published in 2024 by
Darton, Longman and Todd Ltd
Unit 1, The Exchange
6 Scarbrook Road
Croydon CR0 1UH

© 2024 Charles Moseley

The right of Charles Moseley to be identified as the Author of this work has been asserted in accordance with the Copyright, Designs and Patents Act 1988.

ISBN 978-1-915412-15-7

A catalogue record for this book is available from the British Library.

Frontispiece: Fifth-century mosaic of St Ambrose, Basilica of Sant'Ambrogio, Milan. Image: Sailko/Wikimedia.

Designed and produced by Judy Linard

Printed and bound in Great Britain by
Bell & Bain, Glasgow

Make a joyful noise unto the L<small>ORD</small>,
all ye lands.
Serve the L<small>ORD</small> with gladness: come
before his presence with singing.

P<small>SALM</small> 100, K<small>ING</small> J<small>AMES</small> V<small>ERSION</small> (1611)

Contents

	Thanks	9
I	How this Book Started	11
II	Clearing the Throat ...	14
III	St Ambrose	28
IV	Prudentius	36
V	Venantius Fortunatus	41
VI	Anonymous and Author Uncertain	49
VII	St Thomas Aquinas	58
VIII	George Herbert	64
IX	Samuel Crossman	76
X	John Mason	86
XI	Thomas Ken	93
XII	Nahum Tate	102
XIII	Isaac Watts	107
XIV	Charles Wesley	117

XV	John Newton	125
XVI	William Cowper	135
XVII	James Montgomery	150
XVIII	Reginald Heber	159
XIX	John Henry Newman	165
XX	Christopher Wordsworth	180
XXI	John Mason Neale	187
XXII	Cecil Frances Alexander	197
XXIII	Catherine Winkworth	203
XXIV	Robert Bridges	209
XXV	Percy Dearmer	215
XXVI	Eleanor Farjeon	225
XXVII	Sydney Bertram Carter	231

Thanks

I owe gratitude to many people for their help with this book: to David Moloney of DLT who believed in it from the first; to Professor Eamon Duffy for his generosity in reading an early draft; to the Revd Dr John Barrett for reading the final MS and being so encouraging; to Canon Professor James Woodward for making many really helpful suggestions; to Bishop Rowan Williams and Rev Fergus Butler-Gallie for their warm encouragement; and to Bishop Timothy Dudley-Smith for listening to me read the first two chapters with apparent pleasure. But above all, first for her acceptance of the idea and then for her forbearance while I was writing, I owe gratitude to Rosanna, my beloved.

I

How this Book Started

ॐ

'I have no idea how I am going to fill next month's *Newsletter*,' she said, looking glumly into her coffee. It had gone cold. Producing every month a *Newsletter* of 24 pages – 21 if you take out fixtures like Vicar's Letter and Notices – for a vigorous Cambridge congregation, which expects things to happen, is a lot of work. It relies on people feeling not only that they have got something to say to the community but also, much less commonly, the urge to write about it. So sometimes an editor's lot, like a policeman's, is not an 'appy one.

I said, 'What about an occasional series on the background to some of the hymns we sing?' After all, I myself have often been curious about the men and women who wrote the words. Sometimes we don't even notice who did, yet to many of those men and women we owe debts we scarcely acknowledge. They deserve more than the obscurity of a right-ranged half-line and a name (with dates) in small caps.

She was showing a bit of interest, if not enthusiasm. I continued, cheerfully: 'Lots of people would join in and write about their favourite hymn.' (I am temperamentally optimistic about people.) I ought to have known better than to open my mouth: lots of people did *not* want to join in, and editors are always short of material. This book is the eventual result.

We all are engaging with the stresses, agonies, joys, ideas

of our own context, and those don't go away when you write a poem or a hymn. So putting the work of, say, Charles Wesley or St Ambrose, J. M. Neale or Fanny Alexander, Percy Dearmer or Isaac Watts, Eleanor Farjeon or Sydney Carter, back into a sketch of their world, their families and contacts, who knew whom, whom they argued with, or listened to, is the least they deserve: and it can make a great deal more sense of why and how they wrote as they did. For example, for a long time 'All things bright and beautiful' was my *bête noire*, but now that I have read up about its author and what she was doing, when and why, I still don't like it, but at least I respect it – and her – greatly. Of course, what people wrote takes on a life of its own on our lips and in our hearts, can even change its meaning in our different context, but it is so much more interesting to see it in technicolour rather than black and white, so to speak. The words are something to which our voices can commit fullthroatedly when singing, and we remember them later in those flashes that come into the mind like sparkles of light on windstirred water. But I am curious to know, and hope you are too, something of *this* man, *this* woman, people who were our fellow pilgrims, who like us had to tackle this puzzle of existence. I hope, too, that that human interest, that curiosity even, may override any lack of interest a prospective reader might claim in hymns as hymns: these people mattered, lived in times just as challenging as ours, and many were good poets choosing to write in a very constrained medium. And just as medieval religious painting and sculpture is as functional as advertising, where artistic quality (as we would see it) serves a purpose *not* artistic, so too with hymns: they may be good poetry, but their aim is something far more august.

I selected whom to discuss from the 1986 edition of *The New English Hymnal*, very largely on personal preference and interest. (Those people I do write about are also represented in *Hymns Ancient and Modern*, 1983 edition, and in the 1933 *Methodist Hymn Book*, and *Hymns and Psalms* of 1983.) But another criterion was people who had been in the thick of things when big changes were happening in liturgy and

How this Book Started

ideology – some of these people, indeed, helped drive those changes. Some will criticise me for leaving So-and-so out or putting Juggins in – just like the readers of the parish *Newsletter*, who could have volunteered, but did not.

The 1986 edition of *NEH,* like *A&M,* has had several impressions and many parishes will not be wealthy enough to abandon that edition in favour of the expected new one. That precluded drawing in some more recent writers of interesting hymns that have become popular. So arbitrarily and somewhat reluctantly, I stopped with Sydney Carter. In any case, the book is not about hymns as such, but about who wrote them in what sort of context, so there was a good case for *not* writing about people living in a 'just yesterday' world with which we are all familiar. This, alas, meant leaving out distinguished and prolific writers of hymns like Timothy Dudley-Smith. Moreover, I have to confess my sketches are not exhaustive: if you want to explore further, there are many websites and reference books to help, and in some cases individual studies. With all its blanks, with all its asides, and stopping to look at things along the way (like on the sort of walk I like) the book is what it is.[1] Humbly I give it as a token of gratitude to my brothers and sisters in Christ at St Mary the Less without Trumpington Gate – which when not in Sunday best everyone calls Little St Mary's, to distinguish it from the University Church, Great St Mary's – for their fellowship and for the joyful noise we can (usually) make together to the Lord.

CWRDM
Reach, Corpus Christi, 2023

---

[1] Footnotes – asides, if you prefer – are a pleasure I find irresistible. Purely coincidentally, as I finished this paragraph, I looked at the *BBC Music Magazine* for November 1, 2021 (accessed 9.2.2022). There I found several prompts: 'What are the lyrics [*that* word is a sign of the times!] for "At the name of Jesus"?' and the same question for 'Onward Christian Soldiers', 'Jesus Christ is risen today', and several more. The words have become invisible, and even more their authors: which is what I hope in this book in some measure to redress.

II

CLEARING THE THROAT …

※

'IT'S A LONG WAY TO Tipperary/ It's a long way to go', sung by filthy, tired men, some wounded, marching to or from the noise of battle … A crowd in Wembley Stadium at a Rugby League Cup Final in a swelling chorus of 'Abide with me, fast falls the eventide' … An elderly widow, singing her heart out to Arthur Sullivan's grand march for Sabine Baring Gould's 'Onward Christian soldiers' …

Those men statistically had a chance of dying very soon. Few would have known where Tipperary lay, let alone have left their hearts there. The Final crowd is not thinking about death; but H. F. Lyte was, when he wrote that hymn on his deathbed.[1] 'Onward Christian soldiers' – really? Old Mrs X in that hat, worn since the time when hats were fashionable? Is she really thinking of Ephesians VI as Sullivan sets her spirits high? In all these cases words are merely scaffolding on which rests the communal euphoria driven by singing together. Interestingly, a recently discovered video of The Beatles in the Abbey Road Studios working on a song, shows John Lennon saying, 'Forget about the words, get the music right.'

---

[1] The tune to which it is now always sung, 'Eventide', is by W. H. Monk, Musical Editor of the first edition of *Hymns Ancient and Modern* (1861): Lyte's own tune was thought dull. Poignantly, Monk's three-year-old daughter had just died.

Clearing the Throat ...

An army may march on its stomach, but often sings when it does so. For singing, *together*, is a very important human activity – and how we missed it, having been deprived of it during the Locust Years that Covid hath eaten! Singing together makes you temporarily invincible, despite all evidence to the contrary. Singing together can cement an ideology, for good or, indeed, ill: during the Nazi era Goebbels' propaganda machine constructed the myth of Horst Wessel complete with a catchy tune in 4/4 time to go with it, a second National (Socialist) Anthem. Singing together enhances individuality of contribution and smooths it into communality, a common spirit. It is about bonding, about a sense of shared belonging, where each individual becomes caught up in something, like a dance, which can *only* be made by many people together. When we join in praise and worship, the 'I' or 'We' of a people or congregation becomes other-centred, not self-centred. I suspect that one way music works its mysterious power, especially in worship, is to insist that reality is much more than what we can know or understand at the moment.

Words enhanced by tune and rhythm can become ingrained in the mind. C. S. Lewis remarked in his autobiography *Surprised by Joy* (1955) that in the horrors of the Flanders trenches men would remember lines from hymns that they had sung at home, never really having thought about what those words meant before the world went mad. Fat lot of comfort 'We have a king who rides on a donkey', repeated three times then 'And his name is Jesus', to the tune of 'What shall we do with a drunken sailor?' – I jest not! – would be in those circumstances!

For when words are well crafted, seriously designed to say something, they can work in the mind like leaven in dough, even if they are hardly noticed first, or fifth, or tenth time round. A skilled writer can pack much doctrine or spiritual insight into a well-constructed hymn – as witness Charles Wesley, or Isaac Watts, or St Thomas Aquinas' hymns for Corpus Christi, or Prudentius' for the Nativity.

But, first, we need to consider the traditions they inherited and to which they responded. I'll try to be succinct ...

You can skip this bit if you wish, or come back to it later.

A Joyful Noise

The word is Old English, via Latin, from Greek ὕμνος (*hymnos*), 'ode or song in praise of a god or hero'. Aquinas has a lovely definition of what a hymn ought to be – and perhaps too rarely is – in the introduction to his *Commentary on the Psalms:* 'A hymn is to praise God in song; a song is the exultation of the mind when, dwelling on eternal things, it bursts forth in voice.' Praising God in song, singing together ... an impulse far older than the Church, reaching back into the worship that Jesus and his disciples would have known.

For the Temple worship used the Psalms as a sort of hymn book – fifteen of them for ascending the fifteen steps up to Solomon's Temple[2], for example. Hebrew poetry – which the psalms are – works on a structure of parallel clauses,[3] often saying the same thing in different ways (technically, the figure is called *expolitio* or *exergasia*), and this structure easily transposed when translating into Latin prose. The reading and singing of the 150 psalms of the

---

[2] In Hebrew the Psalms are *Tehillim*, 'praises'; the Greek ψαλμοί, 'psalmoi', means 'words accompanying music.' Music and song included in worship is suggested by Amos 5:21-23, Isaiah 38:20, and Jeremiah's description of the Temple ritual (Jer. 33:11). Pss. 119-133 in the Anglican Psalter are 'Psalms of Degrees', as the Psalter notes of some of them (a degree, *gradus,* is a step), originally sung as pilgrims mounted the wide steps of the Temple in Jerusalem.

[3] *The Jewish Encyclopaedia* succinctly puts it: '... parallelism is the fundamental law, not only of the poetical, but even of the rhetorical and therefore of higher style in general in the Old Testament. By parallelism in this connection is understood the regularly recurring juxtaposition of symmetrically constructed sentences. The symmetry is carried out in the substance as well as in the form, and lies chiefly in the relation of the expression to the thought. The same idea is expressed in its full import—that is, in its various aspects and turns—not in a continuous, uninterrupted sentence, but in several corresponding clauses or members with different words. Hence the name *parallelismus membrorum* or *sententiarum*.'

CLEARING THE THROAT ...

Western Psalter (the number is different in the Orthodox Churches) in a monthly cycle became central to medieval devotion.[4] In services they were chanted in the manners attached to the names of St Ambrose and Pope Gregory the Great:[5] chanting was monophonic, with syllables given equal length, which is ideal for communal *a capella* singing, as in a monastery. When with the sixteenth-century Reformation came the translation of Bible and liturgy into tongues understanded of the people, many of Martin Luther's own first publications were psalms and hymns, but now put into metrical forms derived from the vernacular, popular, song tradition: get people singing and they remember! John Calvin in Geneva also made metrical translations for congregational singing, to instruct while giving pleasure.[6] In Reformation England, metrical versions of the psalms, starting with Thomas Sternhold's *Certayne PSALMES chose out of the PSALTER OF DAVID, and drawe into English metre, by Thomas Sternhold grome of Ye Kynges Maiesties roobes* (that Majesty was Edward VI), became central to Protestant congregational worship. (In 1562 John Hopkins supplemented Sternhold's work, and 'Sternhold and Hopkins' became standard Anglican fare until 'Tate and Brady' (see p. 104) appeared in 1700. From this period we still sing William Kethe's version of Ps. 100, 'All people that on earth do dwell.' In that period, most poets with any ambition had a go at translating some of the psalms: Sir Thomas Wyatt, Henry Howard, Sir Philip Sidney and his sister, and we still sing John Milton's version of 136, 'Let us

---

[4] In the west, Roman Catholics follow the Greek numbering (via St Jerome) while Protestants follow the Hebrew numbering. Thus Anglican psalm 23 is Catholic psalm 22.

[5] Gregorian chant certainly has links to St Gregory, but, as *we* know it, was much affected by changes during and after the reign of Charlemagne two centuries later.

[6] He also wrote an extensive *Commentary on the Psalms*, praising them for presenting an 'Anatomy of all the parts of the Soul'.

with a gladsome mind'.[7] Richard Hooker (1554-1600) only repeated what Christian writers had said since St Basil, in the fourth century, when he asked, 'What is there for man to know that the Psalmes are not able to teach?' So too his younger contemporary John Donne, who called the Psalms the 'Manna of the Church' since, just 'as Manna tasted to every man like that that he liked best, so doe the Psalmes minister Instruction, and satisfaction, to every man, in every emergency and occasion'.[8]

But the Church has things to say, and celebrate, that are indeed a New Song of the New Creation in Christ: the wisdom and passion in the Psalms do map much of the human condition, but not the whole of it. One of the oldest things in the liturgy – Greek λειτουργία means 'work for, or service to, the people' – is the *Te Deum Laudamus*, certainly no later than the fourth century. Strictly speaking it is a hymn, but not quite as we understand the term after at least a dozen centuries of verse in various patterns. It's a rhythmic prose: the clauses are breath length, very suitable for emphatic communal chanting, and its outline of the even older summary of the Faith, the Apostles' Creed, is melded with a vision of the heavenly host joyfully singing in overflowing love and praise. Good to sing together ... Sixteen centuries later, a treble me in our village choir at Mattins got to know it in several settings – not a bad introduction to choral music, as it happens. What it was all about rather escaped me then – indeed, I don't think I worried my head about that. But the chanted words stuck, and certainly came to make sense later.

By Ambrose's time, towards the end of the fourth century, singing together in some form was clearly part of worship – and the unlearned as well as the learned still spoke Latin, even though the latter might have had classier accents. Ambrose himself composed many hymns: at least four of what went into the *Hymnal* named after him were his. That hymnal was used,

---

[7] In 1648 he translated from Hebrew Pss. 80-88 and in 1653 1-8.

[8] Sermon 66, 29 January 1625.

Clearing the Throat ...

in one form or another, for a millennium. Ambrose may have been one of the first to give hymns a stricter metrical pattern than rhythmic prose: the Ambrosian strophe has four verses – lines, if you prefer – of iambic tetrameter (eight syllables), e.g.:

> *Aeterne rerum Conditor,*
> *noctem diemque qui regis,*
> *et temporum das tempora*
> *ut alleves fastidium.*

> (Eternal King, of all the source,
> who day and night dost rule,
> and to the seasons sets their times,
> that so our weariness may ease...)

It's simple to construct, dead easy to memorize – which before the age of cheap writing materials mattered – and has a good punchy rhythm that adapts easily to walking in procession or marching or to unison singing, and small wonder that some people think popular tunes of the Roman legions were taken over into worship.[9] (What would happen if we sang something to *Colonel Bogey*...? There's a challenge to budding poets! After all, it's a catchy tune, and General Booth of the Salvation Army wisely remarked that the Devil need not collar all the best ones.) It is instructive to go through *NEH* and *Ancient and Modern* or any of the major hymn collections and note just how many hymns we sing are indeed translations, of varying dates, of very ancient

---

[9] We only have two fragments indisputably from the songs of the legions, one, clearly obscene, which Suetonius records the soldiers singing at one of Julius Caesar's four triumphs. To what tunes they were sung we don't know: one plausible suggestion is that rhythm was key, and the words were sung rather like speeded-up plainchant, with only minor movements of pitch. I can't help thinking of the almost hypnotic effect many people seem to find in modern rap. One clue is in Prudentius' *Psychomachia* (see later) where he says that Roman soldiers marched to a metre of three groups of four syllables followed by a group of three syllables (totalling fifteen syllables per line).

texts. Two of the best Passiontide hymns were written at the Merovingian court in France in the sixth and seventh centuries, and the processional used on Palm Sunday, 'All Glory, Laud and Honour' (*NEH* 509, *A&M* 328) was written for the court of Charlemagne.[10] Of course, as Latin over the slow centuries came to be understood only by the clergy and learned, many hymns, however fine, would have been neither known nor sung by laity. So this book must do due honour to the translators, above all John Mason Neale, who, late in time, made poems locked away for centuries in Latin singable by people who were ignorant of the language. A revolution – yes, it really was that – in Anglican worship was precipitated by *Hymns Ancient and Modern* (1861), which contains no less than 58 of Neale's translated hymns. And that revolution could probably not have happened without the remarkable, and emotional, growth of Methodist hymnody when the CofE's voice was silent.

It is hard now to imagine worship without hymns. But at the beginning of the eighteenth century, the Church of England allowed only the singing of metrical psalms, or the chanting of lines of Scripture – prose, from the King James Bible.[11] Apart from the translations from Latin, most of the older hymns we sing do come from the Dissenting tradition, the Congregationalist, the Moravian, and especially the later Methodist communities. The CofE only approved the singing

---

[10] In 810, by one of that learned king's favourite scholars, Bishop Theodulph of Orleans. Theodulph worked closely with another of Charlemagne's protégés, Alcuin of York, founder of the Palace School at Aachen, from which the educational revival of Europe could be said to begin. (There is another book in that ....)

[11] Which is sometimes set to music with a breathtaking ingenuity and beauty: e.g. Purcell's 'Rejoice in the Lord always', which is a chunk of one of the Epistles, or – a late example – S. S. Wesley's 'Blessed be the God and Father of our lord Jesus Christ', which sets words from I Peter (itself quoting Isaiah XI). But it's not for congregational singing.

of hymns in 1821 and old customs died hard: not every parish could afford new books[12], or was willing to change old custom. Moreover, the formal patterns in metrical psalms affected many later writers, often because they were using an old tune: they could write in four-line units of Common Measure, with lines of 8, 6, 8, 6 syllables (Bottom in *Midsummer Night's Dream* says he will have Peter Quince write the ballad of his dream in that form), Long Measure (8, 8, 8, 8), Short Measure (6, 6, 8, 6) or Poulters' Measure (12, 14: i.e. 6 + 6/8 + 6) – those numbers at the head of the music for each hymn puzzled me mightily as a choirboy – and for a long time setting was isosyllabic (one note to each syllable) and even ploddingly isochronous (all syllables the same length). Good examples are Kethe's Old Hundredth (Ps.100), 'All People that on earth do dwell', or Thomas Ken's 'Glory to thee my God this night' (*NEH* 244, *A&M* 10) which is set to the much older tune now called 'Tallis' canon'. Some poems not written as hymns, like William Cowper's or Isaac Watts' or James Montgomery's, were written to the familiar verse patterns of Long Measure, Common Measure, etc. When someone decided to sing them they conveniently fitted tunes that in more than a few cases already existed.

Hymn writing and singing in England, in fact, goes through several phases. Take Isaac Watts' huge, ground-breaking opus (see p. 112ff.) as the start of the first. Here, hymns aid, make memorable, scriptural exposition. With the Wesleys comes hymn singing as aid to Christian doctrine. Watts, Doddridge and others in the Calvinist tradition paraphrase Scripture, while Charles Wesley, you might say, paraphrases the Prayer Book and versifies theology.

Third stage is when an Anglican hymn book becomes explicit companion to the services of the *Book of Common Prayer*. This grew from the coinciding of the legalizing of hymns (1821) with the Oxford Movement (see below, p.170).

---

[12] Some collections of hymns were available in 1821: for example, among recent ones the *Olney Hymns* (1779) of John Newton and his friend William Cowper.

A Joyful Noise

Hymns Ancient and Modern (1861) has a Table of Contents directly derived from the Prayer Book, with hymns grouped according to appropriateness to office or season. (But there are no hymns for the *Churching of Women* or *A Commination*, both of which are in the 1662 book ...) And given that hymns have this agreed communal function, any question of literary merit, or not, becomes irrelevant. Some are, indeed, awful on that criterion. But more than a few are not.

One thing all these phases share is grounding in biblical, Prayer Book or doctrinal sources. This necessarily excludes those people not – or not yet – of faith or that shared ideology: these are the songs of the elect. But a fourth phase comes in the mid-1800s: using subjects not specifically 'religious' as a means to express religious feeling becomes much more acceptable – indeed, common. This was inevitable given the revolution precipitated by the Romantic poets, who made us recognise 'Nature' as something moral, expressing the Divine. There is a clear line of descent from Wordsworth's *Ode on the Intimations of Immortality* (1804) and *Lines written a few miles above Tintern Abbey* (1798), or Coleridge's *Dejection Ode* (1802) or *Frost at Midnight* (1798) to Gerard Manley Hopkins' visionary theophanies in *God's Grandeur* (1877), or *Pied Beauty* (1877). In the first half of the century, writing a hymn for singing in an Anglican church about natural objects like, say, mountains or rainbows or spring mornings would have been highly controversial. Had it been written a little earlier, Fanny Alexander's 'All things Bright and Beautiful'(1848) would certainly have prompted at least raised eyebrows. But the line from the Romantics through it to Eleanor Farjeon's 'Morning has broken' – a much better *poem* (*NEH* 237) – is clear.

Of course, many poems we *now* think of as hymns were not that at all when new. That we do so encounter them is largely due to the work of Percy Dearmer (see below p. 215ff.) as editor of the *English Hymnal* (1906). One example is that wonderful poem

Clearing the Throat ...

by Samuel Crossman, 'My song is love unknown' which was not written as something to be sung, but like George Herbert's lyrics, simply as a poem: later a tune might be attached to a poem, or composed specially. (For example, John Ireland's for Crossman's poem, or Ralph Vaughan Williams' matching, or adaptation, of music to existing texts in the first edition of *English Hymnal*.)

We ought to be grateful this happened. The singing of the metrical psalms, and their offshoots, would have sounded very odd, even unpleasant, to us: each line was sung or chanted by the Parish Clerk, then repeated by the congregation, and so on, line by line ... and this hardly enthusing custom of 'lining out' lasted in some of the poorer, more remote parishes until at least the very late 1700s.[13] Such singing was one thing that Isaac Watts so deplored that he wrote his own hymns (see p. 111) Furthermore, reminding us just how different was even the recent past, Thomas Hardy's bittersweet picture of the band of Mellstock church in *Under the Greenwood Tree* (1872) demonstrates how painful was change to musicians used to playing in consort with bassoon, flute, hautboy (oboe), viols, serpent, vox humana,[14] in the once common west gallery of a church. Grumbles were the frequent result of a modernising Vicar or Rector introducing a fashionable pipe organ: one instrument was cheaper to maintain than several, and one musician easier to manage than a clutch of them – often, as J. M. Neale complained, independent-minded and awkward.

Forms of Christian worship, after all, are evolving all the time. Ambrose's writing was a response to the Church drawing

---

[13] After all, books were expensive, and many people could not read. (This custom explains why the lines in so many hymns of that period are end-stopped.) My friend and colleague Revd Dr Roger Greeves told me in 2023 that he recalled hearing lining out singing in the Outer Hebrides in the 1970s. Alastair Moffat in *A New History of the Highlands and Islands of Scotland* (2024) describes hearing it in Lewis, with the congregation adding gracenotes to their repetition.

[14] There is a helpful outline of this music, common in the eighteenth and well into the nineteenth centuries at http://www.rodingmusic.co.uk/

closer to the structures of Roman secular power after the Edict of Milan in 313, when much of Roman culture was still pagan. This evolution continued in the following centuries as the church rituals became more and more central to the community, and affected not only architecture, vestments, painting, statuary and the decoration of the building but also music and song. The vestments a priest wears today at Mass echo the court dress of a Byzantine gentleman; the shape of a basilica like Old St Peter's in Rome or the Church of the Redeemer at Trier (the actual Aula Palatina commissioned by Constantine) replicates the judgement hall of a Roman magistrate – and that affected how the authority of the clergy came to be perceived, when often the only stable institution in a society in turmoil was the church; the huge size of many later church buildings, when the population was far, far smaller than it later became, was needed because processions of clergy and laity were embedded in the developing liturgy, in what was effect an acted-out metaphor of the pilgrimage of human life – a metaphor explicit in Hebrews XI. And processions, almost of their nature, like marching, demand singing. When, singing 'All Glory, Laud and Honour' on Palm Sunday (as it has been sung since the early 800s), we at St Mary the Less process – when it is not wet – from the bridge over the river Cam, through the Cambridge streets, with mystified tourists taking photos, and into church – we are not simply acting but *becoming* the crowd at Jesus' entry into Jerusalem: times elide. The Eucharist[15] is inherently dramatic, acting out an Event. The elaboration of ritual in that necessarily communal activity led to the need for more and more singing: processional introits for the day are one example. Another crucial area was the procession down the church between Epistle and Gospel, for which Sequences (literally, 'Followings')

---

[15] Much of the redevelopment of Western drama after the General Crisis of the sixth century, which destroyed so many of the structures and customs of late Antiquity (including public drama) stems from the innovative splitting of the Easter Gospel between two speakers at Vienne (Isère), sometime in the 800s. I could go on about this, but won't.

were written, to be sung after the Alleluia.[16] Often like the *Te Deum* in rhythmical prose (like the Lent Prose in *NEH* 507), only later were they normally in verse. Many sequences are fine poems on a biblical theme, that can stand apart from their original function. Many of the mediaeval hymns translated in *NEH* were originally sequences – the Rosy Sequence (385, *A&M* 126), the Golden Sequence (139 and 520, *A&M* 92), and so on. The best capture that sense of wonder and gratitude at the saving Sacrifice the Mass celebrates which much, much later Charles Wesley felt when after his conversion he gave us 'And can it be that I should gain/An interest in my Saviour's blood' (1738) – possibly his finest poem/hymn, which inexplicably is *not* in *NEH* or *A&M Revised*.

But: who is 'I'? The stress in early hymns, when not restating doctrine or reflecting on the narrative and mystery of Salvation, is on 'we', the pilgrim people of God, not on the individual. Even into the late Middle Ages, liturgy was premised on community. But after the 4th Lateran Council in 1215 made it obligatory for every single person to go to confession at least once every year and be examined as to the state of their soul, perceptions of the self naturally began to change, and each change precipitated another. With Reformation and Counter-Reformation came much stronger emphasis on a *personal* relationship with the Lord, and, especially among Protestants, a searching for signs of grace in your soul. The importance of the general, social, effects of this major, pretty universal, shift of sensibility in the West is difficult to overestimate. The marks are there all over the place, in the development of psychology – a word that did not exist in English before the eighteenth century – and in the priority put on the individual, and on subjectivity, by the Romantic movement. You see it even in apparently trivial things like the rise in diary keeping and writing of autobiography. (Perhaps it reaches its *reductio ad absurdum* in mere solipsism – 'if it feels right for you, dear, then that's all

---

[16] In 2002 the revised Roman Missal reversed this order.

A Joyful Noise

right'.) Some of the hymns of Charles Wesley, of John Newton, of Isaac Watts, which though sung in concert with others, are worded, so to speak, for a single mind in a state of high devotion, would have been impossible without it. There is a vast difference between a George Herbert, or a John Donne, each wrestling with his relationship to God in a poem written perhaps simply to try to make sense of that struggle, and to be read later by a single reader, which an editor then hijacks into a hymnbook, and the programmed subjectivity, which many people share at once, of many later hymns.

And now: in the affluent, materialist West, the last sixty years have seen a steady decline in attendance at formal services. In most cases there is sheer ignorance of such things, which until so recently were part of the cement that held a society together: a common myth, if you like. Yet one of the perennially popular programmes on BBC Television is *Songs of Praise*, an hour of watching people, often in close-up, singing hymns – and perhaps singing along 'in the comfort of your own home', as adverts used to say. But the original context of liturgy and doctrine has gone. Moreover, of the 50 most popular hymns in a 2013 survey of the programme 20 were from before 1900; in 2019, in a comparable survey, it was six out of the top ten. This situation presents a wholly different challenge for writers, for you can't count on a common ideology or base of knowledge any longer. 'How shall we sing the Lord's song in a strange land?', lamented exiled Israel (Ps.137) – for it *is* a strange land. How do you write religious poetry in a so-called secular age?[17]

---

[17] That supposed 'secularism' – a concept more difficult of definition that people generally realise – does not however preclude gross credulity in many things, from bogus astrology and 'aliens have landed' to the weirdest conspiracy theories. (As G. K. Chesterton remarked, 'When people stop believe in in Something they believe in anything.') One helpful examination of the religious poet's problem is Peter O'Leary, *Thick and Dazzling Darkness: Religious Poetry in a Secular Age* (New York: Columbia U.P., 2017). And David Jones' poem 'A A A Domine Deus' is exactly on the theme of the silencing of song by the machine age.

Clearing the Throat ...

Like the Salvation Army in the nineteenth century, reaching out to those parts of society that the organised churches did not, *could* not reach, now the hymnwriter has to reach to where people are, in their default scepticism, ignorance perhaps, to draw them into the Mystical Body of a Church they do not know and which, if they do know of it, mystifies them. Song, giving them the joy of being in a community with its whole attention focussed on making a joyful noise *together* – not to an audience! – may be some of the few ways of doing this, and if that means using popular music and forms that some of us might not like, might even abhor, well, nobody ever said that the Holy Spirit had a refined Classical taste. It's a tough job, though. But Ambrose and his successors did it in times quite as tough as ours.

Cut deep into the stone in a formal garden of an ancient house in Cambridge are Edmund Burke's words: 'Nobody made a greater mistake than he who did nothing because he could do only a little.' I have taken many of my pupils to see it.

III

St Ambrose
339–397

THE FIRST MAN TO WRITE hymns specifically for congregational use seems to be St Hilary of Poitiers (d. 367), but apparently nothing of his collection survives. So we start with Ambrose of Milan. Writer of some of the most delicate hymns ever written, he was also much, much more: civil servant, politician, bishop, and saint. He is one of those four people revered for centuries as the Latin Fathers of the Church, whom the Anglican Church of the sixteenth century accepted as authoritative in matters of doctrine. These four changed the Western Church for ever: Ambrose, Augustine (354-430), Jerome (342?-420), and the great reforming Pope, Gregory (540-604). The first three all knew each other, and it was Ambrose whose magnetic influence and preaching finally drew Augustine, a glamorously successful professor of rhetoric in Milan with good hopes of a lucrative job in the Imperial administration, to the faith. Originally Augustine had gone to listen to him to pick up some rhetorical flourishes he might use himself. He got much, much more.

When Ambrose was born, so many things we take for granted were still way in the future. His birth was only a generation or so after the Emperors Constantine and Licinius issued the Edict of Milan in 313 – Milan had been capital of the Empire since 286. This granted Christianity legal status

St Ambrose

and restoration of property confiscated during persecutions – some quite recent.[1] For the pagan altars still smoked, animals were still garlanded and led to sacrifice, as they would be for a good many more years, and many in the higher, educated, echelons of society were pagans – though perhaps in a more refined, philosophical way than many of their lower class contemporaries.[2] Some actively campaigned against Christianity and its claims, and nobody could guarantee that a change in Emperor or his advisers might not bring back the bad old days of persecution: and the church had not yet the power to become a persecutor in its turn. The Empire still functioned. The world crises of the fifth and sixth centuries, which triggered huge movements of peoples and transformed the nature of Europe, were still in the future. Moreover, the Church was riven by bad-tempered arguments, especially over the nature of Christ and the Trinity, which sometimes spilled into open fights in the streets. One must see Ambrose's hymns, with their succinct, even epigrammatic, summaries of doctrine and the faith, as something his community *needed*: morale boosters in an uncertain world, polemic against heretic and pagan alike, mnemonics for people who had few if any books.

Ambrose – Aurelius Ambrosius – was the second son of the Prefect of Gallia Belgica – roughly, modern Belgium, Luxembourg, Flanders, northwest France and a chunk of land watered by the lower Rhine. He was born in Trier, just around the time when the walls were rising of the basilica Constantine had commissioned in this ancient Imperial city. That basilica, now the Church of the Redeemer, still stands. But his father died soon after his birth, and Ambrose was taken back to Rome.

The family were Christians, well to do, and well connected. He grew up with his widowed mother and his elder sister Marcellina – she later took vows of virginity, dedicating her

---

[1] It only became the Empire's *official* religion with the Edict of Thessalonica in 380. An Edict of Emperor Galerius in 311 gave Christians freedom from persecution

[2] After all, *paganus* means originally 'someone who lived in the village': 'clodhopper', 'rustic'.

life to Christ. Christian priests were frequent visitors at the comfortable house. The boy would have followed the old Roman educational pattern, with a thorough grounding in literature ancient and modern, then in the crucial art of rhetoric – how to use words to best effect, to please, to move, and above all to persuade an audience – and finally dialectic: how to argue. This stress on the verbal arts, and on public speaking, was inevitable when persuading an audience in law court or politics, in addressing a ruler's court or a crowd in the public square, were fundamental to a career. From words grew – grows! – power; the ability to win the sympathy of an audience, to structure your own and demolish an opponent's argument, was indispensable for any man – and it *was* men – who sought any public position. With his background, this was clearly the sort of career which he would have been expected to follow.

His ability was soon noticed, and by 370, aged only about 31, he was made Consular Prefect (i.e. governor) of the province of Aemilia Liguria (roughly Piedmont and a lot of Lombardy) with its administrative centre at Milan. Milan was a rich city, strategically placed where major roads – along which moved trade as well as armies – came together in the richest part of Italy. The Imperial court frequently met there: indeed, it did so well into the twelfth and thirteenth centuries when the Western Emperors – Holy Roman Emperors, after Charlemagne's crowning in Rome on Christmas Day 800 – had long been German. Ambrose was noted for his talent and eloquence, and showed obvious administrative skills.

Milan's Christian community was bitterly split between those who accepted the Nicene Creed promulgated, after much heated argument, by the Council of Nicaea (325), and those who followed the teachings of the ascetic priest Arius, from Cyrenaica, that Jesus was *not* co-eternal with His Father. They needed a new Bishop, but neither side would accept one from the other. Then they made common cause virtually to drag

St Ambrose

Ambrose to the office: he was not even baptised[3] let alone ordained priest, and had never studied theology! But he was known to be a devout man, who although he accepted the Nicene Creed had also been charitable toward Arians. Like any sensible man would have done, he ran away from the awful job: he actually went into hiding, but his whereabouts were leaked by a colleague. So within a single December week in 374, aged 34, he was baptized, ordained and consecrated bishop.

He took his new position very seriously. Among his first acts was to give away all his considerable property to the poor, which made him immediately popular, and his wisdom and skill with his flock reinforced that over the years. He took himself off to Rome for a crash course in theology from the learned Simplicianus, a priest twenty years older than himself, to whom both he and Augustine became very close. (Simplicianus actually followed Ambrose as Bishop.) As governor, a civil servant, for a fixed term, and of an only moderately distinguished family when such things were very important, he could, if need be, be ignored by those in serious power. As Bishop however, a major (what would now be called) 'influencer' of a large proportion of the population, he could *not* be ignored, and he came to dominate the cultural and political life of the region. He was an indefatigable preacher of sermons, to which people flocked. He denounced social abuses – there is one notable sermon on Naboth's vineyard, which could do with preaching to our rulers more often nowadays – and frequently was able to get pardon for men condemned to the nasty sorts of death Romans often went in for. At times his word carried more weight than that of the often absent emperor. Nor was he afraid to stand up to those in power – and here his rhetorical, legal and dialectical training stood him in good stead. Occasionally indeed he came into open confrontation with the Imperial court, and showed, as one biographer puts it, 'a directness that combined the republican

---

[3] Baptism, taken very seriously, could be late in life. Some Christians were baptised only on their deathbeds.

ideal of the prerogatives of a Roman senator with a sinister vein of demagoguery.' (I am not sure about 'sinister'.) Speaking the truth to power always takes courage of a kind which is scarce in all ages. In 388 he dared publicly to rebuke Emperor Theodosius I ('the Great') for having punished a bishop who burned down a synagogue, and in 390 barred him from Milan cathedral[4] and imposed public penance on him for having punished a riot in Thessalonica by massacring its citizens. Ambrose was however so trusted, so useful as an Imperial diplomat and ambassador – in 383 and 386 he was sent to Trier on difficult missions to treat with the usurping emperor Magnus Maximus – that these extraordinary interventions were tolerated. They may have affected his developing ideas about the nature and duties of the ruler.

As I said, in his lifetime, and for a good deal longer, many people, possibly even most, were still pagan. Ambrose's own relative, Quintus Aurelius Symmachus, was spokesman for the pagan party in the Roman Senate.[5] The Church was thus still in the strict sense evangelical: the job of proclaiming the Gospel where it was not known was still to be done, and arguments from the most abstruse theological and philosophical to the practical, political and administrative were everywhere. No bishop at that time could escape polemics, and theological polemic became something at which Ambrose excelled. The split in the Christian community between Arians and Trinitarians was increasingly bitter. (The latter, we know, triumphed in the end, despite several later Western emperors, like Theodoric the Great, being Arian. But nobody then knew that would happen.) Ambrose smote the Arians hip and thigh with every argument he had, and in Holy Week 386 things

[4] The National Gallery houses a bravura painting (1618) by Antony van Dyck of the incident.

[5] Ambrose's eloquence in 384 defeated an appeal for tolerance of paganism by members of the Senate, led by Symmachus. By one of those extraordinary connections that one keeps finding, Symmachus was the grandfather of the great Boethius' adoptive father and father-in-law. It's a small world then ....

came to a very dangerous head when he refused them – and that included the party of the Empress Justina and her son the boy Emperor Valentinianus – use of a church building his own congregation was occupying: in fact, they were almost doing what we could call a sit-in. He was also tentatively developing – perhaps as a result of these quarrels with authority – ideas about the proper relationship between the emperor, the earthly power, and the Church, which in several ways anticipate those of Augustine in the absolutely seminal *City of God*, which is at the bedrock of fifteen centuries of theories of the State. The two may even have talked about Ambrose's ideas. The notion of a Christian Emperor as a dutiful son of the church, serving under Christ and obedient to the advice of his bishop, which Ambrose developed in two funeral orations for dead emperors, anticipates not only Augustine but the whole interminable clash between State and Church, Caesar and God, which rumbled on, often bloodily, through the Middle Ages and right down to the Reformation and beyond. Yet, like all his generation, he was always somewhat insecure, aware that the Faith could still be rejected by a largely pagan nobility and Trinitarianism rejected through the influence of Arian courtiers who had the ear of the Emperor.

He had excellent Greek, not then that common in the West (even Augustine, one of the most learned men of his time, apparently only had it at a rudimentary level). Prompted by Simplicianus, he read deeply in the Eastern theologians and philosophers, ancient and modern: Philo Judaeus, Origen, Basil of Caesarea, and the great neo-Platonist Plotinus. (They all seem so distant from us in time, but then it would have been like us reading the Victorians.) All this learning, especially Plotinus, fruited in eloquent sermons, which were greatly influential in transmitting Greek philosophy and theology to the West.[6] Augustine went to Milan as a sceptical professor of rhetoric in 384. When he left, in 388, as a result of those sermons, he had been baptized by Ambrose and soaked in Ambrose's Catholic Neoplatonism, which gave him a philosophical base that came to transform Christian theology. For Ambrose gave educated Latins a version of the Faith and a language for its discussion which their Classical habits of mind could accept. As Bishop, his letters and visitations strengthened this articulate and intellectual Christianity in those northern Italian towns where once he had ruled merely as Roman governor.

But he was Bishop not only of the educated. His initial popularity lasted, and quite apart from the tireless work he did with individuals finding their way to faith, he gave the community songs to sing and verses of rare beauty which for them became succinct summaries of key elements of the faith. Ambrose's hymns are profound, and their Latin is patterned – as one would expect of a fine rhetorician – most elegantly so that they are utterly memorable. Fine as some of the translations are, you cannot do in English what you can do in Latin: the languages work in different ways. But Ambrose, in giving the people songs to sing that they kept on singing, changed the world, and gave us an inestimable treasure.

It has been suggested that the very first time Ambrose introduced communal singing and chanting was to boost the morale of those of his flock in their long occupation of the Portiana church in defiance of the Empress that Holy Week in 386. (Augustine's mother, Monica, was there.) While it is possible that monophonic chanting, as in plainsong, might then have been one popular way of singing together, where rhythm is basically what matters – think, for example, of work

---

[6] So eloquent were his sermons, apparently, that noble families, whose status and power often depended on useful marriage alliances (poor girls!) were reluctant to let marriageable daughters attend them, for Ambrose urged most austere asceticism and the crowning virtue of virginity.

songs like sea shanties – we don't really know. There are only a few scraps of ancient melody that can be reconstructed. But we should not underestimate the retentiveness of folk tradition over centuries: some melodies may be very old indeed.

The fact remains that though we know they *were* sung, we have no idea of *how*. Some said Ambrose 'bewitched' the people of Milan by introducing new melodies from the Eastern, Greek, tradition, and this might not have been uncontroversial. Some of the early Fathers of the Church deeply distrusted music as a distraction from the words – which, to be honest, it can be – and forbade singing and dancing as part of worship or even of conduct in ordinary life. That sort of disapproval comes round with depressing regularity in most centuries. The great Augustine in the *Confessions* describes how he has himself vacillated between the peril of pleasure and approved wholesomeness, but says how he 'loved the chanting of the sacred words, seeing it as encouraging piety and healing the division of our community'[7] – indeed, drawing voices together in harmony is an undoing of the Confusion of Tongues at Babel.

There is a mosaic, near-contemporary, and therefore probably a recognisable likeness, in San Satiro's chapel in San Ambrogio, Milan – the building of which Ambrose commissioned in 379-86, in an area where many Christians had been martyred. It shows Ambrose as he would have wished: as a simple, humble bishop. It seems to me entirely appropriate that this should be the frontispiece to this book exploring the lives of some of those who are his eventual successors in making the new songs to be sung unto the Lord.

---

[7] *Confessions*, XXXIII, 49-50.

IV
Prudentius
?346–?406

≈

Prudentius is hardly a household name nowadays. Yet to him we owe at least two excellent hymns, *NEH* 33 – *A&M 325* – and 48, which we sing regularly and one (80) which we don't. Number 33, 'Of the Father's heart begotten' ('heart' is right; there are some versions which mistranslate as 'love') is not only a fine summary of good theology, and a great joining with all of Creation in an outpouring of joyful praise, but in *NEH* it is set to a splendid tune, based on a very ancient melody, from one of my favourite Reformation collections, the *Piae Cantiones* which Jaako Suomalainen, head of the Cathedral school in Turku, Finland, published in 1582. It's a joy to sing – especially when the organist adds a few twiddly bits and the choir gets excited – and the last verse has (for me) a spine-tingling descant. You know Christmas has come to Narnia when you sing it.

How did I first come across this man? Decades ago, I was reading the minor (if voluminous) seventeenth-century writer Phineas Fletcher, rector of Hilgay, north of Ely (I did not read *all* he wrote). Fletcher has a sentence that stuck in my mind: '[Prudentius]… brought foorth in his declining age so many & so religious poems, straitly charging his soule, not to let pass so much as one night or daye without some divine song, *Hymnis*

Prudentius

continuet dies, Nec nox ulla uacat, quin Dominum canat[1]. And as sedulous Prudentius, so prudent Sedulius was famous in this poeticall divinity....' That elegant chiasmus never sent me to read Sedulius the Irishman, who is Prudentius' contemporary, though he too makes an appearance in *NEH*.[2] But at the same time I was also being taught by Dr F. J. E. Raby of Jesus College, Cambridge, who wrote a great book on Christian Latin Poetry in which he had discussed Prudentius, and he was a fine teacher. It also chanced that concurrently I was getting excited by study in another area, on medieval allegorical poetry, and there (thanks to C. S. Lewis) I found Prudentius seminal – one indeed, who had no small influence on the way we in the West can think about, and express, our contradictory emotions and psychology. His are some of the foundations on which we now rest.

Marcus Aurelius Clemens Prudentius was born about 348 in Hispania Tarraconensis – the bit of Roman Spain governed from Tarragona. For the Empire's structures still functioned, as it seemed they always had done, and always would do, whatever the trouble at the top with all those people quarrelling for the Imperial diadem. (Does that remind you of anything?) Who could have guessed that less than 100 years later the Goths led by Alaric would sack the Eternal City on its seven hills? Prudentius is contemporary with SS. Jerome, Ambrose and Augustine, when the Church still had to fight its intellectual and social corner against those who regarded it a dangerous movement subversive of old custom and stable rule, and, indeed, in rather bad taste. He became a lawyer – what so many young Romans of good birth would then do, in the hope of winning some place in Imperial administration. He made it to being a provincial governor of some talent in a turbulent century, and was summoned to Milan, to the Imperial secretariat, by Emperor Theodosius I, where he would

---

[1] 'May the day be filled with hymns, let there be no night that does not sing of the Lord.'

[2] A couple of decent hymns extracted from a long 23-verse hymn to Christ (each verse in the alphabetical order of the 23 letters of the Latin alphabet) (*NEH* 20, 46).

have met Ambrose. But in 392 he threw it all up to become an ascetic, devoting himself to prayer, poetry and meditation. He wrote a lot. In 405 he collected his many poems, and wrote a preface for them, and *NEH* 33, 48 and 80 are all gobbets culled from one long one, *Cathemerinon liber* ('The Book of Daily Things', i.e. hymns) which has twelve hymns, six of which are for daily use, then hymns for before and after fasting, for 'all hours', for the Burial of the Dead, for Christmas and for Epiphany. (Incidentally, R. F. Davis, translating *NEH* 33, makes Prudentius' fifth strophe the last, omits his seventh and eighth, and himself adds the rather fine verse 6.)

A lot of Prudentius' writing was topical, and polemical. After all, like Ambrose and Augustine, his were times of intellectual ferment. (For once, the cliché is spot on: heady, intoxicating stuff in times of great political change.) He wrote two polemics *Contra Symmachum* ('Against Symmachus') rebutting, as Ambrose had done, that pagan senator's demands that the altar of Victory be restored to the Senate House in Rome. Three long poems expound Christian doctrine in a style and literary form immediately accessible to those (like himself) soaked in the old classical literary tradition.[3] The *Apotheosis* is vehemently anti-Arian, powerfully supporting the Trinitarian position of the Nicene Creed – and over that issue of the co-eternality, or not, of Son and Father armies marched and blood had been and would be spilt. That hymn we sing at Christmas, 'Of the Father's heart begotten' deals precisely with that issue: its topicality was once urgent. The *Hamartigenia* ('The Origin of Sin') waded into the arguments of Marcion and his followers.[4] But his lasting influence on literary practice and on the way we think about ourselves really stems from the *Psychomachia*

[3] Prudentius often used another popular metre, the trochaic tetrameter, as in *Corde natus ex parentis*. ('Of the Father's Heart Begotten' *NEH* 33.)

[4] Marcion (c. 85-160) had a considerable following for some centuries, despite condemnation in 144 as a heretic. (One of his positions – the Docetist theory – was that Jesus was a divine spirit who appeared to humans in human form, but did not actually take on human flesh.)

PRUDENTIUS

('Battle for the Soul'). The *Psychomachia* is nearly 1000 lines of decent hexameters in the high manner of Virgil, and describes how Faith, aided by the personified virtues of Hope, Temperance, Chastity, Patience, Humility, etc. fights idolatry and the personified vices of Pride, Wrath, Avarice, Unbelief, etc. (Neither the Virtues nor the Vices are quite those with which we are familiar: those categorisations were still being formed.) These personifications have to be women because Latin words for abstract concepts are mostly feminine. Accept the highly artificial premiss, and it's a good read. But what is important is that this is arguably the first really significant use of allegory, a wonderful tool for telling a story that has two parallel meanings, one on the surface and another which the thoughtful mind discovers. Think *Animal Farm*, *Pilgrim's Progress*, Spenser's *Faerie Queene*, Langland's *Piers Plowman* and so on back to the seminal thirteenth-century *Romance of the Rose*, for three hundred years one of the most read of poems, and beyond. (Mischievously, I think of Freud too …) Prudentius may not have invented the form – some argue that the Sceptic philosopher and Sophist Favorinus of Arelate (Arles) (c. 80- 160) used it, but there's no evidence Prudentius knew his work – and I myself think of Rabbinical readings of the Pentateuch. There are hints of it even in Homer. But his poem's elaborate *and systematic* use changed the direction of European literature and thought, for allegory became one major mode of expression in the Middle Ages, used for everything from satire, or the delicate exploration of how we fall in love, to the search of the soul for its Lover, God.

The poem survives in many manuscripts. More have certainly been lost, and 20 of the ones we do have are illustrated. To do that cost money, and therefore suggests the high value and importance put on the poem. Indeed, so well-known was it that an illustrated MS of it may be the source of early mediaeval wall paintings in All Saints', Claverly, Shropshire, and St Nicholas, Pyrford, near Woking. And if you ever wonder why we say, 'Pride comes before a fall', well, it seems that with Prudentius is where it starts. In a ninth-century MS of the

Psychomachia in the Bibliothèque Nationale de France (BNF Latin 8085), is an energetic picture of a very glum-looking Pride falling off her horse and being beheaded by a vengeful Humility, (see *https://gallica.bnf.fr/ark:/12148/btv1b6000032n/f125.item*)

And this one ran and ran: the proud warrior falling off his horse comes up again and again, even when a tired monk a thousand years later tipped up the seat in the choir stalls of Lincoln Cathedral to rest his weary bottom on the misericord on which it was carved, during the long chanting of the Psalms set for the day in the daily Office.

Thank you, Prudentius.

V

VENANTIUS FORTUNATUS
C.530–C.600

ଙ୬

I WROTE THE FIRST version of this piece for the Parish *Newsletter* that was to be sent off on Maundy Thursday and (one hopes) read over the Easter weekend. Not all that many hymn writers have first-class hymns for both the Passion and for Easter. (Cue for someone to write to correct me…) Venantius Honorius Clementianus Fortunatus (c. 530 – c. 600) was one of them. You know him for *NEH* 78 (*A&M* 59) 'Sing my tongue the glorious battle', 79 'The Royal Banners forward go' (*A&M* 58), and 109 'Hail thee festival day'. The first was translated by Percy Dearmer, the second by another hymnodist I revere, J. M. Neale, and the third by 'Editors' – Dearmer and his colleagues. He wrote many others, equally good, which did not make it into *NEH*. Indeed, he has been called the last major Latin poet of late Antiquity.

I remember once writing an essay on him when I was an undergraduate. Thankfully, like many other youthful follies, it is now lost. He was born c. 540, at Treviso, just north of Venice[1], and died just after 600 at Poitiers, where he had become Bishop. His family were pagan, as many people then

---

[1] So was Lorenzo da Ponte, Mozart's finest librettist. Quite irrelevant.

still were: he converted when still quite a young man and we do not know how his family reacted. He grew up, possibly in Aquileia whither some suggest the family had moved to escape the political situation in Treviso after the death of King Theoderic the Ostrogoth in 526 – he is the chap who put the great Boethius to death.[2]

It was a turbulent time: the Eastern Roman (Byzantine) Empire under Justinian had poured resources and troops into reconquering North Africa from the Vandals and Italy from the Goths. The Byzantine commander Belisarius (about whom Robert Graves wrote a fine novel, 1938) may be the figure on Justinian's right in the wonderful mosaic in San Vitale in Ravenna. The Eternal City of Rome had now declined to an importance really only symbolic, and so acute was depopulation that sheep grazed in the streets and on the slopes of the Capitol. The fulchrum of power was Ravenna, on the Adriatic coast. It is hard to imagine that city, now known for petrochemicals and spectacular churches, and in many ways both metaphorically and literally a backwater – for its once grand harbour is now six miles from the sea – as the capital of the Empire in the fifth century. It had been the Ostrogothic capital, and there the Byzantine fleet had its base, whence access to Constantinople itself was easy. The splendour of its churches was no more than becoming to its status. Sometime in the 550s or 60s, soon after Belisarius defeated the Goths, Fortunatus was studying in this metropolis. Somewhere, he got an education in the Roman style, with strong emphasis on rhetoric, that art of persuasion, of using words. (What a gorgeous place to study, when the new church of Sant' Apollinare in Classe was bright with its new mosaics!) He clearly knew the classical Latin poets – Virgil, Horace, Ovid, Statius, and Martial – well, but also the

[2] Awaiting his execution, in 524, in prison Anicius Manlius Severinus Boethius wrote one of the greatest books of the Western world, the *Consolation of Philosophy*. I have had undergraduates sit on my sofa and say, after I had made them read this book of which they had never heard, 'That book has changed my life.' Please do read this beautiful book if you do not know it.

Venantius Fortunatus

Christian poets, including Arator, Claudian, and the Irishman Coelius Sedulius. Moreover, being in Ravenna, where Greek was commonly heard, he could hardly not have known at least some and, like any educated late Roman, would certainly have had knowledge of Greek literature and philosophy.

Young men must earn a living, and a poet needs patrons. Eventually he went north, to the vibrant, somewhat dangerous, courts of those Germanic rulers whom Romans only recently had seen as barbarian. Now they had to be taken seriously – some indeed had become Emperors, like Theodoric – and many aped the manners and style of the Empire their forbears had helped destroy. He turned up at the Merovingian court in Metz in 566, a young man hoping to become one of those people no self-respecting court careful of its reputation could do without: a resident poet and PR man. But he did not go direct from Italy: he took in what would in time be Austria, Germany and France, and later gave two quite different reasons for that route: on the one hand, in the *Life of St Martin,* which he wrote much later, he says he wanted to worship at St Martin's shrine at Tours, but elsewhere he portrays his journey as serendipitous and himself as a wandering minstrel, if not exactly 'a thing of shreds and patches, with ballads, songs and snatches'. Whichever itinerary he took, his journey would not have been easy: while the Roman roads that netted down Europe were still in decent repair, how the efficient infrastructure for travellers had fared as the central authority weakened is much more questionable. The provision of staging posts and accommodation in *mansiones* may well have been much more patchy, and passing through different spheres of authority is always expensive and sometimes dangerous. One can't help wondering how he paid his way – the question that always comes to my mind when you think of late Antique and medieval travel. (And also the problem of finding the way in a world without maps.[3])

---

[3] Travellers on the main Roman roads might have *itineraria*, which gave to the distance to the next way point, such as a town, or (if you were lucky), a *mansio* (inn) or a bridge.

A Joyful Noise

When he got to Metz, the king, Sigebert, was just about to marry Brunhild, and Fortunatus performed a celebration poem before the entire court. (That says much about the Latinity of these erstwhile 'barbarians'.) This was impressive enough to win him several patrons – patronage was, after all, key to getting dinner each day – among the nobles and bishops. About a year later, he moved to Paris, to the court of Sigebert's brother Charibert, and stayed there until that king died (567 or 568). But another brother, Chilperic, was proving a nuisance (those Merovingians did family quarrels rather well), and so Fortunatus moved to Tours, which was in Sigebert's lands, and then to Poitiers, where he met a certain Radegund. Yes, that is the Radegund after whom they named the rather dull road to which the buses go in Cambridge, and the dedicatee of the nunnery which Bishop Alcock of Ely dissolved in the late 1400s to make Jesus College. We need a digression on her to indicate the sort of intermittent mayhem in which Fortunatus lived.

Radegund was a princess of Thuringia, and had been carried off (aged about 11) by Clotaire 1: he had just killed both her father and her uncle. When she was about 20 Clotaire made her one of his six wives, or concubines. (What went on in her head? How did she feel about this husband with the blood of her family on his hands?). Ten years later he killed her last remaining brother. Sensibly, she fled to Noyon, where she became a deaconess. Ten years after that she founded the Abbaye de St Croix at Poitiers to house the relic of the True Cross that she had somehow obtained from the Byzantine Emperor Justin II – a reminder of how extensive were the personal networks of the powerful in those times. And it was for its installation in Radegund's Abbey that Fortunatus wrote a series of hymns, including the famous *Vexilla Regis prodeunt* ('The Royal Banners Forward go', *NEH* 79), one of the most significant Christian hymns ever written, still sung on Good Friday, Palm Sunday, and for the Exaltation of the Holy Cross. He and pious Radegund became very good friends. It may have been she who persuaded him to become a priest, and

VENANTIUS FORTUNATUS

after her death he wrote a verse *Life* which is a main source for our knowledge of her life and history. He wrote many poems in her honour. In Tours and Poitiers he also became friendly with the learned and devout Gregory (whom Sigebert insisted be consecrated Bishop of Tours in 573). For that occasion Fortunatus wrote a panegyric to him, celebrating his learning. Indeed, his *Decem Libri Historiarum* ('Ten Books of Histories', aka *Historia Francorum* -'History of the Franks' – for short), is of great importance in understanding this turbulent period, and what it was like to write in and about it. Near the end of his life Fortunatus was elected bishop of Poitiers, and after he died was revered as a saint.

Eleven books of his poetry survive. He wrote in several genres, each demanding a different rhetoric and set of conventions: epitaph, panegyric, georgic, consolation, and religious poems. Paul the Deacon, who died in the 790s, says, in his *History of the Lombards* (II. 13), *nulli poetarum secundus, suavi et disserto sermone composuit* – 'he wrote in a sweet, elegant style, second to none of the poets.' His long verse epic, the *Life of St Martin* uses many of the tropes of Classical epic poetry. In all, he wrote panegyrics to four Merovingian kings: Sigibert and Brunhild his queen, Charibert (father of Bertha, queen of Æþelberht of Kent, who welcomed Pope Gregory the Great's envoy Augustine to Canterbury in 597), to Chilperic, and to Childebert II and his wife (another Brunhild). The one addressed to Chilperic demonstrates the tactful ambiguity panegyric can deploy. For Chilperic was not an easy man: he was headstrong and hot-tempered, and Fortunatus wrote the poem when the king had his friend Gregory of Tours on trial for treason. But Fortunatus depicts Chilperic as gracious, compassionate, merciful, never hasty in judgement, and even praises the king's poetry. Some argue, cynically, that Fortunatus was simply trying to ingratiate himself with the new patron whom he might need if things went against Gregory. But only fools believe palpably untrue flattery, and it is far more likely that, as in much panegyric, Fortunatus was reminding Chilperic of how the ideal king *should* rule: a public rebuke, yet nobody could possibly take offence. The poem thus becomes a plea for his friend.

If I were being literary-historical, much could be said about his prosody, lexis and other technical things. But far more important to me: I think he was a great liturgical poet, whose verse moves me to a fuller engagement with and understanding of that which is celebrated. You see *through* his poetry. Three poems I love have remained part of the liturgy of the Catholic Church, the *Pange lingua gloriosi proelium certaminis* ('Sing, O tongue, the glorious battle') for Good Friday (which later inspired Aquinas' *Pange lingua gloriosi Corporis mysterium* for Corpus Christi). Then, *Vexilla Regis prodeunt* ('The royal banners forward go'), used for centuries as a sequence for Vespers during Holy Week. Both manage in a few verses to summarise the whole narrative and typology of salvation, and the latter, with its focus on the 'Tree of Beauty, tree of light/ Tree with royal purple dight', has for me more than just a hint of the meditative intensity of the wonderful (possibly eighth century) Old English poem *The Dream of the Rood*. Fortunatus' poem is in trochaic tetrameter, a rhythm ideal for a procession, but more subtly, because of the play on the word *hostia* (= victim/ Host) in line 20 it is also a meditation on the Mass itself. There is also (ll. 20-24) an extraordinary conceit of the Cross as a sort of steelyard in which the Sacrifice is weighed against our sins, and the witty paradox of the last lines – which did not make it into the translation – where life pushes away death and gives life back by death. (I could go on…) The one we don't sing as often as I would like is the great Easter hymn (adapted later for Ascension) *Salve Festa Dies* (109: 'Hail thee festival day', which decades ago was the processional our church always used at Ascension). Actually, it is only a part of a much longer poem, *Tempora florigero rutilant distincta sereno*: 'These bright times blush in the clear weather that brings forth flowers, and the gate of heaven opens with greater light', *(Venanti Fortunati Carmina*, III. No. 9), celebrating the coming of spring and addressed to Bishop Felix of Nantes to honour the newly baptised. The translation in *NEH* is a bit clumsy but does adhere closely

Venantius Fortunatus

to the pattern of the original elegiacs – and Fortunatus was writing just when accentual metre, such as our ears are used to, begins to influence the older quantitative prosody of high Latin poetry. Be all that as it geekily may, Vaughan Williams' tune is a corker – it will fit both the English version and the Latin original – and I do wish I could join in singing it more often.

Fortunatus' poems, indeed, have inspired more than a few composers of first rank: Palestrina, William Byrd, Praetorius, Puccini for example. *O Crux splendidior* ('O Cross, shining brighter than all the stars' – not in NEH) has been set many times, e.g. by Peter Philips in the sixteenth century (fine recording from Winchester Cathedral on the Web) and Orlando di Lasso, and more recently by Knut Nystedt. Anton Bruckner wrote a fine motet based on *Vexilla Regis*. Fine poetry sung to good music – how much we missed that in the COVID years!

But there is one issue that had better be settled now before we go any further in this book. Fortunatus was writing at a time when warfare was a fact of almost daily life: Emperor against pretender, petty (or not so petty) prince against petty prince, people displaced by climate change and war from the vastnesses of Asia pressing on the eastern margins of what had been Roman. Several of Fortunatus' wonderful hymns use imagery that becomes endemic in hymns right down to today. '*Vexilla*' (banners) in 'The royal banners forward go' is quite specific: these are not just any old banners, these are *battle* standards. 'Sing my tongue the glorious *battle* ...'. Imagery of war and conflict, right down to 'Onward Christian Soldiers' and beyond, is inescapable (and for many, nowadays, uncomfortable) in Christian song. Where does it start? Perhaps with the great passage in Ephesians VI where St Paul talks of the breastplate of righteousness, the shield of faith, the helmet of salvation and the sword of the Spirit as the spiritual armour of those who must struggle against the Principalities and Powers, the malign spirits of evil? But Constantine's vision of the Cross before the crucial (ouch!) battle of the Milvian Bridge in 312 also had the legend, *In hoc signo vinces* – 'Under this standard [the Cross]

A JOYFUL NOISE

thou shalt conquer' – and the imagery of war and battle may well receive a boost there. From this is it but an unthinking step to the obscenities of Crusade[4] and the explanatory metaphor becoming a template by which the ambiguity of reality is simplified, made manageable. Of course it remains a metaphor for spiritual struggle, not least against one's own unruly desires – 'Christian, dost thou see them/on the holy ground/How the troops of Midian/prowl and prowl around' (*NEH* 65 – *A&M* 55 – by J. M. Neale) – and of course we really are engaged in a cosmic struggle, but it can so easily translate into the dreadful 'Othering' by which a community reinforces its sense of its own unique rightness and the devilish error of those who do not share its ideology. Examples, regrettably, are all too numerous, and some are too near home for comfort.

Fortunately, for Fortunatus, much of that had not yet happened.

---

[4] It should be remembered, and never is, that there was much principled, and growing, opposition to the idea of Crusade from both churchmen and lay people from the start – almost from the moment Pope Urban II launched the first Crusade in 1096 with that speech at the Council of Clermont.

VI

ANONYMOUS AND AUTHOR UNCERTAIN

ೂ

ANONYMOUS AND AUTHOR UNCERTAIN are among the most prolific of writers. They have a claim on our respect, and often our gratitude, for they often wrote very well indeed. For much, if not most, of the Middle Ages the people who laid the foundations on which we so often unknowingly build simply did not bother to attach their names to what they did, be it in building a cathedral, inventing a wheelbarrow, carving a statue, painting an altarpiece, or writing a poem. They did not think of authorship, or individuality, as we do. Some names we can conjecture; some we shall never know, and can only honour by loving and trying to understand their work and why they made it. They made no distinction, as we do, between 'Art' and 'craft', and it is well to remember that however beautiful it may be, most of the religious art of the Middle Ages is as functional as advertising.[1]

There are many hymns in our hymn books where we know the (modern) translator but not the author of the original Latin (or, more rarely, Greek). Those many include two very well-known ones. *NEH* 97 (*A&M* 69), 'At the Cross her station keeping' is a version of the great poem, *Stabat Mater dolorosa/*

---

[1] See my 'Speaking pictures: mediaeval religious art and its viewers', in Stephen Prickett (ed.) *The Edinburgh Companion to the Bible*, (Edinburgh: Edinburgh University Press, 2014) pp. 175-194.

iuxta Crucem lacrimosa/ dum pendebat filius, on Our Lady at the foot of the Cross watching her Son die. *NEH* 524, 'Day of Wrath and Doom Impending' (as one version goes) aka *Dies irae, dies illa*, with its inseparable plainsong melody, is so well known that its tune is quoted many, many times, often in quite other, non-religious, contexts ranging from Berlioz' *Symphonie Fantastique* to Rachmaninov to Disney's *Frozen II*.

The meditation on Our Lady at the foot of the Cross has been regularly attributed to the Franciscan[2] Friar Jacopone da Todi (?1230-1306) or (less often) to Pope Innocent III, (?1160-1216, born Lotario de' Conti, of the distinguished house of the Counts of Segni). All we can say with absolute confidence, thanks to the discovery in 2010 of a new, notated, MS, is that the Dominican nuns in Bologna in the thirteenth century were using it as a gradual, sung between Epistle and Gospel. However, the emotional and spiritual context of how its writer thought can be reconstructed to some degree, and this is what I shall try to sketch in a moment.

Much the same could be said for whoever wrote the *Dies Irae* (why can I not get the setting in Mozart's *Requiem* out of my head as soon as I think of this poem? I think my bass is almost up to *Tuba mirum spargens sonum* … but only in private). It is originally a sequence, certainly thirteenth-century at the latest, and possibly older, for meditations on the Day of Judgement are not uncommon. Conventionally people ascribe it to another Franciscan, Tomaso di Celano (1190?-1265?). But other names have been suggested: a Dominican, Latino Malabranca Orsini (d. 1294), lector at the *studium generale* at Santa Sabina on the Aventine in Rome (later the Pontifical University of St Thomas Aquinas), or St Bonaventura, biographer of St Francis, or St Bernard of Clairvaux (d.1153), founder of the Cistercian Order.

Jacopo dei Benedetti – Jacopone da Todi is just his nickname – quite plausibly could have written the *Stabat Mater*. But, as he

---

[2] By the later thirteenth century, the Franciscans were splitting into two parties, one far more radical in its embracing of poverty and rejection of status than the other. To this group, the Spirituals, Jacopone belonged.

would have been the first to agree, its existence, and its effect on those who read and sing it, matters more than who wrote it. He was born in Todi, in Umbria, a city that some claim had 40,000 inhabitants in 1290: a place therefore of consequence. He became a lawyer, wealthy and worldly, but probably no more so than most. He was born when the city states of Northern Italy were always quarrelling, and the quarrel between the Pope and the (German) Holy Roman Emperor (whose main base was Milan) drew them into interminable sputtering war, and even civil conflict in individual towns. There was much to be cynical and despairing about when churchmen went to war for power and profit and lay princes ruled in their own interest and not to defend the poor and lowly, who endured, living and partly living, a grim existence. 'How long, O Lord, shall the ungodly flourish?': the Psalmist's cry must have seemed very pertinent. No wonder this was also the time when lay fraternities like the Flagellants, processing hooded and singing, beating each other for the sins of the world, were a regular sight.

An accident brought about complete change in Jacopone's comfortable, selfish life. For he had insisted his devout wife accompany him to watch a tournament – the Church had already made clear its disapproval of tournaments, in which people quite frequently did get killed – and she was most reluctant. Then the temporary wooden staging for the élite spectators collapsed, and she was killed. When her women laid her out, they discovered she was wearing a hair shirt – horrible, scratchy things, and horsehair can be like needles – in penance for her husband's worldliness. His conversion was immediate: abandoning his legal practice, giving away his goods, he lived as a wandering ascetic. Originally the Franciscans, whom he did eventually persuade to admit him,[3] would have nothing to do with him. For many thought him mad, and his controversial, often clowning, behaviour included turning up to a wedding tarred and feathered as a Savage (= Wild) Man, and even crawling on all fours round the Piazza del Popolo in Todi pretending to be a horse. But he was

---

[3] Through one of his fine poems, on the vanities of the world.

a poet, and a good one, and his *Laude* ('Praises'), often satirical about current abuses, written in the common Umbrian speech, seem to have been sung in the towns, and in confraternities, and he was certainly something of a mystic. He was also one of the first people of whom we know the name to have dramatized Gospel subjects, aiming by the immediacy of performance to increase the emotional reaction of those watching. More than 100 of his mystical poems survive.

'At the Cross her station keeping ...' Something of the force of this wonderful meditative poem can be guessed from the enormous number of musical settings (counting only the ones that actually made it into documentation on Wikipedia) from Josquin des Pres to James Macmillan, each composer trying to take on the challenge of what came before. But whoever wrote the words was not thinking of fame. He was steeped in the meditative practices and disciplines of the Middle Ages, which not only clerics but also many lay folk followed: imagining, in minute detail, in every sense – literally – what it would have been like to 'be there', and, having imagined that by will and by memory, to *see* the grief, to *touch* Our Lady's robe, to *smell* the blood, to *taste* the salt of tears on the cheeks of our own compassion – literally, 'feeling with' – to *hear* her sobbing, as she watches her son's agony. 'A sword shall pierce thy heart ...' The goal of this meditative practice was indeed just that: the eliding of time then and time now, the complete apprehension of this terrible moment. And only in the last verse do we get a glimpse of the fruit of salvation that grew on this bitter tree.

> *Sancta Mater, istud agas,*
> *Cucifixi fige plagas*
> *Cordi meo valide*

says the Latin:

> 'Holy Mother, do the same,
> On my heart inscribe the pains,
> Of my Saviour crucified.'

Anonymous and Author Uncertain

A sword shall pierce thy heart...

The poem, properly read and meditated upon, is doing in words what an altarpiece, say, or a wall painting was intended to do to the viewer. (Forget about aesthetics: mediaeval religious art was to do a job. Some of it is awful, but that would not stop it working.) This focus on Our Lady's motherhood, on her grief, we take for granted, as unremarkable, something familiar from a sculptured *pietà*, or a Nativity scene on a Christmas card with Joseph nodding off in the corner or the Virgin giving the breast to her Son. But once that with which we are so familiar would have been revolutionary. Those images which we take for granted depend on massive changes in sensibility, which need not have happened. Sometime in the eleventh century, there began in the West a new attention, in art and in devotion, to the humanity of Christ and the tenderness of his Mother, and of that this emotional plangency is the fruit. More and more in art she becomes not simply the regal – I almost wrote iconic – Mother of God, but in her humanity our bridge to grasping what Incarnation meant for those who shared Christ's years on earth. It shows more and more in the visual arts, where Christ's body becomes twisted in agony, his mother becomes a young woman you could meet in any street. That was a revolutionary move, discernible in so many ways, from the (re)dedication of churches to Mary, to the development of Marian devotion, which became so wildly popular, so approachable, that the more excitable Reformers banned it altogether in their worry that it might make Our Lady a sort of Mother-Goddess maybe? (not that they would/ could have used that term) or co-Redemptress. And when this poem was new, this emotionalism, this excitement, was at its height. Our author must have felt it as the words expressed this passionate sympathy. Nor is this exploration of emotions limited to religious expression. This is the very period when the expression of romantic sexual love begins to find a new voice – which again we take as normal, something that was always there – and when women and the feminine begin to be much more prominent in art and literature, where they often have a power which they did not at that time have in actual life. Nature – or ideology at least – follows art more often than we complacently realise – though ironically tyrants always know that the first thing they must do on getting power is control the arts and media. The fiction of power, the games people came to play in the conventions of love, lead eventually, if slowly, to women no longer being merely legal chattels of their menfolk.[4] But change, though slow, has to start somewhere, and the author of the *Stabat Mater* was one of the agents of that change. And if we reinstate the necessary reciprocity of male and female in our social thinking, surely it will remind us that in the Source of all Being, male and female are subsumed, and that in Christ there is neither male not female, slave nor free: just Love that endlessly gives itself.

༄

For centuries the *Dies Irae* was part of the Roman rite for a Requiem Mass; in *NEH* it is suggested for All Souls.[5] It belongs in the same context as the *Stabat Mater*, a context of intense visualisation, realisation, of an Event (in this case in the future) of fulchral importance. Visualising the last things, or the Apocalypse, in art was not new. The details in the *Revelation of St John* were and are well known, as a moment's search in the

---

[4] It took until the 1590s for a bang up to the minute Shakespeare to dramatize in Juliet the dignity of a woman's passion and the enormity of her being regarded simply as a piece of useful property. It took until 1882 for the British Parliament to pass the Married Women's Property Act.

[5] Several English translations have been proposed for liturgical use. A very loose, and Protestant, version was made by John Newton (see Chapter XV), which opens:

> Day of judgment! Day of wonders!
> Hark! the trumpet's awful sound,
> Louder than a thousand thunders,
> Shakes the vast creation round!
> How the summons will the sinner's heart confound …

Anonymous and Author Uncertain

wilder shores of Google Images will show. The essence of the Judaeo-Christian model of history – quite unlike other models – is that time is linear, that one day there will be an End, an Eschaton, when all shall be revealed, and known for what it is – which is what the Greek word ἀποκάλυψις ('apokálypsis') means. There were many scholars and theologians over the centuries who had used St John's book as a means of interpreting current events, from the shock of Vandal, Gothic and especially the Moslem attacks on what was left of the Empire, to Alcuin of York at the court of Charlemagne writing about the Viking sack of the monastery on Lindisfarne. Many had sought to know the times and the seasons of the Second Coming (as Jesus said they never would) by matching current events to cherry-picked details in St John. What is new in this great poem, the *Dies Irae,* is the *immediacy* of its visualisation – and its personalisation: this terrifies not just everyone, but *me*, this is about *me* being judged, this is *my* appeal to the mercy of Jesus. 'But who can abide the day of His coming? And who can stand when He appeareth?' (Malachi 3:2) This emotionalism is exactly what the great Doom sculptures, vividly carved and originally brightly coloured, were intended to engender as you, or you, or you, walked into the church, the sheltering Ark, through the door that symbolically separated the Christian from the storm without. There are many all over Europe, in paint as well as stone, and it is only the uniqueness of the twelfth-century sculptor, Gislebertus, having *signed* (*Gislebertus hoc fecit* – 'Gilbert made this') his work at Autun that makes me single that one out as especially fine.

That extraordinary vividness, the roundness of vision, the immediacy of expression, the detail of emotion on each person's – and even each devil's – face in *this* situation is exactly of a piece with the emotional vividness of the Stabat Mater. To make you *feel* what intellectually you *know* is the key to so much mediaeval religious art and writing. For only from feeling does change come.

The poet, whoever he was, who wrote the *Dies Irae* knew exactly what he was doing. He makes us focus our minds on details which to mediaeval eyes were familiar, memorable, in the visual arts, making the painting or the bright new sculpture on the church you pass every day suddenly hit you – 'Oh, this is not just a game, just what people say, it's real.' The tramp of his inexorable trochaic tetrameters become almost hypnotic, the piling up of reference upon reference to the details of the End are meant to induce, well, a sort of terror. (Try listening to Verdi's setting after reading that last paragraph.) Yet its later strophes move towards hope, a plea for mercy and forgiveness. But that is given only by grace: 'When this man rises from the ashes, spare him, O God ...'

As Wikipedia ineffably puts it, 'The final couplet, Pie Iesu, has been often reused as an independent song.' Yes indeed: and I have heard it more than once sung, in the setting with which Fauré concludes his Requiem, at weddings, where one hopes the world is all before the couple ... Which seems a bizarre mismatch.

ዕ

Well, suppose it was Tomaso di Celano who wrote it: the poem is indeed full of that passionate emotionalism which is typical of the early Franciscan movement, and Tomaso was one of the first followers and intimates of Saint Francis. He wrote two early biographies of Francis, well before the better known one of Saint Bonaventura. His noble family gave him a thorough education in the liberal arts; he had deep learning, great fluency with words, and he was eventually given great organisational responsibilities by his Order. He and (?)Jacopone show in their writing and their spirituality the stamp of the new confidence of a Church trying to renew itself after a great reforming Council (1215, in St John Lateran in Rome) which stressed personal devotion and spirituality, the need for a regular discipline of self- examination, and *personal* contrition. This is the period when there is a sudden flowering of great mystical writing and poetry which speaks to us across eight centuries as fresh as when it was new. We must be grateful: as perhaps one of the greatest of all the mystical writers of the Middle Ages, the German theologian Meister Eckhart (1260- 1327) once said, 'If the only prayer you said in your whole life was, "thank you", that would suffice.' He also reminds us that, 'Truly, it is in the darkness that one finds the light, so when we are in sorrow [as when we share the Virgin's sorrow, tremble at the approach of the Judge in whose sight no man can stand], then this light is nearest of all to us.'

VII

St Thomas Aquinas
1225-74

⁂

THERE ARE SOME YEARS, when Easter is really early, when every moveable feast also falls early. And so the last major festival before the long green trudge up to Advent can fall only just into June. Corpus Christi is not one of the most ancient of festivals, but it became one of the most loved, and was one of the most missed when the Reformers in England dourly suppressed it. This was the midsummer festival, between getting both the spring sowing and the lambing over, and the unremitting labour of haysel and harvest. It was party time. This was when, in many towns in the later middle ages, the whole community would join in the comedy and pathos, the ritual and junketing, surrounding the annual Corpus Christi processions and plays. Enjoy while you can, for after midsummer the nights begin to draw in, reminding you of the dark that will fall on everything.

What better thing to celebrate than the mystery of the Eucharist, God made flesh and offering himself in food to his people? The doctrine of transubstantiation, after centuries of argument, was only made an article of faith in 1215 at that great reforming Second Lateran Council. Veneration of the Blessed Sacrament, which was not of course new, attracted increasingly popular and often very emotional devotion in

St Thomas Aquinas

that century when everywhere you look in art and writing you see new stress on feeling and emotion. It was St Thomas Aquinas, *Doctor Angelicus*, who persuaded Pope Urban IV that the mystery at the heart of the Mass deserved its own festival. Immediately popular – it fitted perfectly with what was already holi-day time – it was established in 1246. Aquinas wrote one of the greatest of all hymns for it, summarising in succinct and allusive Latin the theology and typology behind the Eucharist. Each Corpus Christi we sing with great reverence the wonderful *Pange, lingua, gloriosi corporis mysterium* ('Of the glorious body telling', tr. J. M. Neale *NEH* 268) to an ancient tune that our forebears in our very church could – would – have known. Sometimes, in that ancient place, I think I can almost hear their voices as we sing. For sometimes the centuries elide and ancient devotion is very present ... Places, like clothes, keep something of the wear, the memory of the people who came before. The hymn's form and words deliberately echo the fine Passion hymn of Venantius Fortunatus which we sing as the Host is placed in the altar of repose on Maundy Thursday: in Corpus Christi, the cycle, the sacrifice, is completed. Now we get on with the old clothes and porridge of Ordinary Time.

Tomaso de Aquino was born in 1224 to a noble family who supported the second Hohenstaufen Holy Roman Emperor, Frederick II, in his war with the Pope. (People called Frederick *Stupor Mundi*, 'the Wonder of the World'.) His brothers were all trained for a military career, but Thomas when only six was sent to the Abbey of Monte Cassino near his home as an oblate: his uncle was Abbot of this, the oldest Benedictine abbey, established in 529 by St Benedict himself. It was quite normal for families then to exert patronage, and his family perhaps hoped Thomas would one day succeed his uncle in that powerful office. However, in that unremitting contest between Emperor and Pope, the Emperor expelled the monks in 1239 because they were too obedient to his enemy, and Thomas returned home. He had no desire whatsoever to be a Prince of the Church – it is said that he was overjoyed when the Lord assured him in a vision he would never have to be a bishop. He went to the University at Naples, and, to his family's horror, joined the mendicant order of friars founded by St Dominic and licensed by the Pope in 1215. This order, vowed like the Franciscans to poverty, chastity and obedience, was specifically a teaching and missionary order: punning on the Latin *Domini canes*, they were the hounds of the Lord hunting down heresy and like sheepdogs guarding the faithful. Their active life of preaching and teaching was far more attractive to him than a monk's life of prayer and manual labour. His mother Theodora, pretty desperate, hurried to Naples, but the friars, fearing she would abduct him, sent him on to Rome, preparatory to sending him to their house in Paris to study in the premier theological University of Europe. But at Theodora's insistence, his brothers waylaid him on the road and imprisoned him in the fortress of San Giovanni at Roccasecca. He was finally released after twelve months, and made for Paris. There he had the extraordinary good fortune to be taught by Albertus Magnus, perhaps the outstanding scholar – *Doctor universalis*, as he came to called – of his age, whose spread of expertise was astonishingly wide. Thomas' brilliance, and learning, prodigious in one so young, were rapidly recognised, and Pope Innocent IV offered him to make him, still only in his 20s, Abbott of Monte Cassino (as his parents might have wished). But he turned this down to go with Albertus when he was sent to be lecturer at the new – well, we would call it university – at Cologne. That says something about the affection between master and student. After returning to Paris in 1256, he was summoned to the Papal Curia as adviser under two Popes, and to teach at Rome. It was during this period in Italy that he began to build out of various theological disputations what eventually became the great *Summa Theologiae*. In 1268 his Order sent him back to Paris as Regent of the Dominican house in Paris in the rue St Jacques. (One of his neighbours in that street would have been the learned Jean de Meung, the clerkly poet who continued and vastly extended Guillaume de Lorris' *Roman de la Rose*, arguably the most read and most

St Thomas Aquinas

influential vernacular poem of the later Middle Ages.) Two years later Charles of Anjou, King of Sicily, summoned him to Naples to reform and in effect to restart the university where his academic career had started.

His work was astonishingly wide, like that of Albertus his master's. But the main reason we now honour him is his brilliant reconciliation with Christian doctrine of the newly recovered (via Moslem Spain) philosophical works of Aristotle, lost in the West since the collapse of the Western Empire, and his reasoned opposition to the implications of commentaries on Aristotle written by the sceptical empiricist Arab philosopher Averroes (ibn Rushd) (1125-98). While there was a period (especially around 1277) when Aquinas' work was opposed as heretical, in 1567 Pope Pius V proclaimed him a Doctor of the Church. His huge (but unfinished) *Summa Theologiae* was one of only two books placed on the altar during the Council of Trent (1545-1563) – the Council which launched the highly effective Counter Reformation. Pope Leo XIII in 1879 declared it the definitive exposition of Catholic doctrine. Dante places Thomas in the sphere of the sun in *Paradiso* X, with the other great teachers of the Faith, and he was canonised in 1323 – just after Dante died. When the cause was being heard, the Devil's Advocate objected that there was scant evidence of miracles, whereupon it is said one cardinal snorted and said that every single article in the *Summa* was a miracle. In the marvellous fresco (painted 1365-8) of the Triumph of the Church on the west wall of the Spanish Chapel of Florence's Santa Maria Novella – the Dominicans' church – Andrea di Bonaiuto di Firenze gave him central position.

This is only part of the story, however, and perhaps to Thomas not the most important. Thomas was not simply a scholar and philosopher. He was by deliberate choice a mendicant religious, influenced both by the passionate evangelism and the ministry to the poor of Francis of Assisi, and the devotion to scholarship of St Dominic. Those two men, who met in Rome in 1221[1], were seen by many as central to the great missionary and reform movement that sprang from the Lateran Council Innocent III had convened. That movement changed Europe for ever. St Catherine of Siena said of them, 'Truly Dominic and Francis were two pillars of Holy Church: Francis with the poverty that was his hallmark and Dominic by his learning.' Thomas' work accomplished more than a brilliant synthesis: that synthesis led to and was itself part of an evangelical awakening to the need for cultural and spiritual renewal throughout the church, in the lives of individual men and women, and reaching to the lowest and poorest in society.

Scholar, polemicist, poet – but also a mystic. He had several ecstatic experiences, and it is said that one reason he never completed his great work was a profound mystical experience of the glorified Lord. He told his friend Reginald of Pipierno, who urged him to get on and finish it, that all he had written reminded him of nothing so much as straw – utterly inadequate in its attempt to encompass the mystery of Creation and the Glory of God. We all, in our measure, know that feeling.

He wrote some of the loveliest and most profound hymns and sequences to survive from the Middle Ages. Quite clearly he was a man of deep feeling, feeling which he can engender in others through his verse. His eucharistic hymns are still part of the Roman Office for Corpus Christi: *Lauda Sion Salvatorem,* 'Laud, O Zion, thy salvation' (*NEH* 521); *Pange lingua, sacris solemniis* (sometimes called *Panis angelicus*, 'Welcome with Jubilee', tr. J. Aylward); *Verbum supernum,* 'The heavenly Word proceeding forth', tr. Neale, *NEH* 269; *Adoro te Devote, latens Deitas,* 'Godhead here in hiding, whom I do adore' tr. G. Manley Hopkins; *O Salutaris Hostia,* 'O saving Victim' has been set many times (Charpentier alone set it six times between 1670 and 1690), and Gioachino Rossini used it as text for a movement in his *Petite Messe Solennelle* (1863).

Enough of the factual: a personal note. I am no theologian,

---

[1] It is often depicted in art. Fra Angelico did a lovely fresco in the church at Assisi.

and most of Aquinas' philosophical subtlety is beyond me, a distant peak I shall never climb. But under the guidance of a remarkable teacher, a young and very ignorant me read a lot of mediaeval Latin hymns and sequences. I was struck then, and am struck now, by the beauty of Aquinas' verse, and even more by how he manages to compress so much into so little, and so memorably. Fully to understand the *Pange lingua* is perhaps impossible, for good poetry is never amenable to prosaic summary – as I always say to my pupils – but as a statement of the mystery of the Eucharist it is approachable on so many levels. But it was written to be sung by those who had Latin, and I can't help regretting that so many of those who have heard it over the centuries simply could not have grasped its beauty and subtlety. So once again we owe thanks to J. M. Neale, who made a glimpse of so much of ancient Latin hymnody accessible to us, late in time.

VIII

GEORGE HERBERT
1593–1633

GEORGE HERBERT DID NOT write any hymns. He wrote some of the most intimate and profound religious poems in English. None was ever printed in his lifetime – though that would not exclude the circulation in MS of some of them among trusted friends – after all, some of them *are* very personal. Yet in *NEH* four of his poems have been re-purposed, as one might say, into well-loved and much sung hymns for singing in community: *NEH* 77 (*A&M* 110), 'The God of Love my Shepherd is' – like pretty well everyone who wrote then (and later), he had a go at turning one or more psalms into English verse; 391 'King of glory, king of peace' (*A&M* 194); 394 'Let all the world' (*A&M* 202); and 456 'Teach me my God and king' (*A&M* 240) The tunes to which we sing them are all much later[1]. Yet for a man so passionate about music as he was, it is entirely possible that Herbert did think of at least some of his poems as incomplete without the music to which he so often refers, a vestige of the harmony of the heavens so faintly heard on earth. Musical imagery fills his poems. Indeed, his first biographer, Izaak Walton, records his saying that '[music] did relieve his drooping spirits, compose his distracted thoughts, and raised his weary soul so far above earth, that it gave him an earnest of the joys of

---

[1] Respectively, 1794; mid-nineteenth century; 1847; 1833.

GEORGE HERBERT

Heaven, before he possessed them', and John Aubrey, writing a generation later, says that a Mr Allen, who knew Herbert, had told him that 'he had a very good hand on the Lute, and that he sett his own Lyricks or sacred poems.' I have loved Herbert ever since a wise schoolmaster introduced my heedless and ignorant youth to the limpid grace of his 'Vertue', one hot June afternoon on the cricket field after A levels, whither a few of us ('we few') who were hoping to read English or Classics at University had accompanied him, officially to watch the cricket. We were far more interested in noticeably and noisily being 'intellectual': but Herbert does not let you get away with that.

I fought shy of writing this piece for a long time. Herbert, for me and many others, is arguably the finest lyric religious poet writing in English, and very near my heart. It is so easy to let one's enthusiasms like an unruly horse carry one off into the wide blue yonder. So let me try to be as factual as one can be. But at the same time let me earnestly recommend the joy and delight one gets from a slow and thoughtful reading of Herbert's *The Temple*. Let his complex limpidity work – yes, I know that sounds like a contradiction, but it isn't: paradox is sometimes the only way of saying the unsayable – let each poem work in the mind like leaven in bread, and perhaps read the poems in the order they appear. As on any journey, there are high and low spots: but the whole journey is much greater than the sum of its parts.

Herbert 's family were at the centre of political, cultural and religious life. They were among the most influential in early modern England. The senior branch were Earls of Pembroke, with their major English seat at Wilton. His aunt Mary, Countess of Pembroke, was Philip Sidney's sister. She was another translator of the Psalms, and herself a good poet: she was niece to Robert Dudley, Earl of Leicester – Queen Elizabeth's 'sweet Robin'. His cousins, William and Philip (both of whom in turn succeeded to the earldom) were the 'incomparable pair of brethren' to whom Hemmings and Condell dedicated the First Folio of Shakespeare in 1623. His father was Richard, Lord of Cherbury, who died young, in 1596, but not before giving his remarkable wife ten children: the eldest, Edward, first Baron Cherbury, was soldier, diplomat, a fine poet, philosopher, musician, and has been called the father of English Deism. George's younger brother Henry became Master of the Revels to Charles I. His mother, Magdalen Newport, was of extraordinary intellectual ability, piety and learning.[2] After her husband died she handled the complex management of a largeish estate for thirteen years, until she re-married: a man much her junior, Sir John Danvers, who became an MP.[3] She was close to men of the calibre of Lancelot Andrewes, who became Dean of Westminster in 1601. He was a regular visitor to her London house in the Strand, and she sent her sons to Westminster School and his care. Andrewes at that very time was deeply involved in preparing the King James Version of the Bible. She was also very close to John Donne, who stood in as godfather when Richard Herbert died – he was not then Dr Donne of St Paul's, but an ambitious, youngish man hoping for a diplomatic or legal career, working as secretary to the Keeper of the Great Seal of England, Sir Thomas Egerton. For her Donne later wrote 'Ascension: To the Lady Magdalen Herbert', and – by then Dean of St Paul's – preached one of his finest sermons at her funeral.[4] In fact, there was hardly anyone

---

[2] George wrote a Latin epitaph for her: *Hic sita foeminei laus et victoria sexus/ Virgo pudens, uxor fida, severa parens* ('Here lies the triumph and the glory of womanhood: modest virgin, faithful wife, strict mother' in 'Memoriae Matris Sacrum'

[3] Danvers as an MP was one of those who signed the death warrant of King Charles. He died in 1655.

[4] Donne and Herbert remained close. Shortly before his death, Donne had many seals made on which were engraved the figure of Christ, crucified on an Anchor (the emblem of Hope), of which emblem Donne would say, *Crux mihi anchora* – 'the Cross is my anchor.' He gave these to many of his close friends. When Herbert died his was found wrapped in a paper with these verses:

> When my dear friend could write no more,
> He gave this *Seal* and so gave o'er.
> When winds and waves rise highest I am sure,
> This *Anchor* keeps my faith secure.

GEORGE HERBERT

of any literary, religious or political standing that she did not know, and who would not have been familiar to her children as a visitor to their home at Charing Cross. As so often, we forget how much smaller society was then than now: anyone who was anybody *would* know everyone else who was anybody in a total English population of about 4 million and a London community of under 200,000. Herbert himself is a case in point, knowing the movers and shakers of his time, often intimately. For example, in 1620, he composed a florid Latin tribute to his friend Francis Bacon, by then Lord Chancellor and Viscount St Albans, on his completion of the *Novum Organum* – one of the seminal works in the history of modern scientific thought – and with Ben Jonson and others helped translate Bacon's *Advancement of Learning* into Latin.

Herbert went up to Cambridge in 1609 and rapidly distinguished himself. Writing verses in Latin and Greek was very much part of the curriculum, and the elegance with which he wrote was soon recognised. He proceeded MA in 1616, and was elected a Fellow of Trinity College. This was a time when at the basis of education were the arts to do with words: the reading of the Classics, filling up your mind with the common frames of reference and the ancient wisdom;[5] the art of rhetoric, using words to best advantage; and the art of argument – dialectic. When in 1618 he was appointed University Reader in Rhetoric, that was no dryasdust 'subject'. It was crucial, up to the minute stuff. Moving, persuading, teaching was done by words and how you used them. The art itself was morally neutral: it could be used, in a lawcourt, or parliament, for example, to argue a

---

[5] Pagan wisdom, of course, which might well be convergent with Christian. It's worth remarking that it is ironic that in a Christian society 90 per cent of its educational materials were pagan and Classical, to which it sat somewhat obliquely: but the conceit of dwarfs standing on the shoulders of giants was a cliché. The giants could not see as far as the dwarfs, but the dwarfs could not see at all without the giants. This cliché is well expressed in the lancet windows in the south transept of Chartres cathedral: it was a twelfth-century Chancellor of Chartres who first made that remark.

case that was honest and true – *causa honesta* – or it could be used to bamboozle, to make the worse appear the better case – *causa turpis*. Knowing the difference might mean life or death. Our forebears took the arts of words, and how they work on the mind, very seriously indeed, and were all too aware of the ambiguous relation words bear to the things to which they refer. To put it aphoristically, words reveal only to conceal: the words are not the thought they try to express, but only its shadow. And shadows can so easily be taken to be real.

Herbert was elected Public Orator in 1620, and stayed in that capacity for eight years, though he was often in London in courtly society, which he seems to have enjoyed. He always returned, however, to Cambridge to welcome the King when he visited after yet another hunting trip to nearby Newmarket or Royston. John Milton, going up to Christ's College in 1625, would certainly have encountered him. (Milton would also have heard Dr Donne preach when he was a pupil at St Paul's School.) Nowadays in Cambridge the Public Orator's job is largely ceremonial. When the University wishes to honour someone with an honorary degree, the Orator has to present them to a Congregation of the University with an elegant, often very witty, Latin address (sometimes the wittier when read in parallel to its English version) celebrating their worthiness of that distinction. In earlier times the job mattered far more. The Orator was the University's official spokesman, who had to present its case as forcefully as possible to those in power at Court or in the lawcourt, irrespective, quite explicitly, of any personal stance he himself might have. He wrote its official letters; he was the man who had to make an address to a visiting dignitary whatever his own views on the matter – or person. When the worlds of Church, politics and academe were so intermingled, this was a crucial post. A man who held it might expect to attract notice, and perhaps to be drawn into the organs of government. Several were: of Herbert's immediate predecessors, Sir Robert Naunton became Secretary of State, and Sir Francis Nethersole Secretary to James' daughter, the Lady Elizabeth, Queen of Bohemia. According to Walton, who

George Herbert

was the same age as Herbert and was writing when his memory was still green, he

> 'managed [being Orator] with as becoming and grave a gaiety, as any had ever before or since his time. For he had acquired great learning, and was blessed with a high fancy, a civil and sharp wit; and with a natural elegance, both in his behaviour, his tongue, and his pen.'

It is difficult to get an idea of that 'natural elegance' and the smart young man who seems to have spent almost as much time in London in fashionable circles as he did in Cambridge. We cannot be certain of what he looked like: yet, as with so many authors who touch our hearts – and Herbert did, and does, touch so many – it is a natural impulse to want to know them (so to speak) through the eye as well as in the heart. The earliest portrait was engraved 40 years after his death by Robert White for Izaak Walton's biography in 1674. Now in London's National Portrait Gallery, it was the basis for pretty well all later engravings, such as those by White's apprentice John Sturt. Sturt's 'The Effigies of Mr George Herbert' has these verses below it:

> *Behold an orator, divinely Sage,*
> *The* Prophet *and* Apostle *of that age.*
> *View but his* Porch *and* Temple, *you shall see*
> *The Body of divine* Philosophy.
> *Examine well the Lines of his dead Face*
> *Therein you may discern Wisdom and Grace.*
> *Now if the Shell so lovely doth appear,*
> *How Orient was the Pearl impryson'd here!*

It is a face curiously like his mother's portrait by William Segar, with the same long nose and broad forehead: except hers is half turned to her right and his to his left. And it is his wisdom and piety that it seeks to memorialise for the reader of the book, that contains 'The Church Porch' and 'The Temple'.

A Joyful Noise

The youthful Herbert, genuinely pious, did indeed hope for some serious secular advancement from King James, but none was forthcoming. He also got involved with the Virginia Company, which traded in the new colonies, an enterprise in which his Pembroke relatives and his friend Nicholas Ferrar (of Clare Hall) were also interested. He and Ferrar, following family traditions, became MPs in 1624. But King James died in 1625, and with him Herbert's hopes of a Court career. Just the year before two of his most influential friends had died, Lodowick, Duke of Richmond, and James, Marquess of Hamilton, and with them their considerable powers of patronage. The result was, as Walton says, that he

> presently betook himself to a retreat from London, to a friend in Kent, where he lived very privately, and was such a lover of solitariness, as was judged to impair his health, more than his study had done. In this time of retirement, he had many conflicts with himself, whether he should return to the painted pleasures of a Court-life, or betake himself to a study of Divinity, and enter into Sacred Orders, to which his dear mother had often persuaded him. These were such conflicts, as they only can know, that have endured them; for ambitious desires, and the outward glory of this world, are not easily laid aside; but at last God inclined him to put on a resolution to serve at his altar.

Herbert was ordained deacon in 1626, and given the living of Leighton Bromswold. The church was in a ruinous condition, and Herbert raised the money – the large sum of £2000 – to restore and rebuild it. (Do visit it: it is almost as it was in Herbert's day.) Also in 1626, Nicholas Ferrar, was ordained by Laud, Bishop of London (and future Archbishop of Canterbury), and set up the devout community at Little Gidding near Leighton Bromswold, which has become a site of regular pilgrimage today. That devout prince Charles I went there three times – the last when in flight after his catastrophic defeat at Naseby.

George Herbert

Herbert's health had never been good, but the few years more he had to live were not unhappy. Laud encouraged his priesting in 1630, and in 1629 he married his stepfather's niece Jane Danvers, ten years younger than he, and the marriage was happy. Probably through the influence of the Pembrokes at nearby Wilton, he was given the living of Fugglestone St Peter with Bemerton, a mile from Salisbury. He again restored the church and parsonage, and rapidly became beloved in the parish. Walton again:

> Some of the meaner sort of his parish did so love and reverence Mr. Herbert that they would let their plough rest when Mr. Herbert's saint's bell rang to prayers, that they might also offer their devotions to God with him; and would then return back to their plough. And his most holy life was such, that it begot such reverence to God and to him, that they thought themselves the happier when they carried Mr. Herbert's blessing back with them to their labour.

And as for Jane, says dear Walton, 'Love followed her in all places as inseparably as shadows follow substances in sunshine.'

Walton recounts the famous story of Herbert's charity and humility. He used to walk into Salisbury to join friends in making music – he was a fine viol player as well as lutanist – and once

> he saw a poor man with a poorer horse, which was fallen under his load. They were both in distress and needed present help. This Mr. Herbert perceiving put off his canonical coat, and helped the poor man to unload, and after to load his horse. The poor man blest him for it, and he blest the poor man, and was so like the Good Samaritan that he gave him money to refresh both himself and his horse, and told him, that if he loved himself, he should be merciful to his beast. Thus he left the poor man. 'And at his coming to his musical friends at *Salisbury*, they began

> to wonder that Mr. George Herbert, which us'd to be so trim and clean, came into that company so soyl'd and discompos'd. But he told them the occasion: And when one of the company told him, *He had disparag'd himself by so dirty an employment;* his answer was, *That the thought of what he had done would prove Musick to him at Midnight, and the omission of it would have upbraided and made discord in his Conscience, whensoever he should pass by that place; for, if I be bound to pray for all that be in distress, I am sure that I am bound, so far as it is in my power, to practice what I pray for. And though I do not wish for the like occasion every day, yet let me tell you, I would not willingly pass one day of my life without comforting a sad soul. or shewing mercy. And I praise God for this occasion: And now let's tune our instruments.*

He died in 1633, of tuberculosis. He left much Latin poetry of great elegance, a MS of a prose treatise on being a priest (published 1652 as *A Priest to the Temple,* as part of *Herbert's Remains, or Sundry Pieces of That Sweet Singer, Mr. George Herbert*) and a MS[6] of poems, many written earlier in his life, when the tension between desire for secular advancement and the call of the Christian life was at its most intense. The dying Herbert sent that MS by a friend to Ferrar:

> Sir, I pray deliver this little book to my dear brother Farrer, and tell him, he shall find in it a picture of the many spiritual conflicts that have passed betwixt God and my soul, before I could subject mine to the will of Jesus

---

[6] Which has not survived. There are two other MSS: MS Jones B. 62 in Dr William's Library in Gordon Square, London, of 78 English and several Latin poems, which has some of Herbert's own handwriting, and, it has been argued, might have been prepared for a group of people connected with Little Gidding. The other is the Tanner MS 307 in the Bodleian Library, Oxford, with 167 poems subsequently published as *The Temple* (Cambridge, 1633). This MS possibly was made to get the licence for that edition.

GEORGE HERBERT

my Master: in whose service I have now found perfect freedom. Desire him to read it; and then, if he can think it may turn to the advantage of any dejected poor soul, let it be made public; if not, let him burn it; for I and it are less than the least of God's mercies.'

Ferrar did publish it, as *The Temple; or, Sacred Poems and Private Ejaculations* (1633) and may have edited the poems' order to suggest a sequence leading up to the poems on the Four Last Things. Ferrar said, 'there was in it the picture of a divine soul in every page: and that the whole book was such a harmony of holy passions, as would enrich the world with pleasure and piety.'

And it did: between the first printing and Walton writing about 1670 more than 20,000 copies sold, and the poems have continued right down to now to give a voice to those to those who themselves have no gift of utterance. Reading the book changed the direction of the poet Henry Vaughan's (1621-95: in *NEH* 412) life and talent, to 'renounc[ing] idle verse': he described Herbert as 'a most glorious saint and seer.' The distinguished Puritan Richard Baxter (1615-91), who also appears in *NEH* (371, 475 – *A&M* 183 and 198 – and 402,) said, 'Herbert speaks to God like one that really believeth in a God, and whose business in the world is most with God. Heart-work and heaven-work make up his books.' Indeed; and Herbert's intimacy expresses itself so often in the language of friendship and love: there can be few poets who can utterly unselfconsciously call God 'my dear'.

Yet Herbert's diffidence in his message to Ferrar is sincere enough. Often in his poems we glimpse that anxiety that any love poet – and religious poetry is a special sort of love poetry – must feel, that in the very art he uses to express something *beyond* art may lie a trap, an end in itself. In Chekhov's *The Seagull* (1895), the playwright Trigorin, passionately, utterly sincerely, talking to his ex-lover Nina, suddenly stops, takes out pencil and jotter, and says, 'I say, that's rather good!' The hardest thing in writing in any devotional sense is to banish that clouding of the vision by the art that tries to reveal it. Several of Herbert's poems, like 'Jordan I' and 'Jordan 2', or 'A Wreath', anticipate Andrew Marvell's 'The Coronet':

> When for the thorns with which I long, too long,
> With many a piercing wound,
> My Saviour's head have crowned,
> I seek with garlands to redress that wrong:
> Through every garden, every mead,
> I gather flowers (my fruits are only flowers),
> Dismantling all the fragrant towers
> That once adorned my shepherdess's head.
> And now when I have summed up all my store,
> Thinking (so I myself deceive)
> So rich a chaplet thence to weave
> As never yet the King of Glory wore:
> Alas, I find the serpent old
> That, twining in his speckled breast,
> About the flowers disguised does fold,
> With wreaths of fame and interest

Herbert knew just what he meant: that when you write in the first person your 'I' may not be you:

> When first my lines of heav'nly joys made mention,
> Such was their lustre, they did so excel,
> That I sought out quaint words and trim invention;
> My thoughts began to burnish, sprout, and swell,
> Curling with metaphors a plain intention,
> Decking the sense as if it were to sell.
>
> Thousands of notions in my brain did run,
> Offering their service, if I were not sped.
> I often blotted what I had begun:
> This was not quick enough, and that was dead.
> Nothing could seem too rich to clothe the sun,
> Much less those joys which trample on his head.

George Herbert

As flames do work and wind when they ascend,
So did I weave myself into the sense.
But while I bustled, I might hear a friend
Whisper, 'How wide is all this long pretence!
There is in love a sweetness ready penned,
Copy out only that, and save expense.'

Copy out only that… the nakedness of the soul before God, where the truest prayer is wordlessness before the Word.

༄

In the centuries since his death, more than ninety of his poems have been set to the music they seem to demand. 'Longing' was set by Henry Purcell, 'And art thou grieved' by John Blow, Purcell's contemporary. Forty poems were adapted for the Methodist hymnal by the Wesleys: 'The Elixir' (aka 'Teach me my God and King') is in 223 hymnals and 'Antiphon' ('Let all the world in every corner sing') in 103. In the last century, 'Vertue' was set ten times, once in French. Edmund Rubbra set 'Easter' as the first of his *Two songs for voice and string trio* (op.2, 1921); Ralph Vaughan Williams used four of Herbert's poems in his *Five Mystical Songs* (1911). Britten and Walton both set him, and most recently Judith Weir's 2005 work *Vertue* includes three poems.

IX

SAMUEL CROSSMAN
1624–1684

◆

ONE OF THE FINEST, most moving, of English Passiontide hymns is *NEH* 86 (*A&M* 63), Samuel Crossman's 'My song is love unknown'. But we know little about Crossman. The longest near-contemporary account of him is in the gossipy and bad tempered (and not always reliable) Antony à Wood's *Athenae Oxonienses* (The entry is under Richard Towgood, Crossman's predecessor as Dean of Bristol). It merely records his birthplace, where educated, sermons he preached before important people, and date of death.

Which was in February 1683/4. His father, also Samuel, was incumbent of Bradfield St George (then Bradfield Monachorum) near Bury St Edmunds, and his son was baptised on 28 September 1625. Of his early life we know nothing. He was admitted to Pembroke College, Cambridge as a sizar[1] in January 1641 – this status suggests the family was not well off, though it may have had some influential connections. He graduated BA in 1645 and MA in 1651 – perhaps the very unhappiest period in England's unhappy seventeenth century. The growing crisis between King and

---

[1] A sizar got some financial help from the College, and often had to perform some pretty humble duties for other students in return. It was a way that poor boys could get an education.

Samuel Crossman

Parliament over taxation and prerogative, rumbling on for the previous twenty years at least, broke into open rebellion in 1642. That Civil War divided father from son and mother from daughter, and its divisive effects are still with us. Add to that the bitter divisions, often driven by ignorant bigotry, in the Church between those supporting Archbishop Laud's attempt to introduce some beauty of holiness, music, and some ritual into the dull round of Anglican worship, and those who saw his reforms as creeping Roman Catholicism[2]. Then add the significant section of the community who argued the English Reformation had gone nowhere near far enough, who wanted to abolish episcopacy and all hierarchy, and in that Dissenting community (as it would later be called) the toxic quarrels between Independents (Congregationalists), Baptists, Presbyterians, Quakers, the Fifth Monarchy Men, the Ranters and so on. Cambridge, then a small town and a small University, was at the intellectual heart of the storm, and leaned if anything more to the side of Parliament and Puritanism than Oxford. Heady times, indeed, for a young man, and times when (so high did theological passions run) that you might quarrel with your barber when he was cutting your hair about, say, infant baptism or the innate, inevitable, inherited, corruption of all mankind. In Crossman's second year at Pembroke, the Parliamentary Army commander, the Earl of Manchester, authorised one William Dowsing to 'cleanse' the churches and college chapels of anything 'superstitious' or 'popish': and Dowsing began a career – which many Fellows fruitlessly resisted – of vandalism and destruction of which we have a full and self-satisfied account

---

[2] Van Dyck's portrait of William Laud in the Fitzwilliam Museum, Cambridge, captures stunningly the energy and quick temperedness of this remarkable man. Laud got many people's backs up by his vigorous, uncompromising reform of Anglican liturgy, with set hours of prayer, the insertion of communion rails, and a much more ritualistic approach to worship. He was also an Arminian, rejecting the Calvinist insistence on predestination (see Article 17 of the 39 Articles), and was hated for that too. Like James I, he recognised Rome as our 'mother church'.

A Joyful Noise

from Dowsing himself.[3] The windows of King's College Chapel survived because on a December day Dowsing and his

---

[3] I can't resist a long quotation from Dowsing's *Journal* to give a flavour of the times. You don't have to read it: 'At Pembroke-Hall, 1643, December 26. In the presence of Fellowes Mr. Weeden, Mr. Mapthorpe, and Mr. Sterne, and Mr. Quarles, and Mr. Felton, we broak 10 cherubims. We broake and pulled down 80 superstitious pictures; and Mr. Weeden told me, he could fetch a Statute Booke to shew, that pictures were not to be pulled down; I bad him fetch and shew it and they should stand; and he and Mr. Boldero told me, the clargie had only to doe in ecclesiastical matters, neither the Magistrate, nor the Parliament had any thing to doe; I told them I perceived they were of Cuzen's [John Cosin's] judgement, and told them I would prove the people had to doe as well as the clergie, and alledged, Acts i.15, 16, 23. (Calv[in]. on Acts i.) The 120 believers had the election of an apostle in the rome [place] of Judas. I cited Calvin, and in his Institutions, in the poynt of ministers elections, and I told them Josiah's reforming religion (1 Kings xxii. 21) with the other godly reforming Kings of Judah proved it; and for the taking down of images, I told them the Book of Homilys did prove it, which they so much honored, and alledged, p. 12, 13, 14, 15, 23 against the Peril of Idolatry [and the Queens Injunctions]. Others alledged cherubims to be lawfull by scripture (Deut. iv. 12, 16 and vii. 5, 25, 26; xii. 2) and that Moses and Solomon made them without any command. I deny'd it, and turned to Exod. xxv. 18, 22. Then they said, Solomon did make them without any order from God. I answered, he received a pattern from David, and read to them, 1 Chron. xxviii. 10, 11 to 18, 19. Weeden said, Reading Paul's sermons was better preaching then now is used, because it was not script[ural]. I told them, God saved by foolishness of preaching, not reading, and alleged, I Cor. i. 21; I told them, if reading was preaching, my child preaches as well as they, and they stared one on another without answere.

'More, Pembroke-Hall, 1643. Ashton: Laws made in time of warr were not of force. I alleged Magna Charta, made in time of warr, between Henry the Third and barrons, that was in force still, and Richard the 2d's tyme the like. Ashton said, the Parliament could not make laws, the King being away, and so many Members. I told them, their practice proved it, that chose Fellowes by the greater number present; and that the King had taken an oath to seal what both Houses voted. Maplethorpe said, he did not think my Lords Covenant was according to the Ordinance, and so I durst not abide by it, but thought I would run away, and used threatning speches ...

crew did not have enough time to do them. Crossman would have been in Cambridge at the time, might even have heard the smashing going on in Pembroke's old Chapel (now the Old Library).

Nobody could have known where all this was leading. The Rule of the Saints on Earth? Nobody had an overall plan: everyone made up the script as they went along, walking backwards, as so very often, into the future. Even to read about it is agonising. Parliament, supposedly standing for the liberty of the subject, was drastically purged in a military coup so that there would be a majority that would agree to behead the King for, save the mark, treason. And then what? All revolutions begin with high ideals, but I can only think of one that has not ended up in repressive dictatorship, as happened with the rule of Cromwell's Major-Generals, and with the suppression of freedom, not least of conscience. In the Protectorate, the diarist John Evelyn records, Anglican services were held in secret, behind locked doors.

We know not what Crossman thought at this time. But he was ordained into the Anglican Church, to whose 39 Articles he would have had formally to assent to be admitted to Cambridge. By 1647 he was Vicar of All Saints, one of the three parishes in Sudbury, Suffolk, and then later Rector of Dalham, Suffolk, and later, in plurality, Little Henny, Essex. And that raises questions about how, young as he was, he got what was a rather plum job, and it may give us a clue about the high profile he had later in the 1660s when there is no trace of any particular activity or publication that would have distinguished him.

Sudbury was an important place, one of the wealthy cloth towns of East Anglia. Like much of that region it was a hotbed of Reforming and Puritan sentiment during the sixteenth and seventeenth centuries. (Many families, like the Winthrops, left for the Massachusetts Bay Colony in 1630.) At the Dissolution, Henry VIII had granted the advowson of All Saints, owned by St Albans Abbey, to Thomas Eden, Clerk of the Court of Star Chamber, whose family held it for many generations. Crossman must have been presented to this living by the then head of the family, another Thomas Eden, and it is possible, as Bradfield is only 15 miles from Sudbury, that there may have been a connection between the Eden family and Crossman's father. Be that as it may: the Eden who presented Crossman to the living was an influential man. He had been at Pembroke, then went to Trinity Hall, eventually becoming Master, but was also MP for Cambridge and sat in the Long Parliament of the Revolution. He was one of those who took the Protestation oath of loyalty to Charles I, but in 1644 he also accepted the Solemn League and Covenant, which would have abolished episcopacy in England as well as Scotland. So Crossman's patron was both Royalist and Puritan, which seems to match his own position.

In 1651 he was given a second living, the Rectory of Little Henny, Essex – a sinecure, for by 1650 the church is recorded as 'fallen down'. (It is good to be reminded that our own headaches about redundant buildings and how (whether) to maintain them, and about declining congregations, are not new.) Meanwhile he had married, and All Saints' Register records baptisms of several children of Samuel and Grace Crossman. He also became minister of the 'separated' – that is, non-conforming – congregation at Sudbury. The practice was not uncommon, but he could not have done it had he not had sympathy with the Puritan position.

But the Restoration in May 1660 brough yet more change to the pattern of English religious life. Crossman must have won some considerable standing among Puritan and Presbyterian divines, for when in April 1661 Charles II called the Savoy Conference by Royal Warrant to consider possible changes in the Prayer Book, Crossman was elected as one of twelve delegates on the Puritan and Presbyterian side. With twelve Bishops, they met to try to make the Book theologically and liturgically acceptable to both sides. Richard Baxter, for the Presbyterian side, presented a new liturgy, but in the end no agreement was reached. The next year a new Parliament, dominated by men who sought no compromise but rather restoration of the *status quo ante* – which is never possible – passed the Uniformity Act, making use of the Book of Common

Samuel Crossman

Prayer everywhere compulsory. The Act enjoined that every clergyman, every schoolmaster, every Fellow of a College, refusing to express by 24 August 1662 his unfeigned consent to everything contained in the *Book of Common Prayer*, was to be prevented from holding any benefice. About two thousand clergy resigned or were ejected, and Crossman was apparently formally ejected from his sinecure living at Little Henny: which fact seems firmly to put him in the Dissenting camp. He was imprisoned for preaching in defiance of the law. In 1665, however, he conformed, and on 28 October was re-ordained deacon and priest by Isaac Barrow, Bishop of Norwich – the man who taught Isaac Newton maths and worked out the basic theorem that Newton would develop into calculus. Crossman was given a curacy of St Gregory and St Peter's, Sudbury's two other churches, and, interestingly, made one of the King's chaplains. It may be that the trend of events in the first four years of the Restoration led Crossman to feel that he could do his work best within the Established Church. Efforts made in Parliament to pass a Toleration Bill had failed, as too many MPs feared the King might try to extend toleration to Roman Catholics. Possibly Crossman felt that to be in any group protected (or not) by any Act that Parliament might or might not pass would be less safe than being within the Established Church. He certainly must have been in touch with the Court through his duties as a King's Chaplain, and in 1667 he was made a Prebendary of Bristol Cathedral. Not only would that certainly have made his financial position more comfortable, but it also indicates that he had friends in high, perhaps the highest, places, in whose gift such preferment lay. But life in Bristol may well have been difficult, for it had a Dissenter community who probably looked askance at his conforming. Several of Crossman's letters to Archbishop Sancroft stress his difficulties with the Dissenters on Bristol Corporation. Perhaps it was these circumstances which prompted him (fruitlessly) to petition Sancroft in 1678 for an Irish prebend. In the end, he became Dean of Bristol in 1684, when the aged Richard Towgood died, but survived less than a year.

A Joyful Noise

He was clearly a divisive figure. Some contemporaries are blunt: the Chancellor of the diocese, Henry Jones, told Sancroft, 'Mr Crossman, our new Deane dyed this morning: a man lamented by few either of the citie or neighbourhood. He hath left a debt upon our Church of 300*l*.' On the other hand, just before he died he wrote *The Last Testimony and Declaration of the Reverend Samuel Crossman, D.D. and Dean of Bristol setting forth his dutiful and true affection to the Church of England as by law established* ... which was published with a preface from Sir John Knight, Sheriff of Bristol, future Tory MP and very anti-Dissenter, who wrote, 'it was this gentleman's lot ... to fall under the lash and scandal of several reproaches: wherein he was so solicitous to clear himself'. Crossman was indeed defending himself and his actions, and praised Charles II for his ‹most admired conduct of the government for our common good', and deplored 'whatever bold insolencies have been lately animated by some to the affronting the true line of succession'.

He published little, so far as we know. The five sermons that have survived, all preached in the 1660s – one before the London's Lord Mayor– do not tell us much. What may be more of a clue to his inner world is *The Young Mans Monitor, or A Modest Offer toward the Pious, and Vertuous Composure of Life from Youth to Riper Years* (London, 1664), written during his wilderness years. This book has all the characteristics of a seventeenth-century devotional work, designed as both moral guide and precept, and offering material, especially in its poems, for serious meditation.[4] The title page makes clear its agenda, with a text from Ps. 119: 'Wherewithal shall a young

---

[4] The practice of disciplined meditation was widespread in all confessions, and the practice and material often crossed apparently rigid boundaries. The egregious iconoclast William Dowsing used Francis Quarles' *Emblemes* (1635), and the sources of the Protestant Quarles' pictures are Jesuit and Benedictine. John Donne used the Ignatian techniques of meditation, as did George Herbert, and much seventeenth-century religious poetry is both fruit of and material for disciplined devotional meditation. Which, as in the case of Herbert (see above, pp. 72-3), raises interesting questions about audience.

man cleanse his way? . . .' Inside is an address to 'Ingenuous Youths ... upon whom the eyes of all are justly set ... May your youth be as the Spring for Loveliness; your riper years as the Summer for real fruitfulness ...' Then come eleven chapters, each with a relevant scriptural text as heading, and then, as if to sum up in a mere 20 pages all the book has been teaching, we come to a title page for a book, so to speak, within a book – the pagination starts afresh – to which the whole previous book has been prologue: *The Young Mans Meditation, or Some few Sacred Poems upon Select Subjects and Scriptures*. Tellingly, the page has a quotation from George Herbert, whose influence is clear in the poems that follow, especially in 'My song is Love Unknown': 'A verse my find him who a Sermon flies'. The nine poems that follow do form a sort of sequence, and 'My song' needs to be seen as part of that whole.[5]

The typography of the first poem, its title in large capitals, proclaims that what the reader has in his hand, this sequence of poems, actually *is* 'THE GIFT' up to which the book has been leading. The supporting epigraph is John 4.10: '*If thou knowest the gift of God*'. The next, untitled, poem addresses the mortality of the flesh – '*All flesh is grass... for ever*'. Isaiah 40:6-8' – and the enduring Word of God. Then comes an anti-Roman poem 'Upon the 5 of November', with the text '*The archers have sorely grieved him, and shot at him ... strength*, Gen. 49:23,24': the Gunpowder Plot, as it came to be called, was a regularly set theme for essays and poems in schools and universities – Milton wrote two Latin poems on it when he was at Cambridge.

---

[5] The poems were republished in 1678 in The Young Man's Calling *or, The whole duty of youth in a serious and compassionate address to all young persons to remember their Creator in the days of their youth : together with Remarks upon the lives of several excellent young persons of both sexes, as well ancient as modern, noble and others, who have been famous for piety and vertue in their generations: with twelve curious pictures...* – there is a lot more! Most of the 276 pages preceding the 20 of the poems mix advice on godly living, with uplifting tales from biblical and historical sources. The book was reissued after his death.

A Joyful Noise

Next comes a moving meditation on Isaiah 53:5, '*He was wounded for our transgressions ... we are healed*', which begins 'Thus died the Prince of life, thus he/That could not die, even died for me.' Then, following the epigraph '*God forbid that I should glory save in the Cross of our Lord Jesus Christ* Gal. 6:14' – which pinpoints the tension between the poet – and he may pun on his own name – creating something which is *his*, and the forgetfulness of self in the Love of God. Then, 'My song is love unknown': the phrase 'Love unknown' is the title of one of George Herbert's most poignant poems. This is a rich poem. Even though utterly overwhelmed at the grace shown him, the speaker is Jesus' 'Friend', and thus in a sense worthy, not one of 'they' who first welcomed him to Jerusalem on Palm Sunday and then 'made strange' and called 'Crucify'. But 'mine the tomb wherein he lay': as if he is identifying with Joseph of Arimathea, the secret follower of Jesus, but who openly honoured Christ's body, as well as recognising that the Lord of Life accepted the mortality of all men: and where is 'here', in the last verse? Is it beside the tomb, contemplating the wonderful life-giving death of his Friend? Or in that out of time moment of contemplation of the mystery?

The next poem's title 'The Pilgrims Farewel to the World', '*For here we have no continuing city, but we seek one to come.* Heb. 13:14', leads on to the Last Things: 'Christs future coming to Judgment, the Christians present meditation' – the theme *Behold he cometh with clouds, ands every eye shall see him.* Rev. 1:7', then the hope of 'The Resurrection', *Though after my skin worms destroy this body: yet in my flesh shall I see God,* Job 19:26' and the joy of '*Heaven*': '*When shall I come and appear before God* Ps. *42:2*', which is in two parts. Each has been turned into a hymn, 'Jerusalem on high' and 'Sweet Place', both popular in America, but less often heard in the United Kingdom. The poems thus form a sort of sequence, with the saving Mystery at the centre, the heart – and in seventeenth-century writing, position often does matter. The poem we love is part of a larger whole, which is designed to lead one through the Passion to the contemplation of salvation, when all tears shall be wiped from all eyes.

Samuel Crossman

These are not the poems of an amateur, new to the game: what *else* did he write? We may never know.

A footnote: Ronald Blythe, who lived near Little Henny, recounted how, soon after the First World War, the composer Geoffrey Shaw[6] took the composer John Ireland out to lunch. He startled Ireland by saying, 'I want a tune for this lovely poem' and handed him a slip of paper with Crossman's poem on it. Ireland read it, became lost in it, took the menu, and wrote on the back of it for a few minutes — 'Here is your tune.' And so the Church in Passiontide can together share Crossman's heartbreak, and joy.

---

[6] He was one of the brothers of Martin Shaw, also a composer, who worked closely with Ralph Vaughan Williams on *Songs of Praise* (1928).

X

JOHN MASON
?1646–1694

ை

JOHN MASON HAS ONLY one hymn in *NEH* out of the many he wrote and published in his *Spiritual Songs* of 1683 – a volume significant as the first collection of verse hymns, as distinct from metrical psalm paraphrases, written by an Anglican priest for singing. But that one hymn has become something of a favourite of mine, not least for musical reasons. Mason's 'How shall I sing that majesty?'(373) the Editors of *EH* quarried from a much longer poem, to include in the first edition of 1906. In *NEH* it has a decent enough tune (Thomas Tallis, after all: Third Mode Melody, rev. Ralph Vaughan Williams) but it is usually now sung to one of the very best of modern hymn tunes, 'Coe Fen', by my friend Ken Naylor (1931-1991). Ken had been Organ Scholar of Magdalene College, Cambridge, and was one of the finest organists – and jazz pianists – of his generation. He was an inspiring Director of Music at The Leys School in Cambridge, which overlooks Coe Fen, and his fine tune (with a grand descant) has become a favourite here and in America. (Did I not remark earlier how foregrounded a tune could be, when the ideal is interdependent with the words?)

Back, though, to Mason, whom the 1885 edition of the *Dictionary of National Biography* calls 'enthusiast and poet'[1]/

---

[1] 'Enthusiast' retains that eighteenth-century distrust of enthusiasm in anything to do with religion because of the traumas caused by it in the previous century.

John Mason

He was an ancestor of John Mason Neale (see Chapter XXI). He was probably the third son of Thomas and Margaret Mason who was christened in Irchester, Northamptonshire, in March 1646. There is a fascinating (and tantalising in what it does *not* say) contemporary account of his life and opinions by Revd Henry Maurice,[2] Rector of Tyringham, whom the Archbishop of York commissioned to investigate thoroughly the scandal that engulfed Mason's later years when he was Rector of Water Stratford. Maurice, who was presented to Tyringham nearby the year after Mason was presented to Water Stratford, must have had to deal with some of the shockwaves his neighbour caused. Maurice did his homework, writing to many people who knew Mason. He mentions young Mason at school in Strixton, and a teacher saying of him, 'if he liv'd, he was like to be a violent Zealot'. Prophetic ... He was admitted a sizar – which suggests no great wealth – of Clare Hall, Cambridge, on 16 May 1661. Maurice quotes a 'Mr Gray, who was his Chamber-Fellow at *Cambridge,* in a letter dated *Sept.* 22. that he was but careless in some part of his Life there, that he would be sometimes starting of Questions, in reference to the usages of the Church of *England* (which seem'd to discover some dissatisfaction) and with greater earnestness, than points discours'd only for dispute sake are ordinarily manag'd.'

He graduated BA in 1664, and MA in 1668, and went as curate to Isham, Northamptonshire, where he lived with Mr

---

[2] AN Impartial Account OF Mr *JOHN MASON* OF *WATER-STRATFORD,* AND HIS SENTIMENTS. By *H. MAURICE,* Rector of *Tyringham, Bucks. (*London 1695*).*The two epigraphs imply much; the one from Romans 12.3, the King James Bible translates,' Let no-one think of himself more highly than he ought to think; but to think soberly', and the other, from Seneca's tragedy about the madness of the hero Hercules, 'Proxima puris/ Sor[s] est manibus, nescire nefas', if put back in context, is very suggestive: *mens vesano concita motu,/ error caecus qua coepit eat:/solus te iam praestare potest/furor insontem; proxima puris/ sors est manibus nescire nefas* – 'Let your mind still race with insanity, may blind error continue as it began: the only thing now that can offer you innocence is madness; after pure hands, the next best fate is ignorance of evil.'

Sawyer the incumbent. There he got a reputation not only for personal probity, but also for obsessive studying, saying 'he had lost his time at the University, and must regain it'.

After a short time at Isham, he was presented in October 1668 as vicar of Stantonbury (Buckinghamshire). There was no vicarage and no congregation, and he may well have given that living to act as chaplain to Sir John Wittewronge, the local notable, who, like Cromwell, was of Independent (i.e. what we would call Congregationalist) views, and had fought for Parliament. But he had recently been given a baronetcy, and with it respectability, by that underestimated King, Charles II. Mason's first published work was a funeral sermon for Sir John's daughter, Clare. For want of his parishioners of his own, Mason used very frequently to minister to the people of Haversham just across the river Ouse and there he became friendly with James Wrexham, a Puritan preacher, who had been ejected as vicar of Kimble Magna and of Woburn for refusing to subscribe to the Prayer Book under the Uniformity Act. Haversham became what he called his 'beloved place'; his affection was returned by its people. While at Stantonbury he married his wife Mary, and as they had their first child, Martha, baptised at Stantonbury, she may indeed have been one of the Haversham people. She could have been a connection of the Wittewronges.

Six years later Wittewronge presented him to the rectory of St Giles, Water Stratford. Initially, his conduct at St Giles' was that expected of a priest of the Anglican Church As By Law Established, if of somewhat Dissenting tendencies. (He could not have matriculated at Cambridge without signing the 39 Articles of Religion, the fundamental identity statement of the Church of England.) A hardworking, moderate cleric, of 'severe morals', Maurice calls him, if 'a rigid Calvinist, and not a little inclining to Antinomianism' and strongly accepting the idea of predestination – which is after all one of the 39 Articles (no. XVII). The distinguished theologian Richard Baxter (who died in 1691, before Mason's tumultuous last years) called him the glory of the Church of England…The frame of his spirit was so heavenly, his deportment so humble and obliging, his discourse of spiritual things so weighty, with such apt words and delightful air, that it charmed all that had any spiritual relish.

He won considerable reputation, too, as a poet. In 1683 a London printer published his collected *Spiritual songs, or, Songs of praise to Almighty God upon several occasions Together with the Song of Songs which is Solomons: [F]irst turn'd, then par[ap]hrased in English verse. To which may be added, Penitential cries.* This book, with some expansions, went through 16 editions before 1761, of which all save the last were published anonymously. Alexander Pope and John Wesley both quote him, and Isaac Watts ('When I survey the wondrous Cross', *NEH* 95, and others) uses him freely. Mason wrote more than 30 hymns, of which quite a few are found in early eighteenth-century collections, and two made it into the *Oxford Hymn Book* (eds after 1908). It may be that Mason's growing anticipation of the Second Coming – in belief in its imminence he was by no means alone – and his interest in the place of music and song in the joys of the new Creation were the spurs to the book's composition. After all, as the Prayer Book version of Psalm 95 puts it, 'Let us come before his presence with thanksgiving, and make ourselves glad in him with psalms', and 96 concurs: 'O sing unto the Lord a new song.' One could take both injunctions very literally.

Two deaths seem to mark an emotional watershed. James Wrexham of Haversham, and Mason's wife Mary (by whom he had four children) both died in 1687. Wrexham, according to Maurice, first 'put him upon *Revelation Thoughts*'; he was deeply affected by Mary's death. His stance became increasingly radically Calvinist and, especially, apocalyptic. In 1690 he preached a sermon on the parable of the wise and foolish virgins – you can see how that would lend itself to an attempt to interpret apocalyptic passages of scripture in the light of recent events personal and political. It was published in the following year as *The Midnight Cry. Sermon on the Parable of the Ten Virgins* (there were 5 editions by 1694) and it made some stir in an age when millenarian ideas and movements (like the Quakers and Levellers and Ranters) were rife and sermons were hot news – what you might read aloud to your family, as was the custom (for example) of the shopkeeper Thomas Turner in Lewes in the 1750s. (Turner subjected them to Archbishop Tillotson's, which are of industrial strength and weight.) Mason became more and more a Dissenter in his ministry, administering no sacraments and focussing simply on preaching. More and more he spoke about the Second Coming of Christ, which he, like so many, was convinced was imminent. Soon he preached only on the personal reign of Christ on earth, which he announced was about to begin in Water Stratford. His eloquent teaching attracted some believers, who accepted his extreme doctrine of predestination – stanzas which the *NEH* editors cut from the final version they printed of 373. Indeed, his followers set up an encampment, in fact a commune, on a plot of common land just outside Water Stratford, which they called the Holy Ground. Noisy meetings took place in barns and cottages, and day and night the parsonage was loud with dancing and singing. But Mason was not well: he constantly suffered headaches, became so sensitive to noise that he retired to an empty house, where the very sound of his own footsteps and even his own voice, low in prayer, caused him pain.

On Sunday, 22 April 1694, from a window in the parsonage, Mason described to a crowd a vision of the Saviour he had experienced, he said, on the previous Easter Monday. Christ appeared 'in a Crimson Garment, his Countenance exceeding beautiful', with a 'deep *Scarlet* Robe down to his feet.' From that time he used no prayers save the last clause of the Lord's Prayer, and announced that his work was accomplished, as the reign on earth had already begun. He died of a quinsy[3] very soon afterwards, and was buried in his own church on 22 May. But his followers remained convinced of the arrival of the Millennium, and of the immortality of their prophet,

---

[3] A rare and often serious complication of tonsillitis.

John Mason

and there were not a few who refused to believe he was dead. The incumbent who succeeded him, Isaac Rushworth, exasperatedly had his body exhumed, and shown to the crowd, but many remained unconvinced, and had finally to be evicted from the 'Holy Ground.' Even so, meetings in a house in the village continued for sixteen years afterwards. Even as late as 1740, there were still some remnants of the group.

Poor man. Rest in peace.

Well, what of the hymn we all know? 'How shall I sing that majesty?', (*A&M* 472) like his other hymns, shows the influence of the wonderful poems of George Herbert in its affective, acutely personal piety and its firm grounding in an exhaustive knowledge of the Bible. But we do sing only the first four verses, with that splendid climax in the last lines of verse four (where the descant rises to a height which silences argument): 'Thou art a Sea without a Shore,/ A Sun without a Sphere;/Thy Time is now and evermore;/ Thy Place is everywhere.' In that imagery, good theology: and in those verses we do perhaps see the best of him, and glimpse the way Mason, like many of his generation, was absolutely soaked in Scripture, indeed used it as an interpretative and predictive model for current affairs. But the editors were wise to prune verses such as

> Unbelief is a Raging Wave,
> Dashing against a Rock:
> If God doth not his Israel Save,
> Then let Egyptians mock...

> Mercy, that shining Attribute,
> The Sinner's Hope and Plea!
> Huge Hosts of Sins in their Pursuit,
> Are drown'd in thy Red Sea ...

Or, despite its biblical source in *Exodus* XXXIII.23,

> Thy bright Back-parts, O God of Grace,
> I Humbly here Adore;

A Joyful Noise

    Shew me thy Glory and Thy Face,
    That I may praise Thee more.
    Since none can see thy Face and live,
    For me to die is best;
    Thro' Jordan's Streams who would not dive,
    To Land at Canaan's Rest?

Even so, I love the hymn we have – as the editors left it. It tries to express (and of course fails) what we have all felt, that awe, and delight, that need to sing, when we are blessed with those brief moments of wild surmise, when we glimpse from our pigmy height the Ocean of Love and the pacific Energy that lies in and through and beyond all Creation.

XI

THOMAS KEN
1637–1711

THOMAS KEN WAS NOT a great poet. His poetical works were published (1721) in four volumes, but rarely leave Library shelves. If you look at *NEH* 182 (*A&M* 310), 'Her virgin eyes saw God incarnate born', you might see why. Yet a few of his poems are among the best known hymns in *NEH* and *A&M*. Of two of them, a morning prayer and an evening one (232- *A&M* 1, appropriately – 'Awake my soul and with the sun'), and 244 (*A&M* 10) ('Glory to thee my God this night' usually sung to Tallis's Canon[1]), Bishop Heber of Calcutta (see Chapter XVIII), remarked on 'the[ir] universal popularity', and said that they were then 'more generally sung, by a cottage fire-side, than any other compositions with which [he was] acquainted', being 'in country parishes, almost universally used'. A few years later, the prolific James Montgomery (see Chapter XVII) said,

> Bishop Ken has laid the Church of Christ under abiding obligations by his three hymns, Morning, Evening, and Midnight. Had he endowed three hospitals, he might have been less a benefactor to posterity. . . The well-

---

[1] Thomas Tallis wrote a hymn in 1567 called 'God Grant with Grace', so often sung, and in canon, that its tune became simply 'Tallis's Canon.' Ken wrote his poem in 1686 for this tune. The *NEH* version has only 5 of Ken's eleven stanzas.

A Joyful Noise

known doxology, 'Praise God from whom all blessings flow,'[2] etc., is a masterpiece at once of amplification and compression. No one stanza of English verse has been so often, so universally, and so heartily, sung in the worship of God.

Fair enough. But why a whole essay in a book with this sort of agenda on someone with so modest an output? When you look at a life (1637-1711) that spans the terrible times of the Civil War and its aftermath – which created a split in English society between what used to be called Whig and Tory, and which is still balefully with us; and then the crisis and revolution that deposed James II; and then the long war over succession to the Spanish throne that sucked in every European Power and for the first time took European conflict to the other side of the globe – well, you remember the force of the old Chinese curse, 'May you live in interesting times'. Ken's times were interesting indeed, and this gentle, peaceable man could not escape their repercussions and the personal anguish that went with them. Looking at him might remind us of what so many of our nameless forebears had to face.

His father – a lawyer, of a Somerset family – married twice; his second wife was Martha Chalkhill, sister of a poet now largely forgotten except by students scrabbling for a PhD topic. Thomas was her younger son. When he was four, she died, and his father followed when he was fourteen. When he was eight, his elder sister, Anne, married Izaak Walton, who despite the forty year gap in their ages became a wise and loving guardian and mentor to Thomas.

That marriage took place as the First Civil War was drawing to its bloody close at Naseby. The chain of consequence that nobody foresaw and nobody could control led four years later to the execution of Charles I – a sixteen year old Samuel Pepys,

---

[2] 'Praise God from whom all blessings flow,/ Praise him all creatures here below;/Praise him above ye heavenly host,/Praise Father, Son and Holy Ghost.'

Thomas Ken

with whom Ken would later, as Chaplain to the Fleet, endure a horridly stormy voyage to Tangier[3] and back in 1683-4, watched it[4] – and to the dour Protectorate of Cromwell. Those years, when Parliament, and then the Rump[5] Parliament, was without any organised opposition, were probably some of the unhappiest in English social history, and rule by the military became usual. They even banned Christmas![6] John Evelyn's diary records how Anglican services had to be held behind locked doors in private houses, with someone watching, for fear of the thought police. Churches were stripped of anything that the bigots could call idolatrous. The schools and universities were purged of those who were not politically correct – for example, many parsons were ejected from their livings, Fellows of Colleges deprived, schoolmasters who did not toe the party line sacked. A popular verse of 1653 ran:

---

[3] It had come to the English Crown as part of the dowry of Charles II's queen, Catherine of Braganza,

[4] Pepys advised Lord Dartmouth, Commodore of the Fleet, to take Ken, not least because a man of 'piety, authority and learning', as senior chaplain of the fleet, was needed to oversee the other chaplains, who were said to be little better than the current decadent state of the navy.

[5] So called because very little but a rump was left of the Long Parliament (1642-1660) after the military coup of 6 December 1648. Colonel Thomas Pride and his soldiers stood outside the entrance to St Stephen's Chapel and, as the Commons convened that morning, arrested 45 MPs and barred from going in a further 186 whom the Army thought were unlikely to support it in punishing the King. 86 more MPs left in protest. This left barely 200 Members. A determined clique forced through an 'Act' on 6 January 1649, to try Charles I for high treason – which carried the death penalty – ignoring the negative vote a few days before of the small number of peers still sitting in the Lords. Yet this Parliament is held up still by many as an example of good British democracy!

[6] Yet Cromwell was not averse to parties, or music, and is recorded as once uproariously pouring a flagon of wine over a lady dinner guest's head. (I have a lot of pity for that man, trapped by circumstance and consequences into actions and positions he would once have abhorred …)

> Wee'l down with all the Versities
> Where learning is professt,
> Because they practice and maintain
> The language of the Beast;
> Wee'l drive the Doctors out of doors,
> And all that Learned be;
> Wee'l cry all arts and learning down,
> And hey then up go we.

And they did. Praise God Barebone's – yes, he was called that – Parliament in 1653 discussed suppressing the Universities entirely. One Herring introduced several motions to that effect, proposing preserving only two Colleges 'for the study of good doctrine'. (A Red Herring ...)

When Ken, aged thirteen, went to Winchester College, its Warden was an eminent Presbyterian, Dr John Harrys, a fine Greek scholar, who had managed to persuade an ignorant Parliamentary visitation in 1649 that the College was being run on principles of which they could approve. So he kept his job. Ken left Winchester in 1656 to enter Hart Hall, Oxford – later Hertford College. However, as a Wykehamist, he had a link with New College, which William of Wykeham (Richard II's Chancellor), Bishop of Winchester, had also founded, and he was admitted there in 1657 as a probationary Fellow. In 1658 Cromwell died, and the University ridded itself, as speedily as it dared, of its recent Puritanism – and the Colleges of many of their Commonwealth-approved Fellows. Whatever his Winchester training under Harrys, Ken graduated in 1661 a thorough High Churchman in the mould of Charles I's Archbishop Laud, who recognised that in holiness there is beauty. Shortly thereafter, he was ordained, and became Chaplain to the wife of William Lord Maynard, Comptroller of Charles II's household. Maynard had suffered much under the Commonwealth for his loyalty to the Crown, and certainly helped confirm Ken in hostility to a doctrinaire Puritanism.

Many men indeed had suffered badly then, denied employment or security simply for being Royalist or Anglican.

Thomas Ken

Izaak Walton (Ken's brother in law) was one, and that situation is one of the shadows on the clear water of *The Compleat Angler*. Another was Walton's close friend George Morley. Deprived of his canonry of Christ Church, Oxford, he had fled to young Charles II's Court in The Hague and at the Restoration a grateful Charles (a monarch far more shrewd and circumspect than his nickname of a famous Newmarket stallion would suggest) made him Bishop of Worcester, and in 1662 translated him to Winchester. In that smaller society (under 5 million or so in all England), where everyone who was anyone knew everybody else who was anyone, Ken's entrée to the circles of the Court, and his friendship with Morley through Walton – Walton had joined his household after Anne Ken died in 1662, and Morley made Ken his domestic Chaplain – led by 1669 to a prebend at Winchester Cathedral and a Rectory which gave him a comfortable living. Morley's generous patronage was some return for the home and safety given him by Anne Ken, at her cottage near Stafford, when he was in real want and prohibited from any employment.

Ken soon became a Fellow of Winchester College, and did much good work among in the town's really poor districts, becoming well known too as a fine preacher. These seem to have been happy, peaceful years, and he is known to have owned a chamber organ and to have played the lute – Antony à Wood's *Athenae Oxonienses* records how he had joined in the musical life of Oxford. In 1674 he published *A Manual of Prayer for the Scholars of Winchester College. (*In the second edition of 1686 he added the three hymns we know.) A year later he made a tour of Europe with Anne's son Izaak – a Grand Tour before that became common – whose education at Winchester and at Oxford he had overseen. Rome's Baroque ecclesiastical grandeur in that year of Papal Jubilee seems to have left him less than impressed – though as Antony à Wood says, some did say, snidely, that he was 'tinged with Popery' on his return.

In 1679 Ken's reputation for wisdom, kindness and learning brought him appointment as Chaplain to the seventeen year old Mary, Charles II's niece, who in 1677 had been married

A Joyful Noise

to her first cousin, William of Orange: a fateful match indeed. She had asked for an Anglican chaplain as some relief from the dour, strict Calvinism of her dour husband: an interesting sidelight on the marriage. Ken was 'horribly unsatisfied' with William, and told him off more than once: about the way he treated his wife, for example. Once he insisted, to William's great displeasure, that a promise of marriage, made to an English noblewoman by one of the Prince's relatives, was morally and legally binding. After a year, though, he returned to England, to Winchester, and Charles made him a Chaplain in Ordinary.

Those rebukes to William show a moral toughness in Ken that few would have suspected from his eirenic demeanour. An example: in Winchester he had a decent house in the Close. But when Charles and his raffish court visited Winchester in 1683 to inspect the new palace Christopher Wren was building, Ken refused to lend the house to Nell Gwynne, then reigning mistress. Charles gave way, and bore no ill will, for two years later, when the see of Bath and Wells fell vacant, the King exclaimed, 'Where is the good little man that refused his lodging to poor Nelly?' and decided he must be Bishop.

That moral courage, and physical courage, was called onto the full during the voyage with Pepys to Tangier. The weather was awful on both the going and return. In Tangier, Ken courageously preached in the Anglican church ‹particularly in reproof of the vices of this town›, sometimes in the presence of officials including the governor, Colonel Percival Kirke, a capable soldier but one who was also described as a 'foul-mouthed, drunken, bullying sensualist'. Dining quietly in Pepys's cabin Ken and Pepys one evening discussed the ‹viciousness of this place and its being time for God Almighty to destroy it›. Another time they confronted an angry Kirke about the ‹excessive liberty of swearing and blaspheming we observe here›. With Kirke, an uncongenial and inescapable companion on that crowded small ship, they embarked, after long delays, on the long and in the event dangerous return journey, in one of the worst gales for decades.

Almost immediately after his consecration as Bishop

in January 1685 he was summoned to the King's deathbed. He demanded that Lady Portsmouth (Louise de Kérouaille, another mistress) and the Catholic Father Huddleston remove themselves, but Charles was adamant that he would receive the Sacrament only from Father Huddlestone, and die a Roman Catholic.

As Bishop, Ken took the oath of allegiance to James II, openly Roman Catholic while yet as King legally Head of the Church of England. It is clear that they respected and liked each other: James called him 'the best preacher among the Protestants', despite Ken's preaching against the growing influence of Roman Catholicism at Court. But it was an explosive situation. James, Duke of Monmouth, Charles's illegitimate son by his early love, Lucy Walter, rebelled and was heavily defeated. Ken stood by him, which cannot have been easy, when he was beheaded on Tower Hill by the notorious Jack Ketch[7]. He then returned to Somerset. He appealed to James to stop the dreadful carnage visited on the rebels by the Royal commanders, Feversham, and Ken's old *bête noire*, Kirke. He did what he could for the prisoners, held in dreadful conditions in the jails of Taunton, Bridgewater and Wells, even in the Cathedral cloisters, and interceded fruitlessly for them with the appalling Judge Jeffreys, Lord Chief Justice and then Lord Chancellor.

But this was only the start. In 1688 James issued a Declaration of Indulgence to Catholics and Dissenters. Fearing that by publishing it they would give episcopal recognition to Roman Catholicism and that the Declaration unilaterally set aside decisions made in Parliament, Ken and six other bishops (including Sancroft, Archbishop of Canterbury) refused to publish it. James, advised badly by his Chancellor, Jeffreys, committed them to the Tower, and put them on trial: they were

[7] Evelyn's *Diary*: 'He would not make use of a cap or other circumstance, but lying down, bid the fellow to do his office better than to the late Lord Russell, and gave him gold; but the wretch made five chops before he had his head off; which so incensed the people, that had he not been guarded and got away, they would have torn him to pieces.'

acquitted to popular delight. The Seven Bishops became the subject of a portrait print by an unknown artist that was copied and reissued many times over the next year or so. But feelings, already high, now ran higher, and Parliament invited Dutch William and his wife, James's own daughter, to invade – she might have not had much choice in the matter. (Had the wind, the 'Protestant Wind', not stayed stubbornly easterly, William would not have got his troops down the Channel, and James's fleet – his justifiable pride and joy, which Pepys had thoroughly reformed – would not have been bottled up in the Thames unable to clobber the Dutch … another of those 'what ifs?' of history.)

Ken was one of those who felt that an oath was absolutely binding. He had sworn the oath of allegiance to James, and despite his growing unease at the King's religious policies felt that he could not simply forget it and swear allegiance to the new joint sovereigns.[8] Of what value would such an oath have been? Inevitably, he was ejected from his see, deprived of his income, and reduced to near poverty. He never accepted his deposition, and used the episcopal signature, 'Thomas Bath and Wells' until well into Anne's reign. For the next 22 years, until his death, he found a home at Longleat with his friend Thomas Thynne, Lord Weymouth, whom he had known since Oxford.

❦

Assessments of Ken have varied. Gilbert Burnet, Bishop of Salisbury, in his *History of His Own Time*, which he began in 1683, is quite guarded about the man he knew: Ken was

---

[8] There were many honest men in office who felt the same. Up to 400 clergy refused the oath, and were deprived of office under the Crown. Similarly, when George of Hanover, 'in pudding time came o'er' there were many who felt that his legitimacy as King, even though he was conveniently Protestant, was compromised when the lawful, lineal heir was alive. There were, however, as there always are, many Vicars of Bray – a song with a good tune we were taught as a class to sing at primary school. I did not then understand what it was all about.

Thomas Ken

> of an ascetic course of life, and yet of a very lively temper, but too hot and sudden. He had a very edifying way of preaching; but it was more apt to move the passions, than to instruct. So that his sermons were rather beautiful than solid; yet his way in them was very taking.

By contrast, the High Church party saw him as saintly, able to move in a 'licentious' court while remaining 'unspotted' himself, a paragon of piety. William Lisle Bowles, in his biography of Ken (1831) quotes a poem typifying this view. I quote, you will be glad to read, only the first of eleven stanzas on Ken...

> Dead to all else, alive to God alone,
> KEN, the confessor meek, abandons power,
> Palace, and mitre, and cathedral throne,
> (A shroud alone reserved), and, in the bower
> Of meditation, hallows every hour
> With orison, and strews, in life's decline,
> With pale hand, o'er his evening path, thy flower,
> O Poetry! pouring the lay divine,
> In tributary love, before Jehovah's shrine.

What are beyond question are the courage, honour, patience and charity with which he negotiated the strains and troubles of his lifetime, as uncertain and morally confusing as ours. Some of his prayers survive: 'Teach me, O my God, to use this world so not to abuse it, to receive and manage all thy temporal blessings with thankfulness to thee, sobriety to myself, and charity to all besides.' We can say Amen to that. And sing his hymns with the humility and gratefulness they teach.

XII

NAHUM TATE
1652–1715

'WHILE SHEPHERDS WATCHED THEIR Flocks by night' must be one of the best known (and most parodied) Christmas hymns; it has even been translated into Esperanto – twice. As a metrical resetting of the Gospel's account of the Annunciation to the Shepherds it is elegant and succinct. At Easter we often sing, 'Jesus Christ is risen today, /Our triumphant holy day.' So to whom de we owe these two old warhorses?

Naming him after one of the less read Minor Prophets might not seem the most auspicious start to your son's literary career. Perhaps you could not know he eventually would be a writer. Nahum's father, Faithful Teate the Younger (his son later dropped the first 'e'), the author of a long poem, *Ter Tria*, on the Trinity, was the (very) Puritan Rector of Castlereagh in Kilmore, until his house was torched because he had told the government of plans for the Catholic (and vehemently anti-Puritan) 1641 uprising. He fled, followed by his family, to Dublin. Briefly, the family lived in the Provost's lodgings in Trinity College, Dublin, where he and his father (another Faithful) had been students and he was Vice-Provost. Around 1648 he had moved to England, to an appointment at Salisbury Cathedral, and in 1650 he took the living of East Greenwich. (His eldest son, yet another Faithful, was sent to Pembroke College, Cambridge, and eventually became 'Preacher of the

Nahum Tate

Gospel' at Sudbury from 1654-6, where he must have known Samuel Crossman). Faithful the elder was back in Ireland, invited by Henry Cromwell, then Lord Deputy, by 1658.

Nahum, his second son, followed the family tradition in letters and religion: he graduated BA from Trinity, Dublin in 1672. (In his final year he had been made a Scholar.) By 1676 he was in London writing for his living. And golly, what an output! By the end of the decade he was writing furiously: in passionate support of Charles II, (and later, to start with, of James II's accession despite his Catholicism), and he was deep in the frantic, precarious world of writing for the theatre – pretty much the equivalent of modern young graduates scrabbling to get into 'the media' and a chance of fame and fortune. Some made it; many, many more did not. John Dryden, who became a friend, wrote a prologue for one of his plays, and the two men collaborated on the second part of *Absalom and Achitophel*. Later, they collaborated again on *The Satires of Juvenal and Persius* (1692). Tate's *Brutus of Alba, or The Enchanted Lovers* (performed 1677–8; printed 1678), was a tragedy in blank verse based on Book 4 of Virgil's *Aeneid*. Heavily influenced by Dryden's *All for Love*, it became immortal as, adapted, it furnished the libretto for Purcell's *Dido and Aeneas* (1689). His, too, is the text for Purcell's Birthday Ode for Queen Mary, 'Come Ye Sons of Art '(1694). He also translated, into heroic couplets, *Siphilis, sive Morbus Gallicus* (1530), Girolamo Fracastoro's Latin epic on the disease of syphilis – the only disease named after a character (a shepherd boy) in a poem, so far as I know. He made adaptations of many earlier plays – for example Shakespeare's *Richard II* he turned into *The Sicilian Usurper*, *Coriolanus* into *The Ingratitude of a Commonwealth*. But his now most notorious (but for long hugely admired) adaptation was *The History of King Lear, Revis'd with Alterations*. The great Betterton played it in 1681. The Fool is omitted, Cordelia has a confidante, Arante, and has her own major scene on the heath. Tate concludes with lots of happy endings: Lear gets his throne back, Kent is rewarded, the lovers Cordelia and Edgar marry after the end of the play. Joseph Addison did indeed protest at thus mutilating Shakespeare, but the great Samuel Johnson himself defended Tate's adaptation both as 'poetic justice' – the phrase is first used a generation or so earlier by the critic Thomas Rymer – and as a restoration of the usual story of Lear (stemming from Geoffrey of Monmouth's account in 1136), which Shakespeare had indeed radically altered: it had been a successful play about what people then believed to be actual British history before Shakespeare ever wrote his version. The shock of those who saw Shakespeare's play about a well-known story when it was brand new might be neatly balanced by the shock of those who first saw Tate's: neither expected the story they got. Tate's was the only version of *Lear* staged till 1823, when Edmund Kean restored the original ending.

But besides this dramatic work, and much else besides, he wrote a long poem on tea (*Panacea*, 1703) and *A New Version of the Psalms of David Fitted to the Tunes used in Churches* (1696, 1698,1700). The expanded 1700 edition was a collaboration with Nicholas Brady. One easily forgets how central the psalms were to Anglican and Dissenting worship throughout the long eighteenth century, and that most people in the pew would know them and sing them in 'Tate and Brady'. Most of us will have sung *NEH* 467 (*A&M* 209), 'Through all the changing scenes of life' (their version of Psalm 34). Tate had a facility for translation into a verse form of 8.6.8.6 (Common Measure), eminently singable to popular tunes, and its two couplets express neatly the parallelisms that are a feature of the Hebrew Psalms. Some of the versions, like as 'As pants the hart' (Psalm 42) are more than workmanlike. A supplement was licensed in 1703, when non-psalm (but still biblical) material like 'While Shepherds Watched' is first included, with other hymns (in all some 120) by Tate – mostly now forgotten.

The 1700 edition of 'Tate and Brady' was designed to replace the versified psalter produced by Thomas Sternhold and John Hopkins in 1562 (see p. 17 above). The *New Version* was designed to remain compatible with the well-known psalm tunes, but to be more 'modern' and elegant in its language –

after all, in 150 years language and idiom does change, and both the Tate and Brady project and the sometimes negative reaction to it ought to be familiar experiences for us. 'Tate and Brady' came under fire from William Beveridge, Bishop of St Asaph, in *A Defence of the Book of Psalms* (1710). He disliked their freedom in translation and what he called 'light and airy' modishness. But Tate could defend himself: his vigorous *An Essay for Promoting of Psalmody* (1710) made a good case for their formal variety and liturgical usefulness.

Dr Johnson's dictum 'No man but a blockhead ever wrote, except for money' (April 5, 1776), is not far from the truth. (It is not all of it.) Tate spent most of his life in unhappy pursuit of popular favour, especially through writing for the fickle stage, and the wealth and security it might bring. But he was never really in tune with the intellectual or indeed social temper, rather 'libertine', of the times. People do seem to have liked him, though. Contemporaries found him learned – most certainly! – and courteous, modest and moral: according to the antiquary and minor poet William Oldys (1696 – 1761), 'a free, good-natured fuddling companion'. He retained the friendship and patronage of Charles Sackville, earl of Dorset, who, when he became Lord Chancellor, got for him the post of Poet Laureate. That post carried prestige, £300 a year, and a butt of Canary wine. It must have been about then that the only portrait, and engraving, we have of him, was made. It shows him wearing the periwig that denoted pretty high social status, and the Laureateship would have given him that. His tenure falls between the now unread Thomas Shadwell,[1] of whom John Dryden, the first Poet Laureate, bitchily remarked

> The rest to some faint meaning make pretence,
> But Shadwell never deviates into sense.

---

[1] Yet if you are of my vintage, you will remember almost every amateur choir singing Purcell's setting of 'Nymphs and Shepherds, come away', which comes from Shadwell's *The Libertine* (1676).

and Nicholas Rowe, whose poetry is forgotten but whose illustrated edition of Shakespeare (1709) was genuinely groundbreaking. Tate is luckier: even though Alexander Pope talks of 'Tate's poor page' in *The Dunciad* and the old (1885) *DNB* dismisses him as 'poetaster and dramatist', each Christmas and Easter we sing his hymns, which are favourites to many, and we might spare a thought for him.

He died within the precincts of the Mint, Southwark, in 1715, one of the Liberties where he could be safe from creditors. For he died poor and in debt. Writers often do.

XIII
Isaac Watts
1674–1748

❧

IN SOUTHAMPTON, LOOKING IN perpetual expectancy at the Civic Centre, is a statue of Watts. The bells of the Centre's clock, every four hours through the day, play the tune 'St Anne' always associated with Watts' hymn, 'O God, our help in ages past.' As well they might ...

In 1660, after the unhappy years of the Commonwealth, General Monck, at the head of an unpaid army, had engineered the exiled Charles II's recall to the throne. Charles II was no fool, and knew the country's divisions needed healing. In his Declaration of Breda, which there is no reason not to take to be as sincere as it was politic, he promised pardon to all except those who had signed his father's death warrant, and religious toleration when it did not disturb the peace of the kingdom. His promises were torn to pieces by the vengeful Cavalier Parliament. By 1665 a raft of repressive Acts of Parliament, named the Clarendon Code after Charles' Lord Chancellor,[1] imposed swingeing penalties on those who would not conform to the 39 Articles and the Prayer Book of the Church of England. It excluded them from holding any public office,

---

[1] And James Duke of York's father in law, and so grandfather to Queens Mary and Anne. Clarendon, a wiser man than the MPs, recognised that nothing but ill could come of this legislation.

from the Universities, and forbade them meeting in any group larger than five. Much of the Code remained in force for the next century, and perpetuated divisions opened up by the Civil War, and before that by repercussions of the Reformation. When Isaac Watts was born, in Southampton, his own father (a clothworker, as many 'Puritans' were) was in prison as a Dissenter – he was deacon in the Above Bar Congregational Church – and Isaac later recalled his mother's story of nursing him, her second baby, sitting on a stone by the gaol gate.[2]

The boy showed prodigious ability with languages. By 4 he was learning Latin – not in itself that unusual, for to get any sort of serious education you needed Latin, that being the international language in which most discussion, legal, historical, religious or philosophical, was conducted. Before he was six he was writing verse. Some people do have the gift, like Alexander Pope, almost before talking properly, of 'lisp[ing] in numbers [verse] for the numbers came' – one of my oldest friends has it – and clearly Watts did. It can be annoying. I can well believe the young Watts might have been irritating to a degree. Once, when he had to explain why his eyes were open during family prayers, he said: 'A little mouse for want of stairs, ran up a rope to say its prayers.' On another occasion, about to be punished for something by his father, he exclaimed, 'O father, do some pity take, And I will no more verses make.' The promise was not kept. When his mother discovered some verses he had written, she was so struck by their quality she questioned whether they could be his. In answer he turned out this acrostic poem on his name:

> I am a vile polluted lump of earth,
> So I've continu'd ever since my birth;
> Although Jehovah grace does daily give me,
> As sure this monster Satan will deceive me,
> Come, therefore, Lord, from Satan's claws relieve me.

---

[2] Isaac Senior was eventually freed and there were seven more children.

Isaac Watts

Wash me in thy blood, O Christ,
And grace divine impart,
Then search and try the corners of my heart,
That I in all things may be fit to do
Service to thee, and sing thy praises too.

There are many anticipations here of the concerns of his mature poetry: the corruptness of mankind, salvation by grace alone. The boy's Calvinist upbringing was going deep.

Unsurprisingly, this prodigy, at King Edward VI Grammar School in Southampton, by age nine was tackling Greek, and by thirteen, Hebrew. French came almost casually, for the family had French neighbours – Huguenot refugees from the increasingly anti-Protestant and repressive government of Louis XIV's minister, Cardinal Mazarin, and his successors. In fact, the hardening of religious division in England was mirrored in France: in 1689 the Edict of Nantes, by which Henri IV had granted toleration to Protestants, was revoked by Louis.[3] Several rich townsfolk, impressed by his ability, offered to pay for Isaac's education at Oxford or Cambridge, a path which normally led to ordination as an Anglican clergyman. But, with views not dissimilar to his father's, Isaac refused and at 16 went to one of the foremost Dissenting (i.e. Nonconformist) academies, run by Dr Thomas Rowe in Little Britain, just outside London Wall. Rowe was one of the most up to date of tutors, especially in philosophy: he was a follower of Descartes when Aristotle was still what was normally taught, and an early supporter of John Locke: heady stuff for a young lad. Watts left in 1694, and two years later became private tutor to the family of Sir John Hartopp, a notable Dissenter and MP – his father had raised a regiment for Parliament in the Civil War – at his house in Stoke Newington, then a village some five miles from the City of London, and at his estate at Freeby,

---

[3] Samuel Pepys' wife was a Huguenot refugee. Many settled in the area round Spitalfields in London, bringing with them their skills in the working of cloth, especially silk.

Leicestershire. Sir John had been MP for Leicestershire, and had been heavily fined under James II, for whose exclusion from the throne on the grounds of his Roman Catholicism he had argued strongly. Clearly the relationship was happy, for Watts preached the funeral sermon in 1722 for Sir John and his wife years after he had left their household.

In 1699, Watts was made assistant to the minister of the Independent (i.e. Congregational) Chapel in Mark Lane, in the heart of London, near the Tower. In actual fact, his religious opinions were more non-denominational, indeed what we might call ecumenical, than was then common for a Nonconformist; he seems to have had a greater interest in promoting education and scholarship than preaching for any particular ministry, as his scholarly work demonstrates.

In March 1702 he became the Mark Lane Chapel's pastor. For ten years people flocked (the cliché is for once just) to his inspiring sermons, in an age when connoisseurship of sermons was commonplace: you might take your friends to hear a particularly fine, dramatic, preacher.[4] His congregation outgrew the Mark Lane meeting-house, moved to Pinners' Hall, and finally, in 1708, to a new meeting-house at Bury Street. Yet all was not well. He suffered increasingly from some form of mental illness, and had to pass an increasing amount of work to an assistant. Finally, in 1712, ill once more, he resigned, and went to stay, intending only for a week, with Sir Thomas Abney, a former Lord Mayor of London, at Theobalds in Hertfordshire. As it turned out, when Sir Thomas died he remained with the family, living in the manor house at Stoke Newington, which Lady Abney had inherited. With the house went the manor, and Watts assisted her in laying out much of the estate as parkland: some of it is now Abney Park cemetery, one of the 'Magnificent Seven' London garden cemeteries.

---

[4] Audiences could be very large – sometimes, in the early 1600s, 10,000 at Paul's Cross outside Old St Paul's. No wonder the authorities kept a close eye on what was being said! In the years before the Civil War (Parliament closed all the theatres in 1642) the stage and the pulpit were in effect the only forms of mass medium, and could have huge influence.

Isaac Watts

The family generously, and affectionately, supported him for the rest of his life. He was tutor to the Abney children, family chaplain, and also a friend for whom they cared when he was ill. According to Thomas Gibbons' *Memoirs of the Rev Isaac Watts*, D.D (1780), without such generous hospitality he 'might have sunk into his grave under the overwhelming load of infirmities'. Once, when Watts commented to a visitor that a week's visit had extended into a stay of thirty years, Lady Abney interjected, 'Sir, what you term a long thirty-years visit, I consider the shortest visit my family ever received'. In fact, many seem to have to been very attached to him, for it was his former pupil, the younger Sir John Hartopp, who with Lady Abney erected a monument to Watts in Bunhill Fields where many Nonconformists were buried.

The 'Father of English hymnody', say the reference books. Well, rather like calling Chaucer the 'Father of English poetry': true, but a very broad brush stroke. In Germany, Lutheran congregations had been singing hymns – chorales – for well over a century; John Calvin's followers, by contrast, sang only versions of the psalms, and Protestant churches in England, including the Church of England, did the same. But there were signs of change: for example, some of the Independent congregations were venturing outside the usual corpus of metrical psalms. For example, the Baptist Benjamin Keach's congregation at Horsleydown in Surrey was probably the first to sing actual hymns, verses designed to be sung, neither psalms nor paraphrases: Keach's *Spiritual Songs: Being the Marrow of the Scripture, in Songs of Praise to Almighty God; From the Old and New Testament*, (London 1691) caused shockwaves when it appeared. (Watts can hardly not have known it.) In Watts' late teens, he had repeatedly grumbled about the dullness of psalm singing, and his exasperated father challenged him to write something better. A week later Isaac presented his first hymn to the congregation, 'Behold the Glories of the Lamb', (not in *NEH*, but popular today in the USA), which they received with enthusiasm. Years later he was still complaining – and when 'lining out' (see p. 23) was still usual, one can understand both his complaint and the dullness people endured: 'To see the dull indifference, the negligent and thoughtless air that sits upon the faces of a whole assembly, while the psalm is upon their lips, might even tempt a charitable observer to suspect the fervency of their inward religion.'

In 1707, he published *Hymns and Spiritual Songs*. It is here that his best loved and arguably finest hymn, 'When I survey the wondrous Cross' (*NEH* 95. *A&M* 67), first appeared. The fact that he wrote it in Long Measure (see p. 21), one of the forms that fitted the tunes used for metrical psalms, argues that he did design it for congregational singing, and the same is true of his other poems. For original though many of his poems are, he was certainly not rejecting the psalm tradition: he just wanted it done better, with more, well, passion. 'They ought to be translated in such a manner as we have reason to believe David would have composed them if he had lived in our day,' he wrote. After all, David did dance before the Ark of the Covenant and his poems – those of the psalms which he probably did write – are full of passionate feeling.[5] So Watts did it: and published *The Psalms of David Imitated in the Language of the New Testament* in 1719.

He divided *Hymns and Spiritual Songs* into three books. The first was mainly paraphrases of biblical texts, the second poems on general sacred subjects, and the third set were designed for the Lord's Supper or Eucharist. His preface claimed that he had 'sunk the metaphors to the level of vulgar capacities', though he hoped 'not to give disgust to persons of richer sense, and nicer education' (*Works*, 7.122); much could be said about the implications of and attitudes behind that remark. His versions of the *Psalms* were not intended as translation, for, as the subtitle indicates, they were 'Imitated in the Language of the *New Testament* and applied to the Christian State and Worship'. This meant Jesus has to be substituted for Jehovah and Britain for Israel – and indeed, the commonplace correlating of

---

[5] Not all the psalms are by King David, of course.

ISAAC WATTS

Reformed England with ancient Israel, as a Chosen People,[6] was already nearly two hundred years old. Half the joke of Dryden's brilliant *Absalom and Achitophel* lies in the ironic parallels between the politics of Charles II's times and those of King David. One of Watts's best-known hymns, *'Jesus shall reign where'er the sun'*, imitates *Psalm 72*; another, *'Our God our help in ages past'*, is based on *Psalm 90:1–5*. *'Come let us join our cheerful songs'* is based on *Revelation 5:11–13*. Watts was confident of the value of his poetry and the revolution he had stimulated in congregational worship: in the seventh edition of *Hymns* he notes, of his two books of hymns and psalms, 'if an Author's own Opinion may be taken, he esteems it the greatest Work that ever he has publish'd, or ever hopes to do for the Use of the Churches'.

Reception was not unmixed. His versions were, indeed, free. One critic called them 'Watts' whims.' Another grumbled indignantly, 'Christian congregations have shut out divinely inspired psalms and taken in Watts's flights of fancy.' And, indeed, it is not obvious that 'Joy to the World' (not in *NEH*) is Psalm 98,[7] or that Psalm 72, written long before the Incarnation, can be 'Jesus Shall Reign Where'er the Sun' (*NEH* 388, *A&M* 143).[8] 'O God Our Help in Ages Past' (*NEH* 417, *A&M* 99) does not immediately remind you of Psalm 90, 'Lord, thou hast been our refuge : from one generation to another./ Before the mountains were brought forth, or ever the earth and the world were made : thou art God from everlasting, and world without end.'

Watts' Preface did anticipate such criticism, and merits quoting at some length:

[6] An idea readily exported to the new Canaan of America by the Old Testament drenched Puritan colonists.

[7] 'O sing unto the Lord a new song; for he hath done marvellous things: with his right hand, and his holy arm, he hath gotten himself the victory.'

[8] 'Give the king thy judgments, O God, and thy righteousness unto the king's son. He shall judge thy people with righteousness, and thy poor with judgment.'

A Joyful Noise

> I come therefore to explain my own design, which is this, To accommodate the book of Psalms to Christian worship. And in order to do this, it is necessary to divest David and Asaph, etc., of every other character but that of a psalmist and a saint, and to make them always speak the common sense, and language of a Christian ...
>
> Where the Psalmist uses sharp invectives against his personal enemies, I have endeavoured to turn the edge of them against our spiritual adversaries, sin, Satan, and temptation. Where the flights of his faith and love are sublime, I have often sunk the expressions within the reach of an ordinary Christian: where the words imply some peculiar wants or distresses, joys, or blessings, I have used words of greater latitude and comprehension, suited to the general circumstances of men.
>
> Where the original runs in the form of prophecy concerning Christ and his salvation, I have given an historical turn to the sense: there is no necessity that we should always sing in the obscure and doubtful style of prediction, when the things foretold are brought into open light by a full accomplishment ... Where the Psalmist describes religion by the fear of God, I have often joined faith and love to it. Where he speaks of the pardon of sin, through the mercies of God, I have added the merits of a Saviour.

Well, as we know, many of his paraphrases became much loved, and he is very well represented in *NEH* (87, 95, 207, 225, 227, 257, 349, 388, 411, 417, 460). Hymns like 'When I survey', 'Jesus shall reign', and 'O God our help in ages past' are in the Anglophone bloodstream. His work influenced many Nonconformist independents and early religious revivalists, such as Philip Doddridge, who dedicated his own work to Watts. Dr Johnson commented with both his usual elegance and with his oblique acerbity, 'He was the first who taught the Dissenters to write and speak like other men, by showing them that elegance might consist with piety.' In fact, Johnson,

Isaac Watts

in *Lives of the Most Eminent English Poets* (1779-81), writes admiringly of his ability, even as a youth:

> Some Latin Essays... written as exercises at this academy, show a degree of knowledge, both philosophical and theological, such as very few attain by a much longer course of study ...

and

> Every man acquainted with the common principles of human action will look with veneration on the writer who is at one time combating Locke,[9] and at another making a catechism for children in their fourth year.

For the writer of hymns we love, revolutionary in their time, had also become, as schooldays had indicated he would, a widely respected scholar, especially in his later life. Nowadays this is largely forgotten. Yet John Wesley thought him a genius, and he corresponded across the Atlantic with the polymath Benjamin Franklin, who printed his hymnal in Philadelphia, and with Cotton Mather: how much harder such correspondence was when you wrote with a quill and sent it by sea![10] He wrote a textbook on logic – *Logic, or The Right Use of Reason in the Enquiry After Truth With a Variety of Rules to Guard Against Error in the Affairs of Religion and Human Life, as well as in the Sciences* (1724) - that was used for decades; essays on psychology, astronomy, philosophy; three volumes of sermons; some 30 theological treatises; and the first children's hymnal, *Divine and Moral Songs for Children* (1715). (Teach them to sing it, and they remember it all their lives ...) This was one of the first books that acknowledged a need for writing

---

[9] John Locke's *Essay Concerning Human Understanding* (1689), greatly controversial and greatly influential.

[10] Further evidence of the respect in which he was held in America: on his death, Yale University in then-colonial Connecticut acquired his papers.

specifically for children, and anticipated – may even partly have led to – the work of printers, like John Newbery (1713-67; friend of Dr Johnson) who made children's literature a distinct market. Some of Watts' hymns for children became universally known: and won the accolade of parody. 'How doth the little busy bee/Improve the shining hour' and ''Tis the voice of the sluggard' are both spoofed in Lewis Carroll's *Alice's Adventures in Wonderland* (1865).[11]

When writing about someone's achievements it is easy to lose sight of the emotional landscape in which they were made. Sometimes a portrait, letters, a journal may give a clue. There are several portraits of Watts, derived from three originals: an oil in the National Portrait by an unknown artist, several engravings by George Vertue after Isaac Whood, and an engraving by George White. The Unknown Artist shows a face that looks guarded, cautious, somewhat severe. The generous mouth does not smile. Vertue's engraving of Whood's has the legend *musas colimus severiores* – 'I cultivate (or serve) the more austere Muses.' Indeed he did. We know Watts was of small and slight stature, about five foot, with his head disproportionately large. All the portraits show him in a voluminous gown, which may be the artist's attempts to give his slight form a dignity visually appropriate to one of his intellectual standing. We know he was plagued by some sort of mental illness, and that he never married. His courtship of the learned and prolific poet Elizabeth Singer Rowe, the 'ornament of her sex and age' as her obituary[12] called her, came to nothing. But his friendship with the Abneys is only one of the many indications of how people loved him, and he will be alive on people's lips as long as English hymns are sung.

---

[11] 'How doth the little crocodile' and ''Tis the voice of the lobster'.

[12] Obituary in *General Evening Post*, 26 February 1737.

XIV
CHARLES WESLEY
1707–88

THE YEAR TURNS. ADVENT again, and again the yearly cycle of the Liturgy begins. The pattern of our 'bounden duty, that we should at all times and in all places give thanks' to the Lord of all may not change, but we change all the time, and our perspective is always new as the years repeat their pattern. Each Advent we sing Charles Wesley's 'Lo, he comes with clouds descending' (*NEH* 9, *A&M* 28), now almost always to a tune, 'Helmsley', originally by Thomas Olivers (1725-1799).[1] Habitude could make it wearisome. But one Evensong years ago, in College Chapel, for the first time, I heard that magnificent descant by Christopher Robinson (b. 1936) which in the village choir at home (when I still was a treble) we could certainly not have managed. Suddenly the old warhorse's tired familiarity from those childhood Evensongs was stripped away: I sat up and took notice.

And it is a great hymn, full of good divinity. In 1885 James King wrote a survey, *Anglican Hymnology*, in which he examined 52 hymnals from churches in the Anglican Communion. On the basis of those statistics – all but one

---

[1] Some say he derived it from a dance tune heard in the street, originally by Thomas Arne, who wrote 'Rule Britannia', as well as many more interesting things.

included it – he considered it one of the 'Four Great Anglican Hymns', along with 'All Praise to Thee, my God, this Night' (not in the 1986 edition of *NEH*), 'Hark the Herald Angels sing', (yes, also Wesley's[2]) – and another of my own favourites, Augustus Toplady's 'Rock of Ages, cleft for me' (*NEH* 445, *A&M* 135). 'Lo he comes' is, of course, based on the idea of the Second Coming, even echoes (in verse 2) Thomas of Celano's (1185 -1260) *Dies Irae*, and closes with the last words of *The Revelation of St John*, which in the Aramaic form 'Maranatha' was used both as prayer and greeting by the early church: 'Lord come quickly'.

So, to Charles Wesley: 26 hymns in *NEH*, and author of over 6000 more. (Yes, 6000 – some say the total is nearer 10,000.) He became the pre-eminent hymn writer of the new Methodist community. Sometimes he reworked what other people had written – after all, both brothers were familiar with the Moravian hymn singing tradition – and usually for the better. For example, the opening of 'Lo he comes' reworks John Cennick's (1718-1755) 'Lo! He cometh, countless trumpets blow', which is in a different form and metre. Wesley was also clearly influenced by the deeply affective piety of George Herbert – to my mind by far the finest of all English devotional poets – as well as by Francis Quarles,[3] John Mason, and Isaac Watts.

The collections he published in his lifetime include *Hymns on God's Everlasting Love* (1741, 1742), *Hymns on the Lord's Supper* (1745), and *Short Hymns on Select Passages of the Holy Scriptures* (1762), and there were others marking major festivals. His poems are soaked in Scripture, full of

[2] In 1840, Mendelssohn composed a cantata to commemorate Johann Gutenberg's invention of the printing press. It is from this cantata that W. H. Cummings quarried the tune we all know to fit 'Hark! The Herald Angels Sing'.

[3] Quarles' *Emblemes* (1634), in small format convenient for pocket or placket, composed of devotional pictures (by the often clumsy William Marshall) accompanied by verses, was reissued time and time again through the long eighteenth century and into the nineteenth.

echoes of great spiritual poets of the past, and he had great facility with metrical and stanzaic forms. They became very significant in the huge contemporary appeal of Methodism, for something very remarkable happens when people sing together, and Methodism made space for that when the Prayer Book of the Established Church made no provision at all for congregational singing. Taken up by the CofE, they became a major contribution to the massive growth of congregational singing in the nineteenth century. With succinct elegance, the best of Wesley's hymns communicate several doctrines: the personal indwelling of the Holy Spirit, the sanctifying work of the Spirit, mankind's need for salvation, and humanity's personal accountability to God. Of the worst of his verse – e.g. one sugary one to 'Gentle Jesus, meek and Mild', which was framed on my childhood's bedroom wall in a coloured print showing a very clean and androgynous Jesus caressing some unrealistically clean sheep – we shall in charity not speak.

As so often, we take Charles Wesley's work for granted, as if it is has always been there, neatly corralled into tidy black marks on a white page. But it came not only out of a complex social and intellectual context but also out of a complicated personal journey, often highly emotional. His father Samuel was Rector of Epworth in Lincolnshire, where Charles was born in 1707. The parents had 19 children, of whom ten grew to adulthood: a survival rate of just over 50%. Charles' elder brothers Samuel and John were nos. 1 and 15 respectively, while Charles was no.18. His mother Susanna was firm with her children, believing that one needed to subdue the child's will wholly to its parents. (His brother John, later in life, enunciated a similar principle.) Aged nine, Charles was sent to Westminster, where Samuel was usher and could provide lodgings. He was a King's Scholar and later head boy, and by one of those curious coincidences protected a young lad, William Murray, from the school bullies who picked on him because of his family's Jacobite leanings. That young boy became Lord Chief Justice, Lord Mansfield, whose judgement in *Somerset v. Stewart* in 1772, that slavery was contrary 'both to natural law and the principles of the

English Constitution,' was a major step towards the ending of slavery in British dominions. He then went up to Oxford, whither his brothers had preceded him. He was admitted, with a scholarship, to Christ Church. Initially – well, John was soon concerned. Charles told John that he was 'very *desirous* of knowledge but can't *bear* the drudgery of coming at it near so well as you could … My head will by no means keep pace with my heart'. And freed of family restraints, Charles' first year was somewhat, shall we say? relaxed: there were several excursions to London and emotional entanglements with London actresses. To his brother's attempts to make him more serious he objected: 'What? would you have me to be a saint at once?' But, soon he was won over by his own maturing and his serious-minded brothers. The three of them and a few friends – including, later, George Whitefield, who became of one of John Wesley's ablest helpers – met three evenings a week to discuss the classical authors they had been reading and, on Sundays, a theological work. Oxford, like Cambridge at that time, was not noted for the seriousness and piety of undergraduate members, and the group was soon scornfully nicknamed 'The Holy Club', 'The Bible Moths' (think about it), 'The Sacramentarians' and 'The Methodists' because everything was done to 'A Method' – including, unusually for that time when most Anglicans might take the sacrament at most once a month (if that), a search each week for a priest who was celebrating the Eucharist.[4] All three brothers were eventually ordained, and John and Charles went out to Georgia in 1735 on the suggestion of that colony's founder, General Oglethorpe, who strongly supported the Society for the Propagation of the Gospel, to evangelise the Native Americans. It was in Georgia that John and Charles were so deeply influenced by the piety and faith of the Moravian settlers (refugees from an oppressive Catholicism in their native Bohemia). But their mission was not very successful, nor was it very happy in its relations with Oglethorpe, and they returned after two years.

---

[4] John disliked the label, but later adopted it.

Charles Wesley

It is impossible to grasp the significance of Charles Wesley's hymns, or poems – call them what you will – without taking into account the trajectory of John's career and thought after this visit. Though John (like Charles) to his death regarded himself as a loyal son, and priest, of the CofE, his independence, his determination to preach to people of all sorts and conditions in the highways and byways, ignoring the parish structure where the incumbent had control, led to a suspicious coolness with the Established Church, and eventually a breach.[5] After 1739, John and Charles and their growing band of adherents were in fact persecuted: though they were ordained, many other Methodist leaders were not, and John's flouting of the CofE's definition of who had authority to preach was considered a threat to institutions on which social order depended. Clergy attacked them in sermon and in pamphlet, and at times mobs threw stones. Wesley and his followers, continuing to work among those at the bottom of society's heap, were labelled promulgators of strange doctrines, fomenters of religious disturbance, fanatics who, claiming miraculous gifts, led people astray. Many clergy, feeling threatened, were deeply hostile. And they were accused – then the ultimate political insult – of trying to re-establish Roman Catholicism. Moreover, Wesley spoke with a passion that many thought deeply dangerous.

For passion was at the heart of early Methodism. It was precisely that passion and 'enthusiasm' – a word always then used as an insult – that the Established Church deeply distrusted. It recalled all too well where such emotionalism had led in the terrible years of the Civil War and its aftermath. The heart of John Wesley's message was each person's relationship with the risen Lord, who loved each undeserving one of us; it was not simply about morality, good manners and paying your tithes, and charity to the poor – though those might be among

---

[5] It is after 1795 that the Methodists and the CofE were formally in schism over this issue. There is an interesting parallel with how the beneficed parish clergy received the wandering friars, working extra-parochially, in the thirteenth and fourteenth centuries. They too were trying to reach the parts other clergy did not reach.

the consequences of the 'heart [being] strangely warmed' by the love of Christ.[6]

Charles shared his brother's views: they both rejected the Calvinism which marked much of the Dissenting tradition – and for that matter, the CofE's 39 Articles (see X and XVII) have a strongly Calvinist cast – and stressed, with the Dutch theologian Jacob van Hermandszoon (Latinised as Arminius), the universality of God's Love and the importance of our free response to it. The brothers had quite astonishing energy and stamina: it has been reckoned that John on his incessant journeys all over England, when he often read on horseback, preached about 500 sermons a year to often huge gatherings of people – for example, at Gwennap in Cornwall, his audience was some 20,000. Charles, aware of how powerful in building a community and as mnemonic was the act of singing together, ensured with his thousands of hymns that, based on sound biblical doctrine, there was something to sing which reflected the passionate and emotional preaching of his brother. And as for tunes, well, as Charles Booth said later, 'why should the Devil have all the best ones?' Charles had the great gift of encapsulating much of the doctrine that John preached in his innumerable sermons into memorable and singable verse, especially that doctrine of love and of an acutely personal relationship with the Saviour. This does raise an interesting issue, not limited to Wesley: when he wrote

> And can it be that I should gain
> An int'rest in the Saviour's blood?

---

[6] John Wesley's *Journal*, 24 May 1738: 'In the evening I went very unwillingly to a society [The Moravians] in Aldersgate Street, where one was reading Luther's preface to the Epistle to the Romans. About a quarter before nine, while he was describing the change which God works in the heart through faith in Christ, I felt my heart strangely warmed. I felt I did trust in Christ, Christ alone, for salvation; and an assurance was given me that He had taken away my sins, even mine, and saved me from the law of sin and death.' Charles had undergone a similar experience three days earlier.

> Died He for me, who caused His pain?
> For me, who Him to death pursued?
> Amazing love! how can it be
> That Thou, my God, shouldst die for me?
> Amazing love! how can it be
> That Thou, my God, shouldst die for me?

it was very soon after what he regarded as his own conversion – or, if you prefer, that moment when intellectual *knowledge* becomes something you intimately *feel*. But when it is sung (the usual tune is Thomas Campbell's 'Sagina') by people *in a group,* what *is* their relationship to the impulse, the effusion of *individual* feeling, the words describe? My thought is that this group singing of such things can subtly change, perhaps not immediately or even quickly, from a secondary record of experience to experience itself. We borrow someone else's words to know what it is we want to say: like when we quote a favourite love poem to our beloved. The saying and the singing changes us.

※

In April 1749, Charles married Sarah Gwynne, who was only 23. She indefatigably accompanied John and Charles on their tireless evangelising journeys through Britain for the next few years. Their schedule was physically extraordinarily taxing and on top of that Charles regularly suffered from severe depression. Only three of the couple's eight children survived infancy. (It is hard to get one's head round what such a rate of infant mortality must have been like for parents, and the risk childbearing posed to women.) The eldest child, Charles, like his brother Samuel, was gifted musically, and like their father both became composers and organists – Samuel, indeed, was known as the 'English Mozart' and was one of the first people to publish an English edition of J. S. Bach, to whose music he had introduced Dr Charles Burney. Most of Charles junior's career was spent as organist to the Royal Family. To his uncle's consternation and his father's grief, Samuel converted to Roman Catholicism in 1784, and brought up his own son, Samuel Sebastian, in that confession. He, Charles's grandson, was one of the foremost English composers of the earlier nineteenth century, and wrote many fine anthems, many still sung.

When he was dying Charles sent for Rev John Harley – of the family who had recently developed smart, fashionable Harley Street – Rector of St Marylebone, where his son became organist. He apparently said: 'Sir, whatever the world may say of me, I have lived, and I die, a member of the Church of England. I pray you to bury me in your churchyard.' And so it was. Six clergy of the Church of England were his pall bearers.

༄

We owe the Wesleys so much. It is right that the calendar of the CofE from which they so reluctantly broke remembers Charles and his brother with gratitude, with a Lesser Festival on 24 May. In so many ways what they did anticipated the urgency of the Oxford Movement's mission a century later. They reflect how the Church, *semper reformanda,* in almost every century, is challenged to rethink what it thought it knew, to get back to the bed Rock. That challenge is never comfortable and is often resisted. But the music goes on. Charles's poems we can sing with joy as the seasons change through the year and we change, and learn, in them.

XV

JOHN NEWTON
1725-1807

※

THERE WAS A TIME, QUITE recently, when you could hardly switch on the radio, or go to a wedding, or a funeral, without hearing a tune everyone called 'Amazing Grace'. It was originally a folk tune, collected in the Appalachian Mountains. It's in a pentatonic scale, and it originally went by the name of 'New Britain'. You heard it *a capella*, or solo, with lots of grace notes, or on the soupiest organ stops that can make a sensible, well behaved instrument sound like the Blackpool Tower Ballroom Wurlitzer. There is a video of it played by the pipe band of the Royal Scots Dragoon Guards (https://www.youtube.com/watch?v=euWfTiYwRB0) backed by 'Scenes of Bonnie Scotland'. It does sit well on bagpipes, actually, and may well have originated, like so many American folk tunes, in Scotland or Ireland. But what those words meant, their context and import, as in the cases of 'Abide with me', or 'Guide me, O thou Great Redeemer' – 'Jehovah' in some versions – had lost their force, and become mere pegs for a tune.

John Newton did not do things by halves. Going to sea as an eleven year old boy, on a merchantman, then at 18 pressganged into the Royal Navy, then a deserter, then flogged for insubordination, then seaman on a slave ship, punished (again for insubordination) and chained up with the slaves, then himself sold as a slave to an African princess in Sierra

A Joyful Noise

Leone, and eventually captain of a slaver out of Liverpool – all before the age of thirty. And in the fullness of time, an Anglican parson, friend and counsellor of William Wilberforce, and a fervent Abolitionist. With his friend and neighbour William Cowper he was author of the greatly influential *Olney Hymns* (1779),[1] originally written to teach, and as *aide mémoire* of the faith, for his not especially well-educated congregation of Olney in Buckinghamshire. 'Amazing Grace' (which is not in *NEH*) is a sort of spiritual autobiography in verse; *NEH* 362(*A&M* 172), 'Glorious things of thee are spoken', *NEH* 374 (*A&M* 122), 'How sweet the name of Jesus sounds' were all in that book: Book 3, 77 'Day of judgment! Day of wonders!' is a very loose version of the *Dies Irae* (see p. 54ff.).

Unsurprisingly, his life has been made into films: Albert Finney – remember *Saturday Night and Sunday Morning* and *Death on the Nile*? – played him in *Amazing Grace* (2006), portraying him haunted by the ghosts of 20,000 slaves. In the Nigerian film *The Amazing Grace* (2006) Nick Moran played Newton. There have been plays, and even, on Broadway in 2014 and 2015, a musical about his life.

He was born, in 1725, in Wapping, on the marshy north bank of the Thames. In the time of the first Elizabeth, John Stow could describe it as a 'continual street, or a filthy strait passage, with alleys of small tenements or cottages, built, inhabited by sailors' victuallers'. It was a rough place: one inn, 'The Prospect of Whitby', (originally 'The Pelican', which Samuel Pepys visited more than once), was a haunt of sailors, footpads, ne'er do wells and the sort of people who prey on sailors home from the sea

---

[1] 'In Three Books: I. On Select Passages of Scripture.[141 hymns] II. On Occasional Subjects [from Seasons to Funerals, 100 hymns] III. On the Spiritual Life [107 hymns]'. 68 of the 358 hymns are Cowper's. The *Olney Hymns* must be one of the largest collections of sacred verse written in modern times. It was hugely influential, going through many editions. It was especially popular in America during the Second Great Awakening, the Revivalist movement that swept the States in the early-nineteenth century. (It was then, in 1835, that William Walker attached the tune 'New Britain' to 'Amazing Grace'.)

with pay in their pockets. It was also favoured by the notorious Judge Jeffreys. Just off the Wapping shore was Execution Dock, where they hanged pirates on a gallows just below low tide mark for three tides.[2] Newton's father was comfortably off, captain of a small merchant vessel: he had been brought up Roman Catholic, but leaned to Protestantism. His mother, devoutly Independent, and ambitious that her son would become a cleric, taught him through Bible readings and the hymns of Isaac Watts. But she died of TB when he was only six. For the next few years, while his father was at sea Newton was raised by his father's cold second wife, Thomasina. He was sent off to a boarding school, but at 11 he joined his father at sea as ship's boy – literally, learning the ropes. We next hear of him as a midshipman.[3] His father made various attempts to set him up in Jamaica in the sugar business, which he managed to evade by taking himself off to Kent to see the girl with whom he had fallen in love, Mary ('Polly') Catlett, daughter of friends of his mother. He would eventually marry her (in 1750). But in 1743, on one of these visits, he was pressganged into the Navy: Britain was just about to go to war with France and Prussia over the Succession to the Austrian throne, and that European family quarrel spread to all parts of the navigable globe. He was again a midshipman, in HMS *Harwich,* 50 guns, but, with that headstrong disobedience that marked his sea career, he deserted, again to visit Polly. But he was captured, and flogged (98 lashes of the cat o'nine tails) in front of the ship's company of 350 and demoted to common seaman. He thought of suicide, even of murdering the Captain, William Adams, and later said it was only the thought of Polly that stopped him. The ship was bound for a five-year tour of duty in the West Indies, but while she was victualling in Madeira he volunteered for transfer – they were probably glad to get rid of him – to the *Pegasus,* a slaving ship bound for West Africa, the first leg of the

---

[2] The last such execution was in 1830.

[3] Not at that time an officer in training, as the term implied after about the 1790s, but an experienced seaman whose station was amidships.

A Joyful Noise

Triangular Voyage – Britain (often from Liverpool, Lancaster and Bristol) to West Africa with trade goods, to America with slaves, and back home with sugar or rum, tobacco or cotton. It was a very profitable trade, and it is hard, now, to recognise that for most of Newton's contemporaries, slavery as an institution was quite uncontroversial and the trade perfectly respectable. For years after he left the sea, this man who would become one of the most bitter opponents of the trade still put money in it – it is hard to think of anyone who did not, directly or indirectly. Indeed, even after his conversion, he had still sailed as a slaver. There had been, and were, dissenting voices about it – mainly from those seventeenth-century radicals, the Quakers, and some of the men and women of the eighteenth century who were influenced by new and developing ideas of human rights[4].

As on the *Harwich*, so on the slaver. Once more, insubordination: a wicked wit and the way with words that one day would go in quite a different direction had him composing obscene lampoons about the captain, and the crew anarchically loved it. Unsurprisingly, he was punished: put in irons like a slave, and denied food. He abandoned the *Pegasus* when she sailed for the West Indies with her human cargo, deciding to stay in Sierra Leone, which he quite liked. But he was himself enslaved: his employer, Amos Clowe, who owned a plantation of lemon trees, *gave* him to his wife, Peye, a princess of the Sherbro people. She and Clowe treated him no less harshly than any of the other slaves.

However, Newton's father had asked people to search for him, and he was rescued. In early 1748 he returned on the Liverpool-bound *Greyhound*. Again, Newton stuck out as one of the most profane men the captain had ever met. Sailors habitually swore, of course, but Newton's linguistic ingenuity shocked even a hard-bitten sea captain used to obscenity.

---

[4] General James Oglethorpe, Dr Johnson's friend, for example, banned slavery in his province of Georgia. In that same social circle was Hannah More. What is astonishing is how quickly – some 40 years – law, politics and opinion turned, slavery was made illegal, and the British Navy was being used to stop the slave trade by other nations

JOHN NEWTON

A severe storm – March is not a good time in the north Atlantic – caught the ship off the Irish coast. She almost foundered. Only ceaseless work at the pumps, and the cargo shifting and partly blocking the hole in the hull, saved her. After a fortnight or so, ship and exhausted crew made it into Lough Swilly in Donegal. This experience Newton later saw as a crucial turning point in his life. He described it in *An Authentic Narrative* (1764),[5] and kept its date as the anniversary of his conversion – in his eighties, a note in its commemoration was the very last entry in his diary. But he did not immediately leave the sea, or the slave trade: he saw both as the station in which God had placed him. He made several more slaving voyages to West Africa and America, and became a slaver captain himself. But he had married his Polly (despite her parents' unease at his reputation as a tearaway) in 1750, and was finding it harder to leave her each time he sailed.

The very year he married he was master of the slaver *Duke of Argyle,* treating his crew humanely and leading the services he required they attend on Sundays. Between October 1753 and August 1754 he captained the slaver *The African.* Whilst she was in port at St Kitts, he met Alexander Clunie, captain of the *Saint Kitts Merchant*, 12 guns. Clunie was a member of the Dissenters' Chapel in Stepney, and it's a curious picture, these two earnest men, the one a devout evangelical and sailing as a privateer – i.e. preying on the merchant ships of Britain's enemies – under letters of marque, the other a pretty hard operator who had seen the worst of the Middle Passage, yet finding his way to faith, sitting talking in the velvet darkness of the tropics, discussing prayer, faith and the Bible under the bright stars.

ರ್

---

[5] It was something of a bestseller: 'An Authentic Narrative of Some Remarkable and Interesting Particulars in the Life of John Newton, Communicated in a Series of Letters to the Reverend Mr Haweis' (1764). It went through 10 British and 8 American editions before 1800.

A Joyful Noise

No experience of near shipwreck is easy, and as someone once said, there are few atheists on a deathbed or when the ship is foundering. As his ship was filling with water, that day off Ireland, Newton recalls in his *Narrative* that he called out 'Lord have mercy upon us!', almost as a mere figure of speech. Yet for most of his life he had rejected Christianity. Early upbringing seemed to have left no mark, and he had abandoned any faith after discussing with a shipmate *The Characteristics of Men, Manners, Opinions, Times* (1711), by Antony Ashley-Cooper, 3rd Earl of Shaftesbury[6] – a fact, incidentally, which says a lot about the literacy of the lower deck and the availability of printed material. He had mocked others who showed any faith, scoffing at the idea of God as mere myth. In a letter much later, inevitably with hindsight, Newton wrote, 'Like an unwary sailor who quits his port just before a rising storm, I renounced the hopes and comforts of the Gospel at the very time when every other comfort was about to fail me.' Yet, oddly, this man whose reputation was for profane speech and disorderly conduct says he had been reading, for several weeks *before* the storm, *The Christian's Pattern*, which summarised Thomas à Kempis' *Imitation of Christ* (c.1420). One has to ask what was going on, and admit we can never now know. 'God moves in a mysterious way/ His wonders to perform', as one of Cowper's poems in the *Olney Hymns* puts it (*NEH* 365, *A&M* 122). He says that he never forgot his desperate cry of 'Lord have mercy', and he began to ask if he was worthy of God's mercy: which is a logical nonsense, as mercy by definition cannot be deserved.

In 1755, still only 30, he suffered what commentators variously call a 'fit' or 'collapse': probably what we might call a TIA. He never sailed again. Friends and influence mattered: his father's friend Joseph Manesty, a Liverpool merchant, got him appointed one of the tide surveyors – i.e. tax collector – for Liverpool port. His job included inspecting imported

---

[6] Cooper could be called a Deist, denying the Incarnation and Resurrection but accepting the idea of a remote Creator.

cargoes, and checking for smuggled goods. But the Seven Years' War meant that traffic had seriously dropped off, and he had spare time to give to learning learn Greek, Hebrew and Syriac, determined on serious religious study. He attended religious meetings, and was drawn into the revival spearheaded by the Wesleys and George Whitefield. Two years after his collapse, he sought Anglican ordination. It took more than seven years for him to be accepted. Eventually, in 1764, he was introduced to William Legge, Second Earl of Dartmouth, who recommended him to Bishop Markham of Chester. He was ordained deacon in April, and priested two months later. He was given the parish of SS. Peter and Paul, Olney, near Buckingham in the gentle, rich soil of the Ouse valley, about as far from the sea as you can get in England, where he spent the next sixteen years. The parish carried an adequate stipend of £60 per year, but the immensely rich John Thornton[7] gave him a further £200 pa to help with 'hospitality and provision for the poor'.

Newton soon became known for eloquent sermons, of a cast strongly 'enthusiastic' – not always a compliment then – in an age that appreciated the art of sermon, and did not mind the turning of the hourglass. His preaching was so popular that a gallery was added to the church to accommodate the crowds who came on foot and by carriage and horse to hear him. 'Amazing Grace'[8] was probably written about this time, and like his preaching it has all the Calvinist stress on God's generous Grace as the *only* means of salvation. But he was also widely respected for his generous pastoral care and use of the money Thornton gave him: after all, the parson was then one of the richer and more influential people of the parish, and how

[7] Thornton had turned a handsome inheritance from his father, a Hull merchant, into quite immense wealth – some said he was one of the richest men in Europe – through wise investment in the Russia trade. After his conversion, he devoted his energies and his wealth to innumerable good causes and charities.

[8] In fact, in the *Olney Hymns* it is called 'Faith's Review and Expectation'.

A Joyful Noise

he did his job affected the rural poor significantly. This was the time when the common fields of England, which from time out of mind had allowed the poor a measure of independence and dignity, were divided up among the rich by an accelerating tide of Enclosure Acts. (Olney's came in 1803.) Without Enclosure, agricultural innovation was impossible, and the swarming populations of the new towns of the Industrial Revolution demanded an increase in food production – which the Agricultural Revolution made possible. It was not all bad. But within a generation the Acts turned the independent peasant into a landless pauper on a day wage – if he was lucky. A conscientious parson could make things just that little bit easier; a slack one much worse.

In 1779, at Thornton's invitation, he moved to London, as Rector of the fashionable parish of St Mary Woolnoth, Lombard Street, in which incumbency he died. Again, his 'enthusiastic' – why are many people so afraid of the passion in the Faith? – strongly Evangelical preaching drew crowds, and many folk, many but not all of real influence, who were struggling with faith, sought his counsel. The list is long. It includes Hannah More, writer, playwright, philanthropist and very much part of the circle of Samuel Johnson, David Garrick and Joshua Reynolds.[9] Then there was the young William Wilberforce MP, friend of William Pitt the Younger and, according to Mme de

---

[9] She was one of the original Bluestockings, groups of women, mostly well-to-do, who met to discuss social and educational matters with men. This was unconventional, even radical, for the time, when scant allowance was made for female education. They got the name 'Bluestockings' because when they invited the brilliant but impoverished polymath Benjamin Stillingfleet to one of their gatherings he protested he had no formal clothes, and so no black silk stockings. According to Fanny Burney, another Bluestocking, Elizabeth Vesey replied: "'Pho, pho," cried she, with her well-known, yet always original simplicity, while she looked inquisitively, at him and his accoutrements; "Don't mind dress! Come in your blue stockings!"'

Staël, the 'wittiest man in England'.[10] (Wilberforce was also the friend and cousin of Henry, John Thornton's son.) Like many – like Newton himself – Wilberforce had become convinced of the evils of the slave trade and of the institution of slavery itself, and was to devote most of his energies to its abolition. (He died in 1833 just as he heard that Parliament was abolishing it throughout the British Empire.)

In 1788, thirty odd years after he had retired from the sea and his career as a slaver, and in the same twelve months that Josiah Wedgwood issued his anti-slavery medallion, 'Am I not a man and a brother?', Newton published *Thoughts Upon the Slave Trade*, vividly describing the conditions on ships during the Middle Passage to America. Sometimes in a storm slaves might be chucked overboard to lighten the ship, and on many voyages 30-40 per cent mortality was usual. He apologised for

> a confession, which ... comes too late ... It will always be a subject of humiliating reflection to me, that I was once an active instrument in a business at which my heart now shudders...So much light has been thrown upon the subject, by many able pens; and so many respectable persons have already engaged to use their utmost influence, for the suppression of a traffic, which contradicts the feelings of humanity; that it is hoped, this stain on our National character will soon be wiped out.

He sent it to every MP, and the pamphlet sold so well that it was swiftly reprinted. He was already working with the Committee for the Abolition of the Slave Trade, which Thomas Clarkson and Granville Sharp had formed in 1786. The tide was indeed running strongly against slavery: Lord Mansfield's judgement

---

[10] Wilberforce had recently contemplated leaving politics, after a crisis of conscience and religious conversion. Yet he was a remarkable orator: James Boswell saw him, a little man, in Parliament: 'I saw what seemed to be mere shrimp mount about the table, but as I listened the shrimp grew and grew and became a whale.' Newton encouraged him to stay and 'serve God where he was'. Good advice ...

A Joyful Noise

in the James Somerset case of 1772, which made a slave a free man once he landed in England, restated that slavery had no place in English law. Newton did live to see the British Empire's abolition of the African slave trade – the first empire, ever, to do so - in March 1807, just months before his death.

A full life, indeed.

XVI
WILLIAM COWPER
1731–1800

WHEN IN 1767 WILLIAM Cowper, suffering from severe, and recurrent, depression, moved to Olney in Buckinghamshire, he became one of John Newton's parishioners. Newton, that energetic cleric, became not only friend and mentor, but a great influence on this exceptionally talented, and, equally exceptionally, troubled man. They co-operated on writing the *Olney Hymns* (1779) – Cowper contributed 67 to the massive collection – and while Newton was incumbent, Cowper wrote many of the fine poems that made his name. He published *Poems of William Cowper, Esq., of the Inner Temple* in 1782 – a volume that included the comic ballad *The Diverting History of John Gilpin,* which, with Barham's *The Jackdaw of Reims* and Keats' *Meg Merrilies*[1] was a regular standby when I was a lad for Miss Murphy, my tired primary school teacher, to read to us on wet Friday afternoons.

Some claim Cowper as the most influential English poet between Pope and Wordsworth. Certainly, for several decades, he was probably one of the most read, for between 1782 and 1837, when Robert Southey completed his *Life and Works of Cowper*, more than 100 editions of his poems appeared in Britain and almost 50 in America. But 'God moves in a mysterious way/ His

---

[1] The poem refers to the character in Scott's *Guy Mannering*.

wonders to perform' (*NEH* 365): for now, alas, this interesting and profound poet, whom Coleridge called 'the best modern poet', hardly anyone except specialists reads. People who quote 'Variety is the very spice of life,/ That gives it all its flavour' with or without the second clause, rarely know it is from Cowper's 'The Timepiece' in his popular *The Task* (1785), II, 606-7. 'God made the country, and Man made the town' comes from 'The Sofa' in the same poem (I, 749). 'Strength join'd with beauty, dignity with grace,' is from *Tyrocinium*, 1784.[2] When we see his name at the end of a hymn it may rarely ring any bells. But his hymns – *NEH* 390 'Jesu, where'er thy people meet/There they behold thy mercy seat', *NEH* 414 (*A&M* 231), 'O for a closer walk with God,/ A calm and heavenly frame', and 'Hark my soul, it is the Lord, 'Tis thy Saviour, hear his word' (not in *NEH*) – all regularly appear in current hymnals. They, and others, are sung across the Anglophone world: in the bloodstream, so to speak. As a very small choirboy the last, and its tune, St Bees, in A flat, by the gloriously named Revd John Bacchus Dykes, always made me feel like crying, because I *would* have tried to love the Lord if I could only have known how you *could* if you could not see Him, and I felt very guilty. That sort of immortality in the songs on people's lips may be worth more than heavy books on library shelves.

Cowper loved the countryside round Olney and wrote about it lovingly. His sharpness of vision, far from any conventions of literary or artistic pastoral, anticipates Wordsworth and, in its realism, George Crabbe. But it is in East Dereham, Norfolk, that he died and was buried: he had spent some happy times in his childhood there and thither he retired in his sad last years. Many have visited the grave and written about it. One tribute, 'Cowper's Grave', came from Elizabeth Barrett Browning, Robert's wife, who found herself deeply moved not only by his delicate poetry and his tenderness to wild animals like

[2] 'It is not from his form, in which we trace
Strength join'd with beauty, dignity with grace,
That man, the master of this globe, derives
His right of empire over all that lives.'

WILLIAM COWPER

> Timid hares [he drew] from woods to share his home-
> caresses,
> Uplooking to his human eyes with sylvan tendernesses

but also by the deep, sometimes nearly suicidal, mental illness he suffered.

> It is a place where poets crowned may feel the heart's
> decaying;
> It is a place where happy saints may weep amid their
> praying;
> Yet let the grief and humbleness as low as silence can
> languish:
> Earth surely now may give her calm to whom she gave
> her anguish.
> O poets, from a maniac's tongue was poured the
> deathless singing!
> O Christians, at your cross of hope a hopeless hand was
> clinging!
> O men, this man in brotherhood your weary paths
> beguiling,
> Groaned inly while he taught you peace, and died while
> ye were smiling!

From that alembic of pain much of his poetry was distilled.

༄

His father John was Rector of Berkhamsted. The Cowpers were a cultured family: John's sister was the poet Judith Madan, who wrote an elegant reply for Abelard to Alexander Pope's *Eloisa to Abelard* (1717); William's mother descended from John Donne. She died when he, her seventh child, was six, and, to judge from a poem he wrote after seeing her picture in 1790, this loss troubled him all his life. His uncle Robert Donne and his wife became close to the child, and gave him his first books – John Gay's *Fables* and

A JOYFUL NOISE

Bunyan's *Pilgrim's Progress* – a book of genius,[3] but whose implicit Calvinism would profoundly and morbidly affect him in later life. He was educated first in the basics at a dame school, then by Revd William Davis at Aldbury. Then came two traumatic years at Dr Pittman's boarding school at Markyate on the Hertfordshire/Bedfordshire border. Writing in the 1760s, in his *Memoir of the Early Life of William Cowper, Esq.* (only published in 1816), he recalled bullying so severe that he knew his tormentor 'by his shoe-buckles better than any other part of his dress'. At 11 he was sent to Westminster. The Master then was John Nicoll, famous both for his use of the birch and his success in turning out excellent Classical scholars. Then came preparations for a career in law: membership of the Middle Temple, and articles to a solicitor, one Chapman, in Ely Place, Holborn. But he was never much drawn to law, and though called to the Bar never practised much as a barrister. (He did serve later as Commissioner of Bankruptcy Courts, a sinecure obtained by family interest.) In Southampton Row – then a broad thoroughfare of newly built, elegant houses, leading to open countryside – near where he was lodging, lived his uncle Ashley Cowper and his daughters Theodora and Harriet. The 21 year old Cowper spent a lot of time at what he recalled as this happy house, and he and Theodora fell in love. Her father, however, forbade any match. She apparently never got over this blow. Cowper seems to have done, but his initial devastation sparked off a sequence of poems to '*Delia*' (published only in 1825). This moves from clever amorous compliment like one finds in the Cavalier poets of the 1600s, and self-observation, in a style often playfully colloquial, to imagined scenes of pain and frustrated desire. Here Cowper first shows that image of himself, characteristic in his later writing, as subject to a fearful doom, an outcast who 'vainly strives to shun the threat'ning death.'

Indeed, this young man about town, and as casual about religion as any of his age, in 1752 sank into paralyzing depression

[3] My friend the cultural historian Victor Neuburg demonstrated that in pretty well any but the poorest cottage in Victorian England you would have found three books: the Bible, one of the cheap editions of Shakespeare that were becoming common, and Bunyan's.

William Cowper

— the first of four major battles with mental breakdown lasting weeks, even months, at a time. Struggle with despair, fuelled by fear that he was not one of those souls elect to glory from before the world began, came later to be the theme of his life. Later, in his *Memoir* he wrote:

> [I suffered] such a dejection of spirits, as none but they who have felt the same, can have the least conception of. Day and night I was upon the rack, lying down in horror, and rising up in despair. I presently lost all relish for those studies, to which before I had been closely attached; the classics had no longer any charms for me; I had need of something more salutary than amusement, but I had not one to direct me where to find it.

He came through this with the help of *The Temple: Sacred Poems and Private Ejaculations* of George Herbert. The dying Herbert had told his friend Ferrar to publish the poetry only if it might 'turn to the advantage of any dejected poor soul ... If not, let him burn it; for I and it are less than the least of God's mercies.' God moves in a mysterious way ...

Recovering, for some years he seems to have been happy enough, in friendly contact with other young men of literary and politically Whig bent whom he had known at Westminster. The Nonsense Club, as they called themselves, met to dine every Thursday. It included Robert Lloyd, Bonnell Thornton (who wrote cruelly witty parodies with the playwright George Colman), and the poet Charles Churchill. Some of the group's meetings may also have included William Hogarth: he and Churchill in the end fell out bitterly, and Hogarth published a print, 'The Bruiser', in 1762, caricaturing Churchill as a bad-tempered bulldog. All of these men could turn a decent verse: after all, that then was a gentleman's expected accomplishment. From the perspective of his retired and gentle later life, it is hard to imagine Cowper in this somewhat raffish group, some of whom became decidedly dissolute. The group soon had some notoriety, and waged not only many virulent literary and theatrical battles, circulated many biting satires, but also, combining with the radical and scandalous John Wilkes[4], engaged in some of the most important mid-century political debates. Cowper began contributing satirical pieces to *The Connoisseur,* a weekly newspaper started by Bonnell and Colman.[5] But these topical pieces have been lost; only the few, commissioned, translations, of Horace *Satires* (1759) and Voltaire's 1728 *La Henriade* (1762) are what survive from this time. The choice of those two works, of course, both critical of a status quo and – as Horace put it – *ridentem dicere verum quid vetat,* 'what stops me telling the truth with a smile?' – is not without significance.

Another major breakdown came in 1763. His father died in 1756, leaving only a small inheritance for William and his only surviving sibling John. Ashley Cowper again used his influence to appoint him to the lucrative sinecure of Clerk of the Journals in the House of Lords, but when a rival political faction challenged his uncle's right of appointment – such rights were then essential parts of the game of politics – Cowper was summoned for examination about his fitness for the post at the Bar of the House. He panicked at the prospect of this ordeal, and descended into a melancholy in which thrice he attempted suicide.

> All the horrors of my fears and perplexities now returned. A thunderbolt would have been as welcome to me as this intelligence [=interrogation] ... Those whose spirits are formed like mine, to whom a public exhibition of themselves, on any occasion, is mortal poison, may have

---

[4] Wilkes was ejected from Parliament – he was MP for Middlesex – several times and was associated with Sir Francis Dashwood's Hell Fire Club at Medmenham. (So were many men in politics: and the Club makes the Cliveden Set of the 1960s look like models of rectitude.)

[5] Boswell says in his *Life of Johnson:* 'I mentioned the periodical paper called THE CONNOISSEUR. He said it wanted matter. – No doubt it had not the deep thinking of Johnson's writings. But surely it has just view of the surface of life, and a very sprightly manner. His opinion of THE WORLD was not much higher than of THE CONNOISSEUR'. (Johnson in the same decade was producing *The Rambler* and *The Idler.*)

some idea of the horror of my situation; others can have none. (*Memoir*, 114).

For more than half a year his feelings were those 'of a man when he arrives at the place of execution.'

So he was sent to Dr Nathaniel Cotton's Collegium Insanorum, an asylum at St Alban. He was confined there for 18 months, plagued by religious doubt and persistently dreading that he was predestined[6] to damnation.

6   As it is so little read nowadays – once upon a time every new incumbent had to 'read himself in' by reading the 39 Articles of Religion of the Church of England on his induction to his living – I quote in full XVII 'Of Predestination And Election', which is thoroughly Calvinist:
'PREDESTINATION to Life is the everlasting purpose of God, whereby (before the foundations of the world were laid) he hath constantly decreed by his counsel secret to us, to deliver from curse and damnation those whom he hath chosen in Christ out of mankind, and to bring them by Christ to everlasting salvation, as vessels made to honour. Wherefore, they which be endued with so excellent a benefit of God be called according to God's purpose by his Spirit working in due season: they through Grace obey the calling: they be justified freely: they be made sons of God by adoption: they be made like the image of his only-begotten Son Jesus Christ: they walk religiously in good works, and at length, by God's mercy, they attain to everlasting felicity.

As the godly consideration of Predestination, and our Election in Christ, is full of sweet, pleasant, and unspeakable comfort to godly persons, and such as feel in themselves the working of the Spirit of Christ, mortifying the works of the flesh, and their earthly members, and drawing up their mind to high and heavenly things, as well because it doth greatly establish and confirm their faith of eternal Salvation to be enjoyed through Christ, as because it doth fervently kindle their love towards God: So, for curious and carnal persons, lacking the Spirit of Christ, to have continually before their eyes the sentence of God's Predestination, is a most dangerous downfall, whereby the Devil doth thrust them either into desperation, or into wretchedness of most unclean living, no less perilous than desperation.

Furthermore, we must receive God's promises in such wise, as they be generally set forth to us in holy Scripture: and, in our doings, that Will of God is to be followed, which we have expressly declared unto us in the Word of God.'

But, slowly recovering, in September 1765, Cowper moved to Huntingdon, within easy reach of the company of his brother John, a Fellow of Corpus Christi College, 16 miles away in Cambridge. Quite soon he met Revd Morley Unwin and his loving, educated and kindly family. Cowper was delighted with the family and they with him, and in October he moved in with them in Huntingdon as a paying boarder. He wrote to his friend Joseph Hill:

> I have added another family to the number of those I was acquainted with when you were here. Their name is Unwin – the most agreeable people imaginable; quite sociable, and as free from the ceremonious civility of country gentlefolks as any I have ever met with. They treat me more like a near relation than a stranger, and their house is always open to me. The old gentleman carries me to Cambridge in his chaise. He is a man of learning and good sense, and as simple as Parson Adams.[7] His wife has a very uncommon understanding, has read much to excellent purpose, and is more polite than a duchess.

Morley and his wife Mary proved a haven where he could convalesce. Unwin had been a Fellow of Queens' College, Cambridge, and the College had presented him to the living of Grimston, near King's Lynn, but, his wife disliking the place and their having sufficient income, he had a curate discharge his duties, and had taken a house in Huntingdon. There he prepared pupils for the University. The Unwins were much in sympathy with the growing Evangelical revival. But in 1767 Morley Unwin was killed in a fall from his horse, and his widow and family, with Cowper, moved to Orchard Side, a substantial house on the market place in John Newton's parish of Olney.

---

[7] The wise and kindly parson in Henry Fielding's *Joseph Andrews* (1742).

WILLIAM COWPER

Newton encouraged Cowper in a life of practical evangelism, and bolstered his growing opposition to the slave trade, forcefully expressed in Book II of *The Task* (1785), and in the dramatic monologue of *The Negro's Complaint* (commissioned in 1788 by the Committee for the Abolition of the Slave Trade). However, Cowper's mental health was weak, and his religious doubt and melancholy, his terror of damnation, returned in full force: for he feared that having once doubted Christ, he had committed the sin against the Holy Ghost (Matthew 12:31), in Calvinist dogma the 'unpardonable sin'. In a poem of 1774 called 'Hatred and vengeance, my eternal portion' he sees himself as 'Damn'd below Judas,' for that long ago rejection of Christ. He did recover, but the black moods periodically returned. He kept busy with gardening, woodwork, and taming and keeping animals, including his beloved hares.

For as he was emerging, still shattered, from fifteen months of illness, he was given a leveret. A shepherd's dog had found it in its form – hares often leave their young for long periods – and the shepherd gave it to the parish clerk, as a pet for his children. As young children will, they neglected it when the novelty was over, and the compassionate clerk offered it to Cowper. He says he was glad 'of any thing that would engage my attention without fatiguing it ... in the management of such an animal, and in the attempt to tame it, I should find just that sort of employment which my case required.' Soon he had two more. He ended up with three, Puss, Tiney and Bess, and in a letter to *The Gentleman's Magazine* (June 1784) describes how

> Puss grew presently familiar, would leap into my lap, raise himself upon his hinder feet, and bite the hair from my temples. He would suffer me to take him up and to carry him about in my arms, and has more than once fallen asleep upon my knee. He was ill three days, during which time I nursed him, kept him apart from his fellows that they might not molest him (for, like many other wild animals, they persecute one of their own

species that is sick), and, by constant care and trying him with a variety of herbs, restored him to perfect health. No creature could be more grateful than my patient after his recovery; a sentiment which he most significantly expressed, by licking my hand, first the back of it, then the palm, then every finger separately, then between all the fingers, as if anxious to leave no part of it unsaluted, a ceremony which he never performed but once again upon a similar occasion ...

As it happens, young hares can sometimes be trained to be affectionate, but they cannot be domesticated, and they will run away: which is why the front door at Orchard Side was never opened. Moreover, while the hares were with him, he also had five rabbits, two guinea pigs, a magpie, a jay, a starling, a linnet, two goldfinches, two canaries, two dogs, and sixteen pigeons.

Two people living in the same house and not married to each other would then perhaps have caused some comment in a village, even had this menagerie not done, and by 1772 it seems Cowper had arranged to marry Mary Unwin. To her indeed he owed, bluntly, his life. On suicide watch during his worst depressions, she slept on the floor of his bedroom; in the parlour she entertained their friends, played the harpsichord, worked at her embroidery. She made every room safe, and Cowper repaid her dedication with his. But the idea of marriage came to nothing: he was ill again, and John Newton looked after him at the vicarage for a time.

During this time at Orchard Side, Cowper became friendly with a widow, Lady Austen, who had come to live nearby. She told him the true story that became the ballad 'The Journey of John Gilpin', and then, complaining that he lacked a big subject for his talent, she playfully suggested the biggest piece of furniture in his parlour. *The Task* starts as a mock-heroic account of a wooden stool metamorphosing into a sofa: it eventually became a major poem in six Books, 'to recommend rural ease and leisure'. Later in it Cowper

WILLIAM COWPER

meditates on the world immediately around him (his parlour, village, garden, animals), and that leads on to much bigger religious and humanitarian concerns: for Cowper is one of the first poets to express the intuition that Wordsworth and Blake knew, that everything is connected to, and affects, everything else, that the world – Nature, if you like – is inescapably a moral force. A long passage in *The Task* denounces any insensitivity or cruelty to animals. He would not have as friend, he says, 'the man / Who needlessly sets foot upon a worm'. More, he avoids any sentimentality or the facile idealization of animals that often gush from later Romantic poetry. He describes animals affectionately but as they naturally are, and he strongly opposed hare coursing:

> They love the country, and none else, who seek
> For their own sake its silence and its shade.
> Delights which who would leave, that has a heart
> Susceptible of pity, or a mind
> Cultured and capable of sober thought,
> For all the savage din of the swift pack
> And clamours of the field detested sport,
> That owes its pleasures to another's pain,
> That feeds upon the sobs and dying shrieks
> Of harmless nature, dumb, but yet endued
> With eloquence that agonies inspire
> Of silent tears and heart-distending sighs!
> Vain tears alas! and sighs that never find
> A corresponding tone in jovial souls.
> Well-one at least is safe. One shelter'd hare
> Has never heard the sanguinary yell
> Of cruel man, exulting in her woes.
> Innocent partner of my peaceful home,
> Whom ten long years experience of my care
> Has made at last familiar, she has lost
> Much of her vigilant instinctive dread,

A Joyful Noise

Not needful here, beneath a roof like mine.[8]
From 'The Garden' (1785)

The west wing of Orchard Side remained his home till 1786. But then Cowper, now a literary figure of real eminence, moved with Mrs Unwin and all his animals to Weston Underwood, about a mile away. The Throckmorton family of Weston Underwood Hall, whom Cowper affectionately called 'Mr and Mrs Frog', put their gardens, and a summer house as a writing retreat, at his disposal. For some time things seemed easier and indeed, the 1790s opened promisingly with new publishing commissions, popular success and the invitation, which delighted him, to edit the works of Milton. But there is a pastel portrait of Cowper done by George Romney done at this time, in 1792. It is, to my mind, Romney at the top of his bent as a psychologist. The face, guarded, eyes wide and anxious, mouth full-lipped, firm set, captures the brilliance of the man and at the same time an almost tragic melancholy. This

---

[8] In *Venus and Adonis* (1593) Shakespeare arouses pity for Wat, the hunted hare. And Alexander Pope, in *Windsor Forest* (1713) captures both the excitement and the pity of it all:

> Nor yet, when moist Arcturus clouds the sky,
> The woods and fields their pleasing toils deny. [120]
> To plains with well-breath'd beagles we repair,
> And trace the mazes of the circling hare:
> (Beasts, urg'd by us, their fellow-beasts pursue,
> And learn of man each other to undo.)
> With slaught'ring guns th' unweary'd fowler roves,
> When frosts have whiten'd all the naked groves;
> Where doves in flocks the leafless trees o'ershade,
> And lonely woodcocks haunt the wat'ry glade.
> He lifts the tube, and levels with his eye;
> Strait a short thunder breaks the frozen sky:
> Oft', as in airy rings they skim the heath,
> The clam'rous plovers feel the leaden death:
> Oft', as the mounting larks their notes prepare,
> They fall, and leave their little lives in air.

is the face of a man who does not trust fortune, a man whom fear stalks. And all was not to be well: Mrs Unwin, on whom he had relied 'as a Mother' had a stroke in 1795, and died soon after, and Cowper, inconsolable, himself died of dropsy in April 1800. The old fears and depression returned. A year before he died he wrote:

> No voice divine the storm allay'd,
> No light propitious shone;
> When, snatch'd from all effectual aid,
> We perish'd, each alone:
> But I beneath a rougher sea,
> And whelm'd in deeper gulfs than he.
> *(The Castaway)*

An extraordinary career, and extraordinary influence on contemporaries and successors. But Elizabeth Browning was right: it came at a price: he could not have written as he did without the suffering, the fear, and the sharpening by that fear of the perception of the beauty and holiness of this world. His hymns, which we sing so blithely and often unthinkingly, have a subtext of uncertainty, the great Calvinist worry of never conclusive search for the signs of grace in the soul. 'The Contrite Heart', one of the *Olney Hymns* (though it works better as a poem) movingly realizes the terror of being outside the company of God's elect:

> Thy saints are comforted I know
> And love thy house of pray'r;
> I therefore go where others go,
> But find no comfort there.

That stanza, in its simplicity of language and form and the complexity of its thought reminds me of some of George Herbert, and his struggles in his soul. In fact, George Herbert seems to have been the only poet in English whom Cowper valued highly. In his *Memoir of His Early Life* (c. 1752) he wrote,

> ... I yet found in [Herbert's poems] them a strain of piety which I could not but admire. This was the only author I had any delight in reading. I poured [*sic*] upon him all day long and though I found not there what I might have found, a cure for my malady, yet it never seemed so much alleviated as while I was reading him.

In January 1773, in a dream, Cowper had heard a voice say, '*Actum est de te, periisti*' ('It is all over with you, you have perished'). 'God moves in a mysterious way' as a hymn had made magnificently present the Calvinist God who is 'his own Interpreter' who 'will make it plain'; but what He made plain in this dream – how reliable are dreams? – was that Cowper was eternally damned. Cowper continued to hold staunchly to his religious beliefs, but he never again entered a church or said a prayer.

༄

And the hymns? Well, hymns need simplicity of diction and conciseness of statement: which does not always make for great verse. Am I alone in finding in 'He plants His footsteps in the sea / And rides upon the storm', from *NEH 365*, the banal sliding into the comic? Yet the subject, God's inscrutability, is serious enough. Knowing something of Cowper's troubled life really does make the hymns read and sing – I speak for myself – differently. Knowing his dread of his own damnation – well, I can glimpse that in 'Hark my soul, it is the Lord' when I recall how that hymn prompted my own childish anxiety. 'God moves in a mysterious way': as I have grown older I have become more and more aware that God is not tame, does not fit our images and categories with which we too often, and often unconsciously, domesticate the wild passion of Divine Love: 'God is his own interpreter', indeed. But for a man like Cowper, deep in depression and fraught with fear, that mysteriousness could easily be threatening, and the hymn lead far from the cheerful, and (to me again bathetic), conclusion of 'Behind a frowning Providence / He hides a smiling face.'

XVII

JAMES MONTGOMERY
1771–1854

ೆ2

'Put not your trust in Princes.' In 1415, at the Council of Constance, Jan Huss, priest, theologian, charismatic preacher, was betrayed by the Emperor Sigismund, King of Hungary. Sigismund had promised Huss safe conduct if he would come to Constance to explain his arguments, both theological and about Church reform, to the Council which sought to heal the schisms in the church and to bring in reforms which everybody agreed were needed. (Alas, as too often, only those that don't affect *my* vested interest ...) He was instead imprisoned. He refused to recant his views on, for example, the nature of the Eucharist, and was burned at the stake as a heretic. They said he could be heard singing psalms as he died.

Huss had a large following in his native Bohemia, a following that fought for decades with sword and shield to defend its position against a resurgent and militant Roman orthodoxy. That resistance is part of Bohemia's national myth: as witness 'Tabor' in Smetana's *Ma Vlast* (1874-9). Like Wyclif in England, only recently dead, Huss questioned much of the Church's teaching on the Sacraments, on confession, on property, and urged a return to a church cleansed to Apostolic purity. Rightly, he and Wyclif have been seen as precursors, the first flaws in the wind, of the great storm of Reformation in the next century, that divided (and still divides) the Western Church. Martin Luther was born 68 years

JAMES MONTGOMERY

after Huss died, and gave yet greater force to many of his ideas.

What have all these 'old, forgotten far off, things, and battles long ago' to do with *NEH* 55 (*A&M* 142), 'Hail to the Lord's anointed', 451 (*A&M* 196), 'Songs of praise the angels sang', or 452 (*A&M* 201), 'Stand up and bless the Lord'? I start this sketch of James Montgomery thus because without some understanding of the enduring influence of Huss and his later followers, the Moravian Brethren (a community born of persecution and martyrdom), there is much that can easily be overlooked in those religious cross currents of the later seventeenth and eighteenth centuries which made the mindset of men like Montgomery. In his lifetime Moravians were engaged in missions in the West Indies, Greenland and Labrador; they colonised and set up communities in the Carolinas, missions in the Low Counties, Denmark, England and Scotland. The Moravians are by no means a historical footnote, as vigorous Moravian communities today attest – like the one I know in Winston Salem in North Carolina. Without the community at the chapel in Aldersgate Street in London, where he went, initially with reluctance, in 1738, would John Wesley's (and Charles Wesley's) career have taken the course it did? For Wesley was much inspired by the spirituality of their community in London as well as Georgia, and it was there that he famously felt his 'heart strangely warmed' during a reading of Luther's Preface to *Romans*. Would the anti-slavery movement have gathered so much support so quickly without the Moravian missions?

James Montgomery's father was a pastor, and missionary, of the Moravian Brethren in the ancient Royal Burgh of Irvine in Ayrshire. He intended James, born in 1771, for the Moravian ministry, and at six sent him off to the School (which still exists) run by the Moravian Brothers and Sisters at Fulneck[1] in Pudsey, near Leeds. In his nine years there,

[1] Happily, the name attested in 1592, Fallneck, was close to that the Moravians gave it when they bought the land in 1744: Fulnek, a town in Northern Moravia, Czech Republic, where there had been a large Moravian community. The Moravians opened schools for both boys and (less usually) girls: they merged in 1904.

Fulneck's curriculum gave James grounding in Latin, Greek, German and French besides the ordinary studies of an English grammar-school. He did complain, however, of 'being driven like a coal-ass' through these subjects: he was no scholar. However, he was also beginning to show some talent for verse, one influential model being the Moravian hymn book, where many of the hymns are in quatrains. In 1779 his parents brought their other two sons, Ignatius and Robert, to Fulneck as well. Then, in 1783, leaving their sons, they went to Barbados as missionaries to the slaves. The Montgomerys stayed there till 1789, then moved to Tobago, where James' mother died a year later. After a year his father died too.

Such missions were often unpopular. There were slave owners who saw them as subversive of their whole way of life – as indeed the Gospel *is* subversive of so many comfortable and accepted things. St Paul had written to the Galatians (3:28), 'There is neither Jew nor Greek, there is neither bond nor free, there is neither male nor female: for ye are all one in Christ Jesus.' It followed, by a sophistry, that if these slaves were not Christian, not 'in Christ', they could be held as slaves. If they became Christian, they had to be freed.[2]

Deciding (to his relief) that he was suited neither for the ministry nor for teaching, the Moravian Brothers, acting as his guardians, apprenticed him at 15 to a baker in Mirfield. Then, one Sunday morning – June 19, 1789 – he abruptly left Mirfield, and went out with no clear idea of where he was going. He trudged along the quiet, summer-dusty roads, all through that day and the next, through Doncaster with its Romanesque church – burned to the ground in 1853 – to Wentworth. He came to Wath, on the river Dearne, and there found a job in a country store—and filled up his spare moments with writing verse. There was a bookseller in the village, who recognised talent. He encouraged him to make a selection of his poetry

---

[2] Katherine Gerbner, *Christian Slavery: Protestant missions and Slave Conversion in the Atlantic World,* 1660-1760, Harvard Dissertation, PhD. 2013, http://nrs.harvard.edu/urn-3:HUL.InstRepos:11095959 (accessed 30 June 2022) p. 34ff.

and try for publication, and himself forwarded it to a London publisher, James Harrison, of Paternoster Row.[3] Montgomery soon afterwards followed in person, with letters of introduction, to see Harrison. Harrison turned the MS down, but took the young man on as a clerk. He stayed a year, well provided for, but repeated attempts to get his work published failed: he offered several publishers poems, novels, books for children, but was turned down each time. At length, fed up with London, he returned to Wath, and took up his old job again. But in 1792 came a major turning point: he saw an advertisement for a clerk's job in Sheffield. He got the job, working for the remarkable Joseph Gales, bookseller, and also founder, printer and publisher of the *Sheffield Register*.

Gales introduced him into the local Lodge of Oddfellows,[4] and was a great influence on him. Unitarian[5] and radical Whig, Gales habitually sailed close to the wind. He had started his paper after meeting the inspiring Tom Paine, already notorious for supporting the rebels in the American War of Independence. Paine's *The Rights of Man* (1791), written

---

[3] Harrison may have been approached because his was an old and well established firm. He printed the *London Gazette,* but also collaborated with Joseph Wenman c.1778-81 on a popular series of reprinted drama, poetry, fiction, and essays: *Harrison's British Classicks* (8 volumes of essays, c.1785), *The Novelist's Magazine, The Lady's Poetical Magazine, The New Musical Magazine,* and others.

[4] The origins of this Society? Brotherhood? can't be traced much before 1730, but by the 1780s there were more than a few local lodges whose members pledged mutual support, and were engaged in charitable work. Members, like John Wilkes or Sir George Savile, advocated civil liberties and even – radical at the time – abolition of laws preventing Catholics and Jews from holding any public office and debarring them from the Universities.

[5] It is remarkable how Unitarians dominated so much of the political and scientific discussions at this time. Erasmus Darwin, Charles' grandfather, was Unitarian, as was his friend Josiah Wedgwood. So too Joseph Priestley, Maria Edgeworth, James Watt, Matthew Boulton, and later Elizabeth Gaskell. They advocated extension of the franchise, education for women, abolition of the slave trade.

as reply to Edmund Burke's *Reflections on the Revolution in France*, many felt to be explosive. Unusually, Gales' *Register* did not simply reprint material from the London papers, but covered local issues as well as major national stories. The paper carried pieces by radical reformers like Paine, William Godwin, Joseph Priestley, and Horne Tooke, and the paper both educated and reflected the views of artisans and the many small manufacturers in the Sheffield area. It carried reports of speeches at public meetings. In 1791 it supported the opposition to an Enclosure Bill to enclose 6,000 acres of Sheffield's common land without any compensation to holders of rights of common. Later that year Gales helped form the Sheffield Constitutional Society, the very first artisan political society. His paper was by this time selling a remarkable 2000 copies each issue, when Sheffield's population was not quite 60,000. Then in 1792 Gales made contact with the recently formed London Corresponding Society, one of the centres of radical thought, which Pitt's government, desperately nervous about a repeat in England of the events in France, rapidly classed as seditious. Provocatively, Gales published a cheap (6d) copy of Paine's *Rights of Man*. In April 1793 he chaired an open meeting on parliamentary reform, starting a petition, which 8000 people signed, for universal suffrage. Sheffield was rapidly becoming seen as the most radical town in England. The following year, Gales fled, with his family, to escape certain prosecution: he ended up in the USA, and eventually became mayor of Washington. In his last issue of the *Register*, he wrote: 'I have committed no crime, but, in these persecuting days, it is a sufficient crime to have printed a newspaper which has boldly dared to doubt the infallibility of ministers, and to investigate the justice and policy of their measures.'

James Montgomery, just 22, now found himself in charge of the paper. He changed the name to the *Sheffield Iris* – for was not Iris the Messenger of the Gods? Inevitably, he was a watched man. He was twice imprisoned on a charge of sedition, first in 1795 for printing a poem (not by him) celebrating the 1789 storming of the Bastille, and then in 1796 for criticising a magistrate's use of force to disperse a political protest meeting in Sheffield. (Later he published the poems he wrote during his sentence, *Prison Amusements,* 1797.) For some time the *Iris* was Sheffield's only newspaper, but though Montgomery produced decent articles each week, he had not got Gales' flair or political clout. Other newspapers started up, and in 1825 he sold the *Iris* to a local bookseller, John Blackwell.

Harrison's declining his youthful verse had not put him off writing poetry, and in 1806 he had some success with *The Wanderer of Switzerland*, in six parts, which discussed the French annexation of Switzerland. When the conservative *Edinburgh Review* in 1807 pronounced it would soon be forgotten, Byron, no less, defended Montgomery in *English Bards and Scotch Reviewers.* No review is a bad review: within 18 months the same presses that had printed the criticism printed a fourth impression of 1500 copies of the poem, and several more followed. This success brought Montgomery a commission for a poem on Parliament's (very recent) abolition of the slave trade, for a celebratory volume. *The West Indies,* in four parts, appeared in 1810. In 1812 came *The World before the Flood*, and then he turned to social issues: he attacked the lottery in *Thoughts on Wheels* (1817), and in *The Climbing Boys' Soliloquies* he took on the socially accepted scandal, the terrible plight of chimney sweeps' climbing boys. William Blake had already written movingly about how children as young as five or six were often sold by destitute parents to their masters and sent to scrub the insides of chimneys. The occupational disease, which killed many of them young, was cancer of the scrotum. His next major poem, much admired, was *Greenland* (1819), which began by describing the ancient Moravian church, its eighteenth-century revival and its mission in 1733 to West Greenland – the area round the modern Godthaab.

Is he a good poet? His *Poetical Works* had four editions (1821, 1836, 1841, 1854), and printers do not print for fun. He certainly had some following. Some reviews of his work were dismissive; on the other hand, *Blackwood's Magazine* could say of *The Pelican Island* (1828), 'the best of all Montgomery's poems:

in idea the most original, in execution the most powerful.' My own view, bearing in mind I could not do half as well? He has a formal assurance in using heroic couplets and blank verse, and can certainly turn a neat line or an elegant quatrain. But there is a somewhat old-fashioned feel about much of his verse, with neatly balanced lines, each noun having its adjective, each verb its adverb, as if nothing much had happened since Pope, and the whole storm of Romanticism had somehow not changed the way he wrote. Of the excitement and wit of Cowper's *Task*, or the elegant ironies, verbal dexterity and tumultuous passion of Byron, or the profundity of Wordsworth's *Tintern Abbey* or *Michael* or *Immortality Ode* – well, no. But this is perhaps unfair. He did not set out to do those things. Montgomery himself expected – hoped – that his name would live, if at all, in his hymns.

Even when a youth at Wath he had been writing hymns. His upbringing had been thoroughly Christian. He had always been interested in the social implications of religion. But for many people there often comes a time when all the assumptions, certainties even, of youth have to be rethought, questioned, when to know and think is simply not enough. Kierkegaard talks about the necessity of going through the dark night of radical doubt, when intellect and knowledge seem like straw, to the full understanding of the faith in emotion and feeling as well as reason – or, to put it another way, to match the template of theoretical understanding to the reality of everyday experience. It is clear from letters to his brother Ignatius, for example in 1803, that he went through exactly this symbolic death and rebirth into faith.[6] This journey, as so often, took years. But late in 1814, he returned to Fulneck and was accepted as a Brother in the Lord, a full member of the Moravian Society. In Sheffield, he worshipped at the Anglican St Paul's, a chapel of ease to Sheffield's only (then) parish Church, St Peter's. St

---

[6] This is well discussed in Robert T. Williamson, *The Religious Thought of James Montgomery*, PhD Thesis, University of Edinburgh, 1950, pp.36ff. (https://era.ed.ac.uk/bitstream/handle/1842/10190/0074214c.pdf, accessed 30 June 2022).

James Montgomery

Paul's had been built by public subscription in 1730 to cater for the town's growing population. A new incumbent, James Cotterill, arrived in 1817, and hoped to persuade his new parishioners to use his own *Selection of Psalms and Hymns Adapted to the Services of the Church of England* (1810). But with typical Yorkshire resistance to change, they were unhappy about it, and bluntly said so. So he asked Montgomery to help revise the collection, and added some hymns by Montgomery. This new edition was sent to be approved by the Archbishop of York, was finally published in 1820, and the congregation accepted it. In 1822 Montgomery published his own *Songs of Zion: Being Imitations of Psalms*, the first of several more collections of hymns – *The Christian Psalmist (1825), and Original Hymns (1853).* Indeed, the Psalms, and the old tradition of singing metrical versions of them, do form a sort of bedrock to many of Montgomery's hymns. *NEH* 55, for example, is based on Psalm 72. Overall he composed some 400 hymns, although not many of them are commonly sung today. *NEH* includes 55 'Hail to the Lord's anointed', 230 (*A&M* 307) 'Palms of glory, raiment bright/Crowns that never pass away' (an Archbishop of York, William McLagan, wrote a tune for it), 270 'According to thy gracious word', 322 'Pour out thy spirit from on high', 406 (*A&M* 227) 'Lord, teach us how to pray aright', 442 'Prayer is the soul's sincere desire', 451 (*A&M* 196) 'Songs of praise the angels sang' 452, 'Stand up and bless the Lord'. Unaccountably, it does not include the fine 'Angels from the realms of glory' or 'Go to dark Gethsemane': they are in *A&M*. If the marks of a good hymn text be a succinct, elegant and memorable statement of devotional insight, and singable, then he does rank high: some of his are equal in these qualities to those of Watts or Wesley, Doddridge, Newton and Cowper. He once wrote:

> If he who pens these hymns knows his own heart he would rather be the anonymous author of a few hymns which should become and imperishable inheritance to the people of God, than bequeath another epic to the world

which should rank his name with Homer, Virgil and our greater Milton.

He died widely respected, indeed beloved. He had been active in promoting Sunday Schools, which of course then really *were* schools, teaching basic reading and writing, as well as the Bible. These were often all the education that many poor children, working long hours in awful, unsafe conditions in the new factories in the industrial towns, ever got. He had supported Bible and Tract Societies, and Mission work generally. This had become very close to his heart – his parents had been missionaries, after all – and in the *Iris* in 1818 he had printed an appeal for support of the Moravian missions in Greenland. He gave lectures on literature to the Royal Institution in London. His standing was publicly recognised in 1833 by Robert Peel's grant of a Royal Pension of £200 p.a. – no inconsiderable sum. When he died he was given a funeral at public expense, and a public subscription raised £1000 for a stained glass window in Sheffield Parish Church (now the Cathedral) and a statue in the precincts. On the granite pedestal of the statue is carved, 'Here lies interred, beloved by all who knew him, the Christian poet, patriot, and philanthropist. Wherever poetry is read, or Christian hymns sung, in the English language, he being dead, yet speaketh by the genius, piety and taste embodied in his writings.'

XVIII
Reginald Heber
1783–1826

As I write, Epiphany is almost upon us, when Christ is first shown forth to the Gentiles. Us, in fact. 'The kings of Tarshish and of the isles shall bring presents: the kings of Sheba and Seba shall offer gifts' (Ps. 72:10). Whom to choose as hymnwriter for this season when we ask the brightest and best of the Sons of the morning to shine on our own darkness?

Reginald Heber's family were wealthy, well-connected, landed, armigerous since the time of the first Elizabeth. His father was both squire and Rector of Hodnet in Shropshire. While at Brasenose College, Oxford, he gained – if only moderate academic distinction – a reputation as a poet of fashionably Romantic cast in both Latin and English. His long poem, *Palestine,* which won the Newdigate Prize in 1803, he wrote with advice from a young Sir Walter Scott, a family friend – this was long before Scott was himself famous as poet and novelist. Heber read it to an enthusiastic audience at that year's Encaenia, and many thought he might make a reputation as a poet. Later *Palestine* was set to music by William Crotch (Professor of Music since 1797), and translated into Welsh by W. Owen Pughe (1822). Heber's biographer, Arthur Montefiore, who himself later held the Bishopric of Calcutta in which office Heber died, called it 'the most successful and popular piece of religious verse of the first half of the

A Joyful Noise

[nineteenth] century'. A later biographer, Derrick Hughes (1986), however, finds this all puzzling: 'It is not a good, not even a mediocre poem; it is leaden.'

Heber graduated in 1805, in December of which year Napoleon won his greatest victory at Austerlitz, crushing the Russian and Austrian forces – but also the year of Trafalgar. A generation earlier it would have been common for a new and relatively affluent graduate to make the Grand Tour through France and Italy and perhaps Greece, but Napoleon's wars stopped that. Instead Heber and his friend John Thornton (the grandson of John Thornton, John Newton's friend and benefactor[1]) travelled for 15 months through Scandinavia, to Russia and its Black Sea coast, and then home through Poland, Austria and several of the little German-speaking states that later made up the Germany we know. Travel for people of Heber's background was eased then by letters of introduction to influential people – he was able to see the Tsar's private apartment in the Winter Place in St Petersburg, for example. Another introduction led to Lord Morpeth's private yacht bringing him home from Hamburg. Back in Oxford, he read for ordination, and was ordained in 1807.

Controversy between the Evangelical movement and the High Church was growing increasingly bitter, and it seems he had not really made up his mind where he himself stood. When he took over his late father's living as Rector of Hodnet – as he put it later, a role that was a 'half-way station between a parson and a squire' – he wrote to John Thornton, 'Pray for me, my dear friend, that I may have my eyes open to the truth ... and if it please God that I persevere in his ministry I may undertake the charge with a quiet mind and a good conscience.' Though by upbringing High Church, he was deeply uneasy about the bitter factional quarrelling, and his own position was eirenic, seeking a *via media*.

He was wealthy enough to pay a curate, and split his time between Hodnet and All Souls', Oxford, of which he had been

---

[1] Heber's daughter, born in Calcutta, married Thornton's son.

Reginald Heber

elected a Fellow. In 1815 he was elected to deliver the endowed Bampton Lectures before to the University, a very prestigious post indeed. For he was a serious scholar: during his sixteen years as Rector of Hodnet, where he was loved as a careful and kindly parish priest, he edited, in 15 volumes, the complete works of the seventeenth-century cleric Jeremy Taylor – whom Coleridge greatly admired – including *The Rule and Exercises of Holy Living* (1650) and *The Rule and Exercises of Holy Dying* (1651). The first is a manual of Christian practice, still read today: the title page offers 'the means and instruments of obtaining every virtue, and remedies against every vice, and considerations serving to the resisting all temptations, together with prayers containing the whole Duty of a Christian'. *Holy Dying* was perhaps even more popular. Heber's edition remained standard for the best part of a century. He also had strong links with the London literary world – he was in Robert Southey's circle, who had been Poet Laureate since 1813, and contributed articles and reviews to *The Quarterly Review* which John Murray started in 1809 as counter to the conservative *Edinburgh Review*. (He wrote on many things, for example the military power of Russia, and Byron's 1821 tragedy, *Cain*.) In 1822 he was elected Preacher at Lincoln's Inn, which meant regular journeys to London. It was during this busy period that he also wrote his large output of 57 hymns, when the Established Church had only just accepted congregational singing of texts other than metrical psalms. The Bishop of London was distinctly cool when Heber asked him for support in publishing a collection of hymns for congregational use, and suggested Heber publish it himself. Yet the *Olney Hymns* of William Cowper (1731-1800), and the hymns of the former slave ship captain John Newton, Evangelical vicar of Cowper's village of Olney, were becoming almost as popular as those of Charles Wesley. John Betjeman (*Sweet Songs of Zion*, 2008) recognised their influence in Heber's work. His style is, in the fashion of the day, consciously literary: as Betjeman put it, 'with careful choices of adjectives and vivid figures of speech: poetic imagery was as important as didactic truth'. His hymns perhaps do not have the scriptural strength of, say, Wesley's, and certainly not the dogmatic force and succinctness of the best Latin ones. But then, they were not so intended. More recent responses (J. R. Watson, for example: *The English Hymn: A Critical and Historical Study*, Oxford 1999), less indulgently, point out Heber's tendency to 'rather obvious sermon', and how he mixes description which can be forceful with 'a rather trite moralism'. Well, nobody's perfect: and though most of those 57 hymns now sound no more, in *NEH* we do have several, composed in somewhat unusual metres which makes the tunes which will fit (if you want to change the accustomed ones) something of a problem – e.g. 146, in 11/12/10/10, or 301 in 10/7/10/7. *NEH* includes the loved Epiphany hymn, 49 (*A&M* 47), 'Brightest and best of the sons of the morning'; 146, 'Holy, Holy, Holy, Lord God Almighty' (*A&M* 95) for Trinity; 187,(*A&M* 311) 'Virgin born, we bow before thee', for feasts of the Blessed Virgin; Verse 1 of 245, 'God that madest earth and heaven' – is it the words or the tune, *Ar hyd y nos* that makes that one so ineradicable in the memory?; 277 (*A&M* 270), 'Bread of the world in mercy broken', and 301 'O most merciful, O most bountiful'. From my old pre-1983 *A&M* I recall with some affection 'From Greenland's icy mountains', which is now not *at all* politically correct and to some lines of which Mahatma Gandhi himself objected. (Its splendid tune, 'Aurelia', which fits its unusual 7,6,76,7,6 metre, is now attached to *NEH* 167, a rather trite hymn for a most *un*-trite figure in Acts of the Apostles.) But it was one of the first great missionary hymns, written when the new Missionary Societies (the Church Missionary Society founded in 1799, the British and Foreign Bible Society, in 1804) were just beginning their efforts in the Empire that had just (1807) abolished the slave trade, thanks to the successful campaigns of British Christian abolitionists – the first formal abolition of slave trading, backed by law (and the British Royal Navy), in the history of the world. Our culture may now think differently of missionary activity, and deplore mistakes our forebears made, but the goodwill and selfless, often courageous, work of so many of those dedicated men and women 'in the Mission field', as it was called, who saw themselves as obeying Christ's own command – not polite advice, for the Lord is not polite – in Mark 16:15-16 deserve some honour and understanding from us.

Indeed, even at Oxford, Heber had shown interest in the Missionary Societies, including the oldest of them all, the Society for the Propagation of the Gospel in Foreign Parts (Royal Charter, 1701). In September 1813, he preached a sermon in Shrewsbury to the British and Foreign Bible Society, which ended with emphatic support for the overseas missions. Clearly, something was maturing in his mind. He could easily have followed a conventional career – the usual range of preferments, ultimately perhaps a comfortable bishopric and a seat in the Lords. While he did accept a canonry at St Asaph, where his father in law was Bishop, he turned down a far more prestigious offer, much better for a career, of one at Durham. It is interesting that while at Hodnet he made notes on a map of India outlining possible journeys long before any possibility of that was in the offing. Indeed, when he was offered preferment as only its second bishop to the new see of Calcutta (which included Ceylon and Australia!), Heber was cautious, enquiring whether there were not a more suitable local man, and expressing doubts about the climate's healthiness for his family. But he did accept, and was consecrated Bishop in Oxford in October 1823. The new prelate's portrait (by Thomas Phillips), in clerical robes and holding a square cap, has a church tower and a palm tree in the background.

Three most remarkable years followed. He travelled right across the sub-continent, and during that pastoral journey visited Benares, most sacred to Hindus, Sikhs, and Buddhists. He spent weeks in a wholly Indian city without any resident Europeans, but with a thriving CMS school and a substantial Christian community. He consecrated a new church, and when he celebrated a Holy Communion in both English and Hindustani there was a large congregation of Hindus as well as Christians. His journeys were prodigious, and he wrote up extensive accounts of them in his *Narrative of a*

A Joyful Noise

Journey through the Upper Provinces of India from Calcutta to Bombay 1824–1825 with Notes upon Ceylon and *An Account of a Journey to Madras and the Southern Provinces, 1826.* He worked to improve the general living conditions of his people. He ordained the first Indian into Holy Orders. He also sharply criticised the way the East India Company managed its affairs, the 'bullying, insolent manner' towards Indians of too many of the Company's employees, and deplored how few Indians had senior roles. On this he got the ear of the Governor General, Lord Amherst, and also wrote to his old friend Charles Williams-Wynn, who was head of the India Board of Control in London. Heber was interested in all aspects of Indian life, busied himself supporting education and the preparation of a Hindustani dictionary. He made friends easily with the local people and with Hindu swamis (with one, Sahajanand Swami, he formed a close friendship), and with members of non-Anglican churches. Occasionally his affability and the generosity of his hospitality scandalised the more puritan and Evangelical of his clergy. Indeed, one Isaac Wilson of the CMS directly attacked Heber, his own bishop, in a sermon after what he considered excessive celebrations following a baptism.

These arduous duties – including that gruelling 16 month visitation across the whole subcontinent – after only three years, a taxing climate and poor health led to a stroke and sudden death. The novelist Charlotte M. Yonge said what many thought when she wrote in, in *Pioneers and Founders: or, Recent Workers in the Mission Field* (1871), 'Heber was one of the first English churchmen who perceived that to enlarge her borders and strengthen her stakes was the bounden duty of the living Church'.

XIX
John Henry Newman
1801–90

❧

Salad days…

In Cambridge in the 1960s and 1970s there was a certain type of High Church Anglican undergraduate – it would be invidious to say which College housed the largest contingent – who would talk familiarly of 'John Henry', seventy years dead, as if they knew him intimately. It went with a certain style, a fondness for claret and chess after dinner, and a distinct leaning towards incense and bells and lace. (They mostly could often not afford gin as well.) It was all a bit *Brideshead*, I suppose, but to a young and ignorant Lancashire lad with a good solid experience of Anglican liturgy of the higher middle sort, its flashiness, and the theatricality of the services they attended, were for a time attractive. One of them became a Minister of the Crown, another a publisher, another an estate agent … I never found out how well they knew Newman's work and background. I certainly did not, and had never heard of the Tractarians, or the Oxford Movement, or its Cambridge near-equivalent the Camden Society. Of Newman I had heard, but only because my godfather, when a very aged Canon of Manchester Cathedral, had spoken of him with something approaching disgust.

Fast forward some dozen or so years. I am in a secondhand

bookshop – David's in Cambridge, to be precise, next to St Edward King and Martyr, from the pulpit of which (still there!) Hugh Latimer preached in the heady days of Reformation. I am browsing as is my Thursday lunchtime wont. I see a paperback with *J. H. Newman: Apologia Pro Vita Sua* on its spine. The title – 'a Defence of My Own Life', I suppose I'd translate it – makes me buy it. And I read it, and am bowled over by the passion it expressed, the beauty of the prose, the rhetorical elegance of the argument – and by the character of the man that shone through it. I finished it thinking, 'Well, there is no more to say.' I expected none of those things, nor the gear change for my low-wattage thinking (if one can dignify it with that word, and excuse the mixed metaphor) about religion and faith. Could this coruscating intellect and palpable goodness be the man of whom those friends had spoken so cavalierly and my godfather so dismissively?

Newman wrote it in 1864. Its subtitle – *Being a Reply to a Pamphlet Entitled 'What, Then, Does Dr. Newman Mean?'* – indicates it was provoked by a passionate attack on him and all he stood for by Charles Kingsley, then newly appointed Professor of Modern History at Cambridge and Tutor to the Prince of Wales.[1] This was an earthquake of a quarrel – Kingsley did eventually apologise ('how deeply I have wronged him!') – which reflected some tectonic divisions in Victorian society. To begin to understand how it came about, we need to look at the trajectory of Newman's whole life.

Newman's father was a banker in Lombard Street. His mother, Jemima Fourdrinier, descended from Protestant Huguenots who had fled France after Louis XIV in 1689 revoked the Edict of Nantes, which had granted toleration to non-Catholics. (It was a Fourdrinier who in the 1790s invented the paper-making machine, which revolutionised the printing industry.) At seven Newman was sent to Great Ealing School, which, founded in 1698, was then considered the best private school in the country and as famous as Eton or Harrow. (George Huxley, father of the T. H. Huxley later nicknamed

---

[1] *Macmillan's Magazine* published the attacks on Newman.

John Henry Newman

'Darwin's Bulldog', was maths master.) At 15, his last year at school, Newman embraced Evangelicalism, and by 1816 he was reading lots from the English Calvinist tradition. (With that went the view that the Pope was the Antichrist.) Though to the end of his life Newman looked back on this conversion as the saving of his soul, he gradually moved away from Calvinism. For, as Eamon Duffy once put it,

> He came to see Evangelicalism, with its emphasis on religious feeling and on the Reformation doctrine of justification by faith alone, as a Trojan horse for an undogmatic religious individualism that ignored the Church's role in the transmission of revealed truth, and that must lead inexorably to subjectivism and scepticism.

The family intended him for the law, but instead of Lincoln's Inn he went to Trinity College, Oxford. He read very widely, but overwork for his final examinations led to him flunking: a lower second class honours in Classics, and unclassed in Maths. But his ability was recognised: in 1822 he was elected to Fellowship at Oriel, a College which had a reputation as a hotbed of fresh thought and a principle of electing on promise rather than past performance. Two years later he was ordained deacon, and in 1825 priest. To these years at Oriel, and the influence there of Richard Whately,[2] Newman later attributed the widening of his mind – and the partial overcoming of his crippling shyness. Newman helped Whately with his popular *Elements of Logic* (1826), and from conversation with him developed an idea of the Church as a Divinely authorised body, independent of the State, and with its own prerogatives and powers.

In 1826 Newman became a Tutor at Oriel, the same year the College also elected Richard Hurrell Froude, who became

---

[2] Interesting chap: rhetorician, logician, philosopher, economist, theologian: then a reforming Church of Ireland Archbishop of Dublin, a leading Broad Churchman, prolific and combative as an author on many topics, and one of the first reviewers to recognise Jane Austen's major talent.

a close friend.[3] Newman thought him 'one of the acutest, cleverest and deepest men' he ever met. The two had a high ideal of a Tutor's role as clerical and pastoral – moral, in fact – rather than secular: this was not universally welcome in the college. Mark Pattison (1813-84),[4] who later became Rector of Lincoln College, had a set of rooms opposite Newman's on the same staircase, and recalls how slack most Tutors tended to be in their teaching, sometime content to keep just one step ahead of pupils, slack in reading essays, and how, by contrast, Newman and Froude really put their back into work with each pupil. Indeed, in 1832 Newman's differences with the Provost, Edward Hawkins, about the substantially religious and pastoral nature of college tutorship became acute, and he, with the other tutors, Froude and John Keble, had to resign – a disagreement and a move that began the Oxford Movement.

This pedagogic position clearly anticipates arguments Newman would develop decades later in *The Idea of a University* (1852). Three themes there challenged many ideas and practices not only in his own time but also challenge – a challenge needed if often unheeded – mainstream twenty-first century education: firstly, his insistence on the nature of knowledge as holistic, demanding that different specialisms – e.g. religious studies or the various sciences — inform each other's work, and not live only in their own discourses; second, that argument – disagreement, debate, questioning – was vital. He saw no conflict between the constant search for truth in what was newly and narrowly called 'science'[5] and in theology

---

[3] He died in 1836, aged 33, and was the brother of James Antony Froude, the historian.

[4] He has a very reasoned take on Newman and the group he influenced in *Memoirs of an Oxford Don* (1885). Pattison, a decade younger than Newman, was in the Oxford Movement, but did not follow Newman when he became Roman Catholic, and deplored the effects of the Tracts on Oxford as a University.

[5] Rather than Natural Philosophy. I think it was Charles Darwin's grandfather Erasmus who first uses 'science' in our narrow sense, a sense that would have been incomprehensible to the Ancients and the Medievals.

John Henry Newman

– rather, like Charles Kingsley, he saw them as complementary. He argued that doctrinaire thought dutifully passed down the generations obstructed any pursuit of Truth and that 'ideas are the life of institutions – social, political, literary.' When Darwin published his *Origin of Species* in 1859, Newman wrote to a friend that he was willing 'to go the whole hog with Darwin.' Second, that religious belief had an important place, especially in higher education. Third, that liberal education – the arts as well as sciences, and *vice versa* – mattered to everyone, especially to university students. In this he clearly rejects the utilitarianism of John Locke's *Some Thoughts Concerning Education* (1693), and this awareness of the importance of the aesthetic to the whole person chimes with his encouragement of the beauty of holiness expressed through colour and music and ritual in worship. His warning is even more needed, now, in face of the crass, reductive, sterile utilitarianism that dominates so much of our own education system.

But this is to anticipate. In the early 1800s, different parties were jockeying for influence in the CofE and no quarrels are more bitter than those driven by theological conviction. Broadly, many, particularly among the higher clergy, were relaxed about differences in theology and forms of worship, while many parish clergy were Evangelicals, with little emphasis on, and indeed sometimes horror of, ritual, the sacraments, and the authority of the clergy. They laid much more stress on individual conversion. In this last, Wesley's influence remained profound even in the church from which Methodism had reluctantly broken. In the Universities, however, desire to restore liturgical and devotional customs which had been lost at the Reformation was growing. And there was a willingness to learn from contemporary Roman Catholic practice.

In 1828 Newman was given the Oriel living of St Mary's, the University Church, with the parish of Littlemore, and in 1832-33 he was Select Preacher before the University. But by the late 1820s, though still associated with the Evangelicals, in, for example, the Church Missionary Society, Newman was fast moving away from his Low Church position. Talk with Froude and Keble led him to emphasise Anglicanism's continuation of ancient Christian tradition, particularly as regards the episcopate, priesthood, and sacraments. It was in these years that he set himself to read the Church Fathers thoroughly. This was bound to alter his thinking on many issues. He broke finally with the CMS in 1830.

In 1833 the High Church Oxford Movement formed. Newman was its intellectual leader. In the next year the High Church *British Magazine* was launched to counter those, particularly in the governing Liberal party that had just passed the Reform Act, who argued for sequestration of much of Church property and attacked the Church's privileged status. John Keble's sermon on National Apostasy (1833) explosively supercharged this controversy. Newman took the *Magazine*'s epigraph from Homer: 'You shall know the difference now that I am back again' – from Achilles' speech in *Iliad* 19. The suggestion is clear: the time is one for battle, and he himself is back from abroad to wage it. (It never does to think that *any* gentle saint of popular myth is not also a bonny fighter.) The Movement stressed the Catholic elements in English religious tradition, and the need to reform the CofE in that direction. From this Movement came the influential series of *Tracts for the Times* – Newman himself wrote 24 – but it was his books – he wrote sensitive and often beautiful prose, which always helps – that really carried most weight: *Lectures on the Prophetical Office of the Church* (1837), the classic statement of Tractarian understanding of authority; the *University Sermons* (1843), on the theory of religious belief; and especially *Parochial and Plain Sermons* (1834–42), which made the Movement's principles available to a much wider audience at a time when reading sermons was something many people, lay as well as clerical, often did. So by the later 1830s Newman's influence in the CofE was considerable, and growing. Many felt his stress on the church's teaching authority was needed in an increasingly sceptical age. There is an authority that comes from a decisive confidence in what one stands for and why, and in Newman's personal devotion it was palpable he practised what he preached.

John Henry Newman

His main contention was that the CofE represented true catholicity – i.e. universality – and that the test of this (as against Rome on one hand and what he termed 'popular Protestants' upon the other) was how it stood up to the doctrine of the ancient, undivided church of the Fathers. After about 1834 this *via media* was attacked for undervaluing the Reformation and its importance, and, when in 1838–39 Newman and Keble published Froude's (he had died in 1836) *Remains,* which attacked the Reformation head on, moderates in the group began to feel their leader was going where they could not follow. Newman's *Tract 90* (1841) which reconciled the 39 Articles of the CofE with the teaching of the ancient church, appeared to many to claim that they were compatible with doctrines agreed at the Council of Trent (1545-63) (which started the Counter-Reformation). Many reacted furiously to this Tract. For example, Rev. Frederick Beasley D.D., called it 'an attempt stealthily and insidiously to vitiate the pure system of our faith with heretical doctrines, and defile our sanctuary with foul superstitions'.[6] The Bishop of Oxford, Richard Bagot, Newman's ecclesiastical superior, asked that the tracts be suspended. A nasty, increasingly bitter, quarrel followed, and distressed by the attacks on him Newman increasingly withdrew into isolation, his confidence shattered. If the CofE did not wish to be universal, then where were those who saw it as catholic to go? He moved out to Littlemore. A few close disciples followed, living a communal, semi-monastic life. He bought a bit of land, turned a row of one-roomed cottages into cells connected by a sort of cloister, and built a library to house his collection of patristic material. Mark Pattison spent a fortnight there in October 1835, and describes in his diary the

---

[6] Rev. Frederick Beasley, D.D., 'Formerly Provost of the University of Pennsylvania, author of the Search of Truth in the Science of the Human Mind, &c., and a Presbyter of the Episcopal Church': *An Examination of No. 90 Of the Tracts for the times* (New York, 1842). Its epigraph is from Francis Bacon, 'But superstition hath been the confusion of many States; and bringeth in a new primum mbile [*sic*], that ravisheth all the spheres of government.'

services at the canonical hours, his spiritual struggles, and how he was 'so anxious for N's good opinion.'

Newman resigned St Mary's in September 1843, and preached his last Anglican sermon in Littlemore a week later. He called it 'The Parting of Friends' – and friendship was a topic close to his heart. It took two years to decide his future course. The modern Roman Catholic Church he could not reconcile with the early Church. But, meditating upon the idea of 'development' – a term used much in discussing biological evolution – as it might apply to Christian society, he tried to show (persuading himself as much as others) that the undivided early Church had rightly developed into the modern Roman Church, and that Protestantism broke from that development in doctrine and in devotion. So, in October 1845, he was received at Littlemore into the Roman Catholic Church. Before the end of that year he published *Essay on the Development of Christian Doctrine,* his justification.

He was ordained as priest in Rome. The more rigorous Roman Catholic clergy always distrusted him for what to them looked like dangerous liberalism, and his early years as a priest had many frustrations. He did manage, after some difficulty, to found the Birmingham Oratory in 1848. Then the Church sent him to Dublin as the first Rector of the new Catholic University. He was not a success in the job, but one valuable fruit was his lectures, published as *The Idea of a University* (1852). He also had several disagreements with another member of the Movement, Henry Manning, who had also converted to Rome. (He would soon be the new Archbishop of Westminster, and later Cardinal.) Manning blocked Newman's attempts to found a Catholic hostel at Oxford. In those years nobody could have foreseen the veneration in which he would come to be held, his cardinal's hat, and his (much later) beatification and canonisation.

The defection to Rome of someone already so prominent in the CofE could only excite anger from many Anglicans, and he was vilified. This came to a head in Charles Kingsley's attacks on Newman, on his intellectual honesty, his morals, his beliefs – asking him, in fact, to justify the honesty of his life as

John Henry Newman

an Anglican: the title of one such pamphlet, which provoked Newman's comprehensive *Apologia*, was *Whether Dr. Newman teaches that Truth is no virtue?* The *Apologia* was very widely read, and the memoir – to class it no higher – has never been out of print. while Kingsley' attack is largely unread now except by specialists. It recovered for Newman much of the stature and standing in public regard that he had lost in the 1850s. It still can – does – change lives.

⁂

In *Apologia Pro Vita Suai*, Newman recounted how he had fallen ill while travelling with Froude in Italy in 1833. He could not travel for almost three weeks.

> Before starting from my inn, I sat down on my bed and began to sob bitterly. My servant, who had acted as my nurse, asked what ailed me. I could only answer, 'I have a work to do in England.' I was aching to get home, yet for want of a vessel I was kept at Palermo for three weeks. I began to visit the churches, and they calmed my impatience, though I did not attend any services. At last I got off in an orange boat, bound for Marseilles. We were becalmed for whole week in the Straits of Bonifacio, and it was there that I wrote the lines, *Lead, Kindly Light*, which have since become so well known.

Yes indeed: *NEH* sets the poem, originally called 'The Pillar of the Cloud'[7] to W. H. Harris's 'Alberta', which Oxford University Press gave it originally, rather than 'Sandon' by Charles H.

---

[7] First published 1834 in the *British Magazine*. Oxford University Press republished it in *Lyra Apostolica* in 1836 – the volume was mainly of poems by Newman (179) and John Keble (46) and the title stakes out a claim to authority trumping that in the title of *Lyra Davidica, or a Collection of Divine Songs and Hymns, Partly New Composed, Partly Translated from the High-German and Latin Hymns* (1708), which spoke to an Anglicanism heavily Calvinist.

Purday (which I prefer), or 'Lux Benigna' composed by John Bacchus Dykes[8] in 1865. (There are also settings by Sir John Stainer and Sir Arthur Sullivan.) It is not the only hymn we sing: from his wonderful Dante-inspired sequence of poems, *The Dream of Gerontius* (1865; set by Sir Edward Elgar 1900), *NEH* takes 360 (*A&M* 118), 'Firmly I believe and truly'. That comes from Gerontius' third speech in Part 1. 439, 'Praise to the Holiest in the Height', is sung by the Choir of Angelicals in Phase 7 (Part 2 in the Elgar). Sometimes it is hard not to hear Elgar's stunning conclusion to his oratorio in your head, but John Bacchus Dykes' tune is also magnificent. The hymn is a profound meditation on 1 *Corinthians* 15:20-47, in which God in Christ, the second Adam, restores by his Incarnation the world which had been lost by the first Adam' sin.

Newman wrote many hymns that are now hardly ever heard. One, written in 1849 at the Birmingham Oratory, is in the 1870 edition of *Hymns for Catholic Children*, p.140:

The Pilgrim Queen of Merry England

> THERE sat a Lady
>   all on the ground,
> Rays of the morning
>   circled her round,
> Save thee, and hail to thee,
>   Gracious and Fair,
> In the chill twilight
>   what wouldst thou there?
>
> 'Here I sit desolate,
>   sweetly said she,
> 'Though I'm a queen,

---

[8] Dykes, a fine musician, is worth an essay himself. His persecution as an Anglo-Catholic by the Evangelical party and indeed by his own Bishop, and the unexpected refusal of the courts to give him a writ of *mandamus* to force the Bishop of Durham to give this overworked man a curate, eventually broke his health.

John Henry Newman

 and my name is Marie:
Robbers have rifled
 my garden and store,
Foes they have stolen
 my heir from my bower.

'They said they could keep Him
 far better than I,
In a palace all His,
 planted deep and raised high.
'Twas a palace of ice,
 hard and cold as were they,
And when summer came,
 it all melted away.

'Next would they barter Him,
 Him the Supreme,
For the spice of the desert,
 and gold of the stream;
And me they bid wander
 in weeds and alone,
In this green merry land
 which once was my own.'

I look'd on that Lady,
 and out from her eyes
Came the deep glowing blue
 of Italy's skies;
And she raised up her head
 and she smiled, as a Queen
On the day of her crowning,
 so bland and serene.

'A moment,' she said,
 'and the dead shall revive;
The giants are failing,
 the Saints are alive;

A Joyful Noise

> I am coming to rescue
> > my home and my reign,
> And Peter and Philip
> > are close in my train.'

For most of the later medieval centuries England was called Mary's Dower, for English devotion to the Blessed Virgin Mary as the country's guardian was profound. Indeed, Archbishop Arundel, about 1400, wrote, 'we English, being ... her own Dowry, as we are commonly called, ought to surpass others in the fervour of our praises and devotions', and by Henry V's reign, the title *dos Mariae* was common. The chronicler Thomas Elmham says that before the battle of Agincourt (1415) the priests sought her intercession. The child who sang Newman's hymn would learn a myth – no derogatory sense in that word! – that would colour their perception of the aridity and shallowness of non-Catholic worship, the growing materialism of mercantile and industrial England, and of their view of history and the operation of the saints. It would also insert 'now' into a story not yet ended.

Of Newman's personal charm there is much evidence. Pattison (to whose deathbed he paid a touching visit) wrote,

> Thin, pale, and with large lustrous eyes piercing through this veil of men and things, he hardly seemed made for this world. But his influence had in it something of magic. It was never possible to be a quarter of an hour in his company without a warm feeling of being invited to take an onward step, and Newman was sure to find out in time whether that onward step was taken. One of his principles was that every man was good for something but you must find out what it was, and set him to work accordingly. He kept a careful account of his pupils, always having his eye on the metal rather than on the dross ... Newman always tried to reach the heart and understanding of those with whom he had to do.

John Henry Newman

A 16-year-old Edward Benson, later to be Archbishop of Canterbury, ignored the advice of his friend Joseph Lightfoot – the future Bishop of Durham – and went in 1845 to hear Newman preach. (By then Newman had broken with the CofE.) He came away, so he wrote, captivated by

> the sweet flowing unlaboured language, the frail emaciated appearance ... the thought that this timid-looking little weak-voiced man had so moved England ... surely if there is a man whom God has raised up in this generation with more than common power to glorify his name this man is he.

But he also continued,

> never turn Romanist if you are to have such a face as that. It was awful, the terrible lines deeply ploughed all over it and the craft that sat upon his retreating forehead and sunken eyes!

So familiar are the photographs of the aged Cardinal, on whose face the years have ploughed their furrows, that it is hard to imagine any other Newman than that. But the portrait done by George Richmond[9] in 1844 – the critical year just before Newman 'went over to Rome' – shows an almost classically handsome face, with a lot of humour in the mouth and eyes, and it is easy, looking at that, to understand Newman's attractive personality – and his gift for friendship. Some of his close friendships were with women, like the gifted and beautiful Maria Giberne, who aged 50 was described by one admirer as 'the handsomest woman I ever saw in my life'. She knew him from youth and followed him into the Catholic Church, and they still corresponded into their eighties. Her portrait was in his room in the Oratory, and she painted several portraits of

---

[9] Hugely influenced by William Blake, Richmond was at the height of his powers, and painted many important people. He was friendly with many of the members of the Tractarian movement.

him. Then there was Emily Bowles, who first met Newman at Littlemore, to whom he wrote some outspoken letters on what he saw as the mistakes of extreme supporters of the new Roman doctrine of Papal Infallibility, and his reasons for refusing to break his silence about them. Visiting the Oratory in 1861, she said she would always remember 'the brightness that lit up his worn face as he received me at the door.'

He had deep friendships with two men particularly: the first with Froude, who died so young, and then with Ambrose St John (1815–1875), who shared community life with Newman for 32 years from 1843. Newman wrote after he died, 'I have ever thought no bereavement was equal to that of a husband's or a wife's, but I feel it difficult to believe that any can be greater, or any one's sorrow greater, than mine.' They were buried in the same grave.

True friendship is not a purely emotional thing, but a matter of reason, discipline, moral judgement and will as well – as the Ancients (Cicero, for example) or mediaevals (Ailred of Rievaulx) or Renaissance (Erasmus) knew.[10] Newman spelt out his Theology of Friendship in a sermon preached on the Feast of St John the Evangelist, traditionally identified with the Disciple 'whom Jesus loved.' Newman said:

> There have been men before now, who have supposed Christian love was so diffuse as not to admit of concentration upon individuals; so that we ought to love all men equally ... Now I shall maintain here, in opposition to such notions of Christian love, and with our Saviour's pattern before me, that the best preparation for loving the world at large, and loving it duly and wisely, is to cultivate our intimate friendship and affection towards those who are immediately about us.

[10] I argue that Good and Bad Friendship is the real issue in Shakespeare's *Merchant of Venice*. It is the only play with so many pairs of friends. The key figure could not have been, for *his* audience, Shylock: after all, he disappears in Act IV, and we know that until about 1800 that was always the clown's part.

John Henry Newman

For Newman, friendship is an intimation of a greater love, a foretaste of heaven. In friendship, two intimate friends gain a glimpse of the life that awaits them in God. ('This is my Friend, my Friend indeed', said Samuel Crossman …) Newman's theory and practice chimes exactly with that wonderful, much copied, treatise *On Spiritual Friendship* by the twelfth-century Abbot of Rievaulx, Ailred, and echoed widely. Wiser ages than our own have recognised that there is an art in all things, including friendship, and the practice of an art takes you deeper and deeper into mysteries and joys lying undreamed of in it.

XX

CHRISTOPHER WORDSWORTH
1807–85

※

I STARTED TO WRITE this on the feast of St Stephen, Protomartyr, for our Parish *Newsletter* that would appear as we approached Epiphany. I wondered how these two things might be brought together. Casting around (as one does) in *NEH*, I found that one man wrote both 56 (*A&M* 53), 'Songs of Thankfulness and Praise', set for Epiphany, and 201, 'Stephen First of Christian martyrs'. Christopher Wordsworth, Bishop, wrote quite a few more, several of which we sing at Little St Mary's, and some of them have grand tunes by people of the calibre of Arthur Sullivan, Walford Davies, Hubert Parry ('Rustington' is a favourite of mine) and Charles Stegall. He also wrote that fine Ascensiontide hymn, 'See the Conqueror mounts in triumph' (132). So there was my problem solved.

To begin at the wrong end: CW writes with great facility. Some have said too much. E. F. Benson, whose father was later Archbishop of Canterbury, knew him as a friend of his family, with a garden delectable for children. (Benson senior was then Chancellor of Lincoln.) He remarks in his memoir *As We Were* (1930) that 'some of these hymns were fine poetry... but Bishop Wordsworth also inherited his uncle's [William's] tendency to lapse into meaner strains ', and gives one leaden example,

CHRISTOPHER WORDSWORTH

> Let us emulate the names
> Of St Philip and St James

where 'emotional appeal is somewhat lacking in such a lyric.' Even so: often using an eight-line stanza which allows for more musical interest in varying the second 4 lines of the tune, CW's verse has a strong rhythm and doctrinal clarity ideal for congregational – well, bellowing. In quieter mood, he can also use a shorter, more reflective stanza, with three 8 syllable rhymed lines followed by a 4 syllable refrain. (e.g. 422, where the song of gratitude has a repeated refrain stressing the generosity of God. But who was he? And how well does his verse stand up to analysis?

The latter point first. As Ambrose knew, hymns have to be singable, hummable if you like, contain deep spiritual truth in simple statement, and stick in the mind – here is where music and rhythm help too. They do not have to be Great Poems: though a few certainly are, that is not their primary job. For hymns are, if I can put it so, 'applied art', like advertising: they have a job to do which *not* primarily aesthetic. Wordsworth at his fine best passes those tests triumphantly.

He was born in 1807, the son of William's brother Christopher, who later became Master of Trinity College, Cambridge. (He called his own son, the liturgiologist, Christopher too, which can be confusing...) His photos show a remarkable likeness to his uncle in that portrait by Benjamin Haydon of William on Helvellyn, and until William's death in 1850 he often visited him at Rydal Mount and the two exchanged frequent letters. (He was William's literary executor.) He grew up partly in Kent, where was then his father's living as Chaplain to the Archbishop, and the family were neighbours and friends of the future Cardinal, Henry Manning. The young Christopher corresponded with Coleridge and George Crabbe. The Mastership of Trinity was in the Royal gift. The Wordsworths were, in fact, thoroughly part of the Establishment, literary, scholarly, ecclesiastical and political, in a much smaller society.

His mother died when he was 8, and in 1820 (when his

A JOYFUL NOISE

father became Master of Trinity) he entered Winchester College, scooping academic prize after prize and distinguishing himself as an athlete as well. He was good at football, fives, and, as one of the cricket First XI against Harrow in 1825, caught out the future Cardinal Manning for a duck. (Later in life he often recounted that story with glee. Who would not?) In 1825 he went up to Trinity, and, as Revd Charles Overton in the old *DNB* says, 'his list of college and university prizes and honours was almost unique'. A Fellowship and Tutorship followed, and before ordination in 1835, travels in Italy and Greece. It was hardly a rest cure. He was the first to decipher the graffiti in Pompeii. He made archaeological deductions about the site of Zeus' shrine at Dodona which were confirmed by excavation half a century later. He learned modern Greek. Crossing the Parnitha range north of Athens in snow, he and his party were attacked by brigands and he, though with a stiletto wound in the shoulder, managed to escape capture and being held to ransom. He wrote a book on Attica which was still authoritative in the early 1900s. He was Public Orator of Cambridge (which position George Herbert had held, when it was more onerous and diplomatic than the composing of elegant orations for graduation ceremonies). That same year, 1836, though young, he was appointed Headmaster of Harrow. With the energy that was his hallmark, he went in as a reformer, resolved to tighten up slack discipline, and the quality of teaching, which apparently left much to be desired. But the eight years that followed before the governors asked him to resign in 1844 were unhappy, if well meaning. Attempts to raise academic standards can only be applauded, and he won the affection of many boys by personal interest in their studies; but building a school chapel so that boys no longer went to the Parish Church upset the local community, as did refusing to accept as foundationers local boys whose parents were not poor. Many boys hated his long sermons on doctrine. Expulsion for misdemeanours was common – one lad so dismissed was a cousin of Gladstone, the future PM. The school roll dropped sharply. He twice failed to get the Regius Chair in Divinity in Cambridge. It was not a happy time.

CHRISTOPHER WORDSWORTH

He was at this impasse when Sir Robert Peel, an Old Harrovian, then Prime Minister, made him a Canon of Westminster Abbey and vicar of Stanford in the Vale, Berkshire. In both roles he was notably successful. In 1868 Disraeli offered him the see of Lincoln on account of his 'confidence in your abilities, your learning and shining example.' He very nearly turned it down, thinking himself too old at sixty-one. It was his friend Edward Benson (1829–1896), then by Prince Albert's design the first Head of Wellington College (near to Stanford), who persuaded him to retrieve from the pillar box the letter of refusal he had already posted.

As at Harrow, he met controversy head-on. He would for example go to law with a patron about a presentation to a living if he did not think the parson fit for it. He opposed any lack of consideration for Church interests – this led to him speaking in the Lords in 1870 against Forster's Bill which became the ground-breaking Education Act: he argued that to set up a State-funded education system would produce 'a race of godless teachers and infidel scholars'. He cared deeply that education should be Christian: at Stanford he had himself taught the village children diligently; in his own diocese, he facilitated the founding of 59 new schools, and a new Theological College (in which endeavour Benson, now Lincoln's Chancellor, helped greatly). In fact, he was a High Churchman of the eighteenth-century type, with a high concept of the nature of the Church. In his view, the problems the early Fathers had encountered with the secular power had not gone away, and could be met by taking a leaf out of their book.

Lincoln diocese had many large Methodist congregations, and Wordsworth yearned for reunion, arguing that the CofE had a mission to bring that reunion about, just as it had a mission to foster reform abroad. But relationships with the Methodists were less than happy. At a time when contact between Anglican and Methodist was usually marked by polite aloofness, he addressed a Pastoral Letter to the Dissenters claiming they threatened the unity of the Church, and his attempts to heal the CofE/Methodist schism got little support from them. Understandably, perhaps.

His career, and personality, clearly have to be seen in the context of the extraordinary evangelical religious revival of the years round 1800. Unusual though, in any age, were his memory, learning and scholarly energy – even among those extraordinarily industrious Victorian clerics, who could classify lepidoptera or excavate a barrow in the morning, write a commentary on Philo Judaeus in the afternoon, turn a few elegant Latin verses before tea, be an entertaining host at dinner, and spend an hour on the Great Book before retiring. It is awe-inspiring even if they did have servants to cut the lawn and do the washing.

CW's output is huge. Revealingly, his daughters made the attic of their dolls' house a study, with a doll sitting at a desk, and when asked about it said, 'Oh, he is writing his Commentary.' CW's monumental Commentary on the *entire* Bible began with the New Testament – for he always insisted that the Old must be read in its light and the light of Christ: that shows in his Epiphany hymn. A less than inspiring verse from one hymn puts it plain:

> What the holy Prophets meant,
> In the Ancient Testament,
> Thou revealest to our view,
> Lord, for ever, in the New.

The revised Greek text and commentary followed (1856–60), then the Old Testament in twelve parts, 1864–1870. One aim in this huge work was to reconcile the new insights of the sciences (Darwin's *Origin of Species* was published in 1859) with the interpretation of Scripture. Many scholars, like him, welcomed the recent revival of interpreting Scripture typologically, an approach flat counter to the reductive approach which descended from ideas like William Tyndale's assertion that 'Scripture hath no sense but the literal'. So to read rejects the ancient Christian, Apostolic and Patristic system of interpretation of the Old Testament as capable of three senses as well as the literal: the allegorical, the moral and the mystical. It is to read it 'with a veil on their heart,' which ... 'is done away in Christ.' (2 Cor. 3.15). Clearly, he found sympathetic the Greek Orthodox approach to Scripture, which sees Christ as the key to all understanding of past, present and future. Interest in the Greek church and what its tradition had to say, supplying something that had atrophied in England, was growing: the Eastern Church Association, which he was tempted to join, was founded in 1853 by John Mason Neale. His hymns – he published *The Holy Year; or Hymns for Sundays and Holy-days, And other Occasions* in 1862 – typological and eschatological as they often are, owe quite a bit to the Eastern tradition. (E. F. Benson again:

> He talked about Uncle William, whose poetical aptitude he inherited, for he wrote a complete hymn book out of his own head... we often sang those hymns at family prayers, accompanied by my mother on a minute harmonium with a tremolo stop which occasionally collapsed with a polyphonic groan ...)

People remembered him with respect and affection – not least some of his Harrow pupils – and he touched many lives. His family and friends recalled affectionately how at table he would be so rapt in his talk as to be quite unconscious of what he ate, helping himself to any dish within reach, crumbling bread over the whole mess, until a daughter signalled to a servant quietly to remove the plate and give him a fresh one. Which he never noticed. People remembered how at a public meeting he would innocently, unthinkingly, quote Greek, and then, suddenly aware that he had lost his audience, apologetically translate it 'for the ladies'. (Gosh, try that today!) Everyone remembered his energy, intellectual curiosity, his physical toughness, his kindness. E. F. Benson recalls how welcome he and his young siblings were made at Bishop's House at Riseholme, and 'that he was kind but was felt to be formidable. At the same time he was enviable because he could skate on one foot, holding the other completely off the ice.' Even when old he could still skate gracefully in the colder winters of that century – and physically he aged well. But he can't have been a restful companion. Physical energy, constant mental activity – well, those things come at a cost. His family mention bouts of depression, and how short was his temper when stressed. His daughter recalled how anxious he could be about public events, and how he never talked down to the children, 'and so we grew up with a rather uneasy sense of impending crisis.' But his marriage to the sister of his Trinity friend John Frere was happy, and when his beloved Susanna died in October 1884 he deteriorated rapidly, and followed her after only a few months.

His vast scholarly and polemical opus is now read only by specialists and historians. Learning, like all human things, passes away. He may be only a name at the foot of a page. But he still gives us, who have not his gifts, a way to make our joyful noise unto the Lord at Epiphany and Eastertide and Ascension, and I for one would not be without any one of the seven hymns *NEH* includes. This is hymn writing of the first order, that stands re-reading: and pondering.

XXI
JOHN MASON NEALE
1818–66

New English Hymnal's Index of Authors credits John Mason Neale with 39 hymns by, or translated by, him, far and away more than anyone else there represented: even the prolific Charles Wesley only has 26 and Percy Dearmer, one of the first editors, 17. How many of us know that Neale wrote, as a St Stephen's day carol, 'Good King Wenceslas'? How many know we owe him 'Christian dost thou see them' (65), 'The Royal Banners forward go' (79), 'Come ye faithful, raise the strain' (106), 'The Day of Resurrection' (117), 'Come thou Holy Spirit come' (139), 'Stars of the morning, so gloriously bright' (193), 'Christ is made the sure foundation' (205), and many others? There are also many we don't often sing and perhaps should. For there is not one that does not have something serious, even profound, to say in decent verse: which is a great deal better than some of the trendy, 'approachable', limping doggerel that has been welcomed into too many modern hymn collections.

The family was intellectually distinguished, and of pronounced Evangelical persuasion. His mother descended from John Mason (1645-94), vicar of Water Stratford (see Chapter X). His father died when he was five years old, and his mother managed much of his education, partly at Sherborne College. A Scholar of Trinity College, Cambridge, he was regarded as the cleverest man of his year, and won the Seatonian Prize for religious poetry eleven times. In his undergraduate years he became drawn to what Newman and Pusey were doing in Oxford, and was one of the founders of the Cambridge Camden Society, which sought to return the Church and churches of England to the religious splendour it saw in the pre-Reformation period. The argument was not only aesthetic – about the peculiar appropriateness, for example, of the Gothic style to church architecture[1] – but also implicitly theological, even though the Society forbade theological discussion in its papers and publications. What it was doing converged with much that Newman and Pusey were arguing, and in a still strongly conservative University this was bold stuff, and as shocking to some as it was in Oxford.

Three years after graduating Neale and Benjamin Webb published *The Symbolism of Churches and Church Ornaments* (1843), translating and editing the thirteenth-century *Rationale Divinorum Officiorum* of Guglielmus Durandus, a thirteenth-century treatise which explains the significance of every detail of church architecture, ritual and furnishing. (It is still relevant – and fascinating reading – today.) By emphasizing chancel and altar, and by removing the three-decker pulpits and comfortable box pews (some, intended for the gentry, had fireplaces!) of the eighteenth century, the young ecclesiologists shifted the emphasis from meeting house to sanctuary, from preaching to sacraments. The subsequent work of the Society (later the Ecclesiological Society[2]) has so marked the physical face of England and of Anglicanism that we hardly notice it. The work later of, for example, Percy Dearmer would not have happened without

---

[1] Something dear to the heart of Augustus Welby Pugin, whose ideas, practice and influence reached far indeed in the design of new church buildings – and part of the Palace of Westminster.

[2] Francis Close (1797–1882), the evangelical Rector of Cheltenham, later dean of Carlisle, pungently attacked the Cambridge Camden Society in *The Restoration of Churches is a Restoration of Popery* (1845), and forced its tactical closure. It was soon reconstituted in London as the Ecclesiological Society.

what Neale did: his *Parson's Handbook* (see p. 218) would have been very different without it.

Cambridge's rule then was that if you were not placed in the Mathematical Tripos you could not take Honours in the Classical. Neale was useless at the maths where his father (of St John's) had excelled. So he had to put up with an Ordinary degree. However, he had won the Members' Prize in Classics, and Downing College, then still a young foundation, made him Fellow and Tutor, and briefly Chaplain soon after his ordination as Deacon in 1841. But he married in 1842 – which meant, under the old Statutes which forbade Fellows of Colleges to marry, that he had to resign his Fellowship. He went to St Nicholas's, Guildford, as curate to William Henley Pearson, but Charles Sumner, the strongly Evangelical Bishop of Winchester, refused this 24 year old, already notorious for his views, a licence to officiate in his diocese, and Neale had to relinquish the parochial ministry he had enthusiastically begun. (We are, after all, in the ecclesiastical climate Anthony Trollope described so wittily in his first two Barchester novels.) In 1843 he was given the living of Crawley in Sussex, but his always poor health now developed into serious lung trouble, demanding a year in the kinder climate of Madeira. From then on his worsening health precluded the considerable physical strain of normal parish ministry; and his open support of Newman and Pusey, and the Oxford Movement, made preferment in the CofE unlikely. His future looked bleak.

In 1846, Mary Sackville, Countess Amherst and her sister Elizabeth, Countess De la Warr presented him to the Wardenship of Sackville College in East Grinstead, a 'hospital' (retirement home) founded by the second earl of Dorset in 1608 for poor men. The stipend was meagre, about £28 p.a. – an agricultural labourer's average wage in 1850. For comparison, the Revd Mr Quiverful, in Trollope's *Barchester Towers* (1857) was indigent on £400 – he did have 14 children to Neale's 5, though – and though soon after 1800 a third of CofE livings were worth less than £150, a living often brought with it glebe land which could be farmed for profit. Nothing like that for

Neale. He made up a very modest living by writing. Standing at his desk – many men did then – in a study crammed with books, he wrote history, fiction, biography, sermons, travelogue, and poetry. He also wrote for children: his income depended on titles like *English History for Children* (1845), *Triumphs of the Cross: Tales and Sketches of Christian Heroism* (1845), *Stories from Heathen Mythology and Greek History for the Use of Christian Children* (1847), *Stories for Children from Church History* (1850, 1851), and *Evenings at Sackville College: Legends for Children* (1852). A fair number of these remained in print for decades.[3]

Somehow he found time to expand Sackville's ministry to include poor women and orphans, and founded the Sisterhood of St Margaret, eventually one of the finest nursing training orders. But his churchmanship, and his radical support of the poor, made him enemies.

The Bishop of Chichester, Ashurst Turner Gilbert, despite his High Church opinions, deplored what he considered 'extreme practices' in church, and when he heard in 1847 how Neale had arranged Sackville College's chapel he forbade Neale to celebrate and suspended him for 16 years from any function in his diocese – even though Neale and the patrons who had installed him maintained that the college itself was a peculiar and therefore outside the jurisdiction of the diocesan bishop. His title of Doctor *honoris causa* he owed to no English University, but to Trinity College, Hartford, Connecticut. There were even those – we'd call them trolls – who circulated unfounded rumours of misconduct and embezzlement about this learned and gentle man. In Lewes, where on Bonfire Night they still burn an effigy of Pope Pius V[4] – and have probably forgotten why they do so – he was all but killed by a mob when he took the funeral, at her father's parish in Lewes, of one of the

---

[3] In 2021 an illustrated version of *Good King Wenceslaus* was available in three versions including Kindle, and some of his scholarly work is still in print.

[4] Pope at the time of the Gunpowder Plot, of which he was wholly ignorant.

John Mason Neale

Sisters of St Margaret, dead from scarlet fever. A rumour had been started – quite possibly by her father, which would explain his subsequent conduct – that she had been pressured to leave all her money to the Sisterhood, and then deliberately sent to nurse someone with the fever. He described what happened in a letter to *The Times* in November 1857:

> ... The churchyard lies, I should think, about a hundred yards from the station. Before reaching it we were joined by Mr. Scobell [the lady's father, Vicar of Lewes] himself and three members of his family, who proceeded to take their places between ourselves and the bier. The service in the church was read by Mr. Hutchinson, of West Firle; the uproar, hooting, and yelling in the churchyard—almost evidently preconcerted, and that with considerable skill—being quite alarming. With some difficulty we made our way to the vault; it is not attached to the church, but is hollowed out of a kind of bank on the north side of the churchyard. Mr. Hutchinson entered the vault, and the service was there concluded; the mob every moment growing fiercer and more threatening. They made way, however, for Mr. Scobell and his family, as well as for Mr. Hutchinson. As the former was passing I stepped up to him and said, 'Mr. Scobell, you see how threatening the mob is; will you not protect the Sisters?' He bowed, and passed on; and that, be it remembered, when his daughter had died in their arms only five days previously. While this was passing the lights were either extinguished, or so flashed in our faces as to make a confusion worse than darkness. There was a cry of 'Do your duty!' 'Now the performance is come off!' and a rush was immediately made upon us. The impression of all of us is that some at least of the bearers and light-men were the ring-leaders of the mob. But the strangest part of all was that men, certainly in the garb of gentlemen, could stand by and see ladies dashed this way and that, their veils dragged off, and their dresses torn, and, far from rendering the least

assistance, could actually excite the dregs of the rabble to further violence. I was myself knocked down, and for a moment, while under the feet of the mob, gave myself up for lost. We were borne along into the street, Mr. Scobell having quietly gone home, and taking no further interest in the matter.

Some of the sisters took refuge in the schoolmaster's house; some, with myself, in a little public-house called the King's Head. Round this inn the mob soon gathered. At last, by the advice of the police, I made my way across gardens and over walls to the station. A larger force having been now got together were sent back with a fly to the King's Head; and thus, after some hard fighting on their part, we were enabled to return to East Grinstead by the next train, the rabble besetting the station to the very last.

Now, Sir, your readers may draw their own conclusions as to the constitution of the Lewes mob – a mob only too notorious in the annals of lawlessness. A lady who had actually laid down her life in the cause of the poor is buried, according to her own wish, in the church of her father, with that father's full acquiescence; is followed to the grave by her executors and by the ladies in whose arms she died; no demonstration is made which could excited any popular feeling, and the result you have seen …

೧൭

Despite his health and shabby treatment, his scholarly as well as charitable work was prodigious. He wrote extensively on liturgy and the history not only of the Latin but also of the Orthodox church: an early book was *The Patriarchate of Alexandria* (1847). For increasing numbers of people (later to be called Anglo-Catholics) were interested in the Eastern church, including Edward Pusey and William Palmer of Magdalen College, Oxford. Palmer, whom Neale visited in 1846, introduced Neale to Orthodox contacts, like Andrey Nikolayevich Muravyov, under-Procurator of the Holy

Governing Synod, and Yevgeny Ivanovich Popov, chaplain to the Russian Embassy. For Neale considered the Eastern church maintained the strongest links with the teachings of the Fathers, unaffected by either Reformation or the claims of papal superiority; moreover, he saw similarities in doctrine between Anglican and Eastern churches, and considered practices like the veneration of icons consistent with his own ecclesiological understanding of the importance of material symbols in matters spiritual. His interest in Greek hymnody is a natural offshoot of this scholarly interest.

The achievement for which we now owe him gratitude is his translations of Greek and Latin hymns from earliest times to the high mediaeval period: he recovered an ancient treasure without which our worship, and perhaps our thinking, would be much poorer. *Medieval Hymns and Sequences* (1851, 1863, 1867), *The Hymnal Noted* (1852, 1854), *Hymns of the Eastern Church* (1862), and *Hymns Chiefly Medieval* (1865) came in quick succession. He claimed no rights in his texts, simply being pleased that they could contribute to the 'common property of Christendom.' Some criticised him for being, in their view, too 'mystical,' especially in his *Commentary on the Psalms* (1874, completed after his death by his friend R. F. Littledale, himself translator of several hymns). Neale anticipated this: his preface stresses 'not one single mystical interpretation throughout the present Commentary is original'. Going back to drink at ancient wells is an important strand in his spirituality and could/should be in ours, a useful corrective to the reductively materialistic tendencies of our age, plagued, not by good science, but by lazy scientism... Neale, an excellent Classical scholar, was also soaked in the mediaeval Latin which many Classicists regarded as slumming it. Père Jacques Paul Migne's *Patrologia Latina*, which collected in 217 volumes *all* the Latin writing between Tertullian (ob.230) and Innocent III (ob.1216) was then appearing (between 1841 and 1855), and so he had available the vast heritage of Latin hymnody. Neale loved the 'noble' task he set himself: to recover a once major component in the worship of the Western Church, abandoned in the storms of Reformation. 'It is a magnificent thing,' he said,

> to pass along the far-stretching vista of hymns, from the sublime self-containedness of S. Ambrose to the more fervid inspiration of S. Gregory, the exquisite typology of Venantius Fortunatus, the lovely painting of St. Peter Damiani, the crystal-like simplicity of S. Notker [Balbulus], the scriptural calm of Godescalcus [Gottschalk of Orleans], the subjective loveliness of St. Bernard, till all culminate in the full blaze of glory which surrounds Adam of S. Victor, the greatest of them all.

For the mediaeval church, even at humble levels, made great use of music – which after all is, we are told, one of the distinguishing joys of Heaven. For example: not just hymns as we know them, but long poems designed for processions; then, also, the complex sung Sequences for seasons and holy days, during the Gospel procession. (They originated in the Alleluia of the Gradual.) Neale tried to copy their exact measure and rhyme, 'at whatever inconvenience and cramping', which made for some difficulties. Many of them had a complex theological underpinning – I think particularly of Aquinas' wonderful *Pangue, Lingua, gloriosi corporis mysterium*, which he wrote for the Feast of Corpus Christi (see p. 59). Neale and Edward Caswall translated it, so we can sing *NEH* 268 with joy and as much understanding of the mystery as we shall get this side of eternity. In his version of St Bernard of Clairvaux's *Iesu Dulcis Memoria* (The Rosy Sequence, *NEH* 291) Neale captured something of the emotional, affective piety that marks that great mystic's writing – and if you don't know St Bernard's little book on the *Song of Songs* you have a treat waiting for you. The Pentecost Golden Sequence, 'Come thou Holy Spirit, come' (*NEH* 139, *A&M* 92) was written either by Pope Innocent III or Stephen Langton, Archbishop of Canterbury. As we sing Neale's longing words, it is ironic to recall the bitter quarrel over Langton's election as Archbishop, resolved only by Innocent's intervention. That was one of the first moves leading to the civil war of King John's unhappy reign, with all England being placed under a Papal Interdict forbidding any sacraments. (There is a story to be told there, but this is not the place for it ... incidentally, Langton it was who divided up the biblical books into chapters – what would we do without that convenience?[5])

Neale's translations were almost universally welcomed by Anglicans, and some were taken up by non-conformists. But some Roman Catholics accused Neale of disingenuousness because he did not point out his softening, or ignoring, of Roman doctrines in those hymns – that, indeed, his translations misrepresented the originals. (Yet *NEH* 268 – *A&M* does seem to me to accept the Real Presence in the Eucharist, which is flat counter to Article 25 of the 39 Articles.) But Neale, as an Anglican, was aware of how Anglicanism claimed descent from Rome as Mother, but rejected some Roman doctrines after the first four Fathers and the first four Ecumenical Councils – First Nicaea (325), First Constantinople (381), First Ephesus (431) and Chalcedon (451). As an Anglican writing for Anglicans, Neale could be properly omit what clashed with Anglican doctrine.

I confess I feel happier considering Neale's work from Latin as I have known many of the originals for decades, and the Greek corpus of sacred writing and liturgy is quite closed to me. So we – I – owe Neale (and others, like Charles Humphrey, 1840-1921) a huge debt for making accessible something of this. In 1862 Neale published his ground-breaking *Hymns of the Eastern Church*. Of it he remarked,

> I had no predecessors and therefore no master ... Though the superior terseness and brevity of the Latin hymns renders a translation which shall represent those qualities a work of great labour, yet still the versifier has the help

---

[5] It was the Geneva Bible of 1560 that was the first English Bible to use chapters and numbered verses.

of the same metre; his version may be line for line; and there is a great analogy between the collects and the hymns, most helpful to the translator. Above all, we have examples enough of former translation by which we may take pattern. But in attempting a Greek canon, from the fact of its being in prose (metrical hymns are unknown) one is all at sea. What measure shall we employ? Why this more than that? Might we attempt the rhythmical prose of the original, and design it to be chanted? Again, the great length of the canons renders them unsuitable for our churches as wholes ...

Many of his translations from Greek, therefore, are extracts from much longer originals. They show great formal resourcefulness, from the rhymed quatrains familiar to English ears, to something resembling the Sapphics of ancient Greek poetry. It is in *Hymns of the Eastern Church* that 'Christian, dost thou see them?' 'The day is past and over', 'The day of Resurrection,' his own Greek-inspired 'Art thou weary, are thou languid', and 'O happy band of pilgrims' appear. This book was warmly admired.

I must close this tribute – a word not used lightly – with 'Jerusalem the Golden' *NEH* 381 (*A&M* 184). Neale crafted this out of verses (ll.290ff.) from a long, long poem (which I first encountered as an undergraduate with much enthusiasm, but only moderate patience) of satire and complaint against the abuses of the twelfth-century church, *De Contemptu Mundi*, by a Benedictine monk, Bernard of Morlaix, later of Cluny. When we sing it to Alexander Ewing's tune, I confess its *sehnsucht*, its longing for that we glimpse but do not see, brings tears to my eyes almost every time. I have asked for it at my funeral. I would so like people to enjoy themselves there.

XXII
CECIL FRANCES ALEXANDER
1818–95

❧

IN AN EARLY *LIFE of St Patrick* (by Muirchú moccu Machtheni, probably seventh-century), the saint and his companions are travelling to the court of the pagan Laoghhaire mac Néill, King of Tara, High King of Ireland, descendant of Niall of the Nine Hostages, from whom the O'Neills of Ulster descend. Waiting in ambush to kill Patrick and his followers was a band of men, henchmen of the Druids. But as the little band walked, they chanted a *lorica* (breastplate) – an incantation, or spell, in Druidic style, for protection on a journey – journeys were dangerous, after all, even without Druids behind bushes. When they passed the ambush, the would-be attackers saw only a herd of deer – hence the Irish title of this *lorica*, Fáed Fíada, 'The Cry of the Deer'.

Hang on a minute: I have sidetracked myself completely. (It often happens.) This chapter is supposed to be about a lady, Cecil Frances Alexander (1818-1895), who perpetrated some verses impeccable (if dull) in their metre but deplorable in their bathos and/or banality. But she also, memorably, gave us the version of the *lorica*, 'I bind unto myself today/ The strong name of the Trinity' (*NEH* 159), which alone would excuse almost anything. But – and to be fair they met

A Joyful Noise

a certain taste of her time – she gave us the gloomy 'Within the churchyard, side by side/ Are many long low graves,/ And some have stones set over them;/ On some the green grass waves… So when the friends we love the best/Lie in their churchyard bed,/ We must not cry too bitterly/Over the happy dead.' (*Hymns Ancient & Modern* 575); 'All things bright and beautiful' (*A&M* 573, *NEH* 264); 'Every morning the red sun/ Rises warm and bright' (*A&M* 570) 'There is a Green Hill' (*A&M* 332, *NEH* 92), and 'We are but little children weak', the concluding verse of which assures us 'There's not a child so small and weak / But has his little cross to take' (*A&M* 331). (Early editions of *Hymns Ancient & Modern* gathered all these in a section entitled 'For the Young': nothing like cheering the little dears up.) She is not to be blamed for 'All things' having become the most popular hymn at funerals, apparently – though I have not recently heard sung the verse, 'The rich man in his castle, / The poor man at his gate, /God made them high or lowly, /And order'd their estate' (That is also in 'For the Young'.)

But she is worth a great deal more than a twenty-first-century Cambridge sneer. She also wrote 'Once in Royal David's City', much loved by so many, and she gave us that version of St Patrick's Breastplate (which is where I came in) after H. H. Dickinson, Dean of the Chapel Royal at Dublin Castle, suggested that she should fill a gap in the *Irish Church Hymnal* with a metrical English version.[1] For she was already

---

[1] There are several versions in Irish of Patrick's *lorica*. The oldest – set down long after Patrick died in the mid-fifth century – is in the early-ninth century Book of Armagh, (MS Trinity College Dublin, 52) along with Patrick's (probably) authentic 'Confession'. Another is in the eleventh-century *Liber Hymnorum*. Scholars better informed than I say its language and style is certainly a much older than that earliest MS, that its form closely echoes a Druidic incantation, and that its sentiment seems authentically Patrician. Personally, I see it as wonderfully elaborating Paul's exhortation to 'put on the whole armour of God' (Ephesians 6:10-18) with echoes of the Song of the Three Children in Daniel 3. And I love singing it as set by Charles Villiers Stanford – another Irishman. Its full version uses two traditional Irish tunes.

known as a poet and hymn writer, and Dickinson sent her a collation of the best prose translations. A week later, she sent him her version.

༄

Cecil Frances ('Fanny') Humphreys was born at 22 Eccles Street, Dublin. (It is of no significance, so far as I can see, that James Joyce's Leopold Bloom was supposedly born at No 7 in that street, then of substantial Georgian houses.[2]) She was the second daughter of Elizabeth Frances Reed, daughter of Captain Reed of Dublin and a second lieutenant in the Royal Marines, later Brigade Major in the Tyrone Yeomanry. (The family soon moved to Tyrone.) She began writing verse as a child, and as she grew up was permanently influenced by the Oxford Movement. She and her friend Lady Harriet Howard, the Earl of Wicklow's daughter, began writing and publishing religious tracts, with Harriet supplying the prose and Fanny the verse. She met some of the Movement's leaders, like Edward Pusey and Henry Manning, and, only just out of her teens, she became very friendly with John Keble. He wrote the preface for *Hymns for Little Children* (1848; and 69 editions before 1900!). The explicit purpose of this volume by a 20 year-old was to explain to children in simple, concrete images the articles of the Apostles' Creed. She had the gift of understanding the questions children ask: 'Who made the world?' is answered by 'All things bright and beautiful' – well, that is the first clause of the Creed dealt with. 'Where was Jesus born?' – easy: 'Once in royal David's city'; 'Why did he have to die?' - 'There is a green hill far away'. The income from these and other early books helped pay for a pet project, building the Derry and Raphoe Diocesan Institution for the Deaf and Dumb. By the 1840s her hymns were becoming very well known, and Church of Ireland hymnbooks were including her work. She

---

[2] No longer so, alas, after the Philistine demolition of so much of Georgian Dublin in the 1970s and 80s. Now it is just a dull street.

also (under various pseudonyms) contributed narrative and lyric poems, and some translations of French poetry, to *Dublin University Magazine*. There were also several books of poetry, well received at the time, of which the least forgotten today is *St Augustine's Holiday and other Poems*. She impressed Tennyson, who himself wrote fine dialect poetry, with the ballad 'The Legend of Stumpie's Brae' in Ulster-Scots.

∽

Then, in October 1850, to her family's consternation, at an age when most women of her generation would have been thought destined to be 'old maids', she married Revd William Alexander, six years her junior, newly appointed to a nearby parish in County Tyrone. The only photographs we have of her in her middle age, very much by then the Bishop's wife in a pose she can hold for the long exposures of those times, show no hint of the impulsiveness that must have led to that action: but the firm mouth and jaw hint at a steely resolve. Her new husband was a strong supporter of the Oxford Movement, and of its social agenda. Later he would become, first, Bishop of Derry, then Archbishop of Armagh, Primate of All Ireland. She threw herself into charitable work in her husband's parish, taking food to the sick in its remoter parts.

∽

When they both visited Oxford in 1853, the reputation her poems and hymns had won her guaranteed her warm welcome. But the parish work to which she devoted herself so assiduously, and some health issues which demanded visits to Dublin, severely sapped any energy for new writing. Her earlier work remained highly regarded: and Sir Henry Baker asked her advice about the structure *Hymns Ancient and Modern* (1861) should take. Including her hymns helped to boost both her reputation and the popularity of that huge, groundbreaking, collection which provides for pretty well everything sanctioned

Cecil Frances Alexander

in the *Book of Common Prayer*. Her verses had an immediate appeal; and their honesty and straightforwardness contributed to the popularity some of them still have.

ം

In October 1867 William Alexander was enthroned as bishop of Derry and Raphoe. The palace in (London)Derry rather than a rural vicarage was now home. She got involved with the Derry Home for Fallen Women, and worked to set up a District Nurses service. Heavy commitments in visiting the sick and in the active role her husband played in overseeing the Disestablishment of the Church of Ireland left even less time for writing. She turned down request after request for hymns and poems, even (in March 1871) from Edward Pusey, who was by now Oxford's Regius Professor of Hebrew.

Work indeed took a toll. She was too poorly to go with her husband to New York in 1891 or to South Africa in 1893 for her daughter's wedding. By 1895 she was really ill, and died at the palace that October. Her husband stayed as Bishop of Derry and Raphoe until the next year, when he became Archbishop. That same year he published a collected edition of his wife's work: *Poems by Cecil Frances Alexander*.

A stained glass window in St Columb's Cathedral, Derry, is dedicated to her, and a blue plaque marks where she was born. And her best hymns are sung, a century and more after they were written, at the beginning of Midnight Mass at Christmas, Trinity Sunday, St Patrick's Day. Many who sing them know not her name, but own her verses as part of their own sensibility. That is perhaps the most convincing, if paradoxical, of all memorials.

ം

Oh, and what happened to St Patrick? He won, of course. He made his way towards the Hill of Tara, seat of the High King and still, even in its now deserted desuetude, where cows graze, a place resonant with ancient memory. On Holy Saturday, he lit a paschal fire on the nearby Hill of Slane, which you can see from the Hill of Tara. This was a challenge and a half to the old religion and to the sacred power of the king: for at that season, Beltane, it was pagan practice to extinguish all fires before the High King himself lit one anew on Tara's Hill. When the Druids saw the light on Slane, it is said they warned Laoghaire that he must extinguish it or it would burn forever. Patrick was summoned to Tara; some say it is on this journey that he chanted the *Lorica*. He warned the king that he must accept the faith, or die. After taking counsel of his people, he submitted, and was baptised. He would do that, wouldn't he?

XXIII

Catherine Winkworth
1827–78

※

In 1907, John Julian, in his *Dictionary of Hymnology* – long a standard reference work, with over 40,000 entries – remarked,

> Miss Winkworth, although not the earliest of modern translators from the German into English, is certainly the foremost in rank and popularity. Her translations are the most widely used of any from that language, and have had more to do with the modern revival of the English use of German hymns than the versions of any other writer.

One can only agree: and we often sing her versions of *Lobe den Herren*, ('Praise to the Lord, the Almighty, the King of Creation' NEH 440 – A&M 207), *Nun Danket alles Gott* ('Now thank we all our God', 313, A&M 205), *Schmücke dich*, ('Deck thyself, my soul, with gladness', 280, A&M 257). And they have very good tunes that reach back into the wonderful Lutheran musical tradition. As will have been apparent in earlier pages, I have a strong interest in the Latin tradition, but the German is almost equally dear to my heart. The Lutheran impetus towards singing as *Gemeinschaft*, a community activity, encouraged hymns – chorales – which were didactic, memorable, as bond-building

A JOYFUL NOISE

as football chants, and Luther, a master of the right word in the right place, had worthy followers in, for example, Philipp Nicolai (*Wachet auf!*, NEH 16) or Paul Gerhardt (NEH 90, 253, A&M 68, 17). And the melodies stick in the mind, whether plain or transfigured in the cantatas of Bach. Catherine Winkworth was born in 1827 – she is the same generation, roughly, as Cecil Frances Alexander – just off Holborn in Ely Place, then (and till much later) a peculiar – with its own 'police' aka beadles – of the Bishopric of Ely. The house was near St Etheldreda's church, and the delectable Mitre pub where Oliver Goldsmith and Dr Johnson and James Boswell were frequent visitors, Goldsmith writing a charming poem to the pretty barmaid. (It is worth a visit, though Goldsmith's barmaid lives only in neat verse. My wife took me there.) Her father, Henry, from Alderley Edge, Cheshire was in the silk business – Macclesfield, nearby, and Manchester were centres of silk weaving in England then – and Catherine and her sister Susanna (also a translator from German) grew up in Manchester. Henry was doubtful about more than art and music for his five girls, but Susanna (the eldest) was insistent that she and her sisters be educated so they were able as teachers or governesses to earn their own living if they had to. Early education was by their mother, but later Catherine studied under William Gaskell, Unitarian Minister of Cross Street Chapel and husband of Elizabeth Gaskell the novelist, and under Dr James Martineau, brother of Harriet Martineau, and they were taken to lectures at the Athenaeum. These connections are important. First, the Martineau family was in the ideological vanguard of social reform: Harriet (1802-1876) is often called the first female sociologist. She wrote copiously from a sociological, religious, domestic and feminine perspective, she translated works by the philosopher Auguste Comte, and her writing earned enough to support her – rare for a woman of her time. Second, it is hard to overstate the influence of the Unitarian community in Manchester. It was the fountainhead of Manchester Liberalism. That community was behind the foundation of the *Manchester Guardian;* it advocated major social and economic reform – with which Mrs

CATHERINE WINKWORTH

Gaskell's *Mary Barton* (1848) and *North and South* (1854) are also involved; and its thinking influenced the city, and the whole nation, for a generation. Catherine Winkworth's association with this circle ensured that she would be well educated, and fully aware of the infant movement for the improvement in the legal and social status of women.

In 1845, the eighteen year old Catherine and her sister spent a year with an aunt in Dresden, a year formative of much of her work later. She immersed herself in German and in art, particularly music. Here she began exploring the rich corpus of German hymnody, using the many hymnals collected by her friend Baron von Bunsen, whom she had met through the Gaskells when he was German Ambassador to the Court of St James. As well as being a busy diplomat he was scholar, philologist, historian and theologian. (I often wonder, despairingly, how those Eminent 'Victorians' got through the amount of work they did with none of the aids we take for granted.) Returning to England they studied logic in James Martineau's class for young ladies, and Susanna later said that for Catherine this had been a time of painful rethinking of many things. Her 'early beliefs had been rudely shattered ... and her philosophy was a chaos', but Martineau's teaching 'fixed for her the intellectual foundations of faith'.

She published nothing until 1855, when the first series of *Lyra Germanica* came out, followed in 1858 by the second. From the collection of hymns made by von Bunsen in 1833 she translated over a hundred for the Christian year. Both books sold widely. The hymns might have been even more widely used had Longmans, the publisher, not refused to allow their inclusion in the many congregational hymnals published in the second half of the century. In translating, she kept the original metres as far as possible, so their German tunes would fit. The Chorale Book for England, with as musical editors the composer William Sterndale Bennett and Otto Goldschmidt (whose wife was Jenny Lind, the Swedish soprano), came out in 1862–3, with a supplement in 1865. *Christian Singers of Germany* (1869) examined German religious poetry at a time when English links with things German were warmest. After all, the English the Queen spoke had a strong German accent, her German consort was of remarkable ability, her eldest daughter was married to the German Emperor and German music was heard everywhere. Although not the first English translator of German hymns (John Wesley, after all, got there first), Winkworth brought German hymn writers into English hymnody, in very good translations. In the 1855 preface to the *Lyra* she said she aimed to sustain the 'deep and true Communion of Saints … among all the children of God in different churches and lands'.

The Winkworths moved to Clifton near Bristol in 1862. Her father's health was concerning, and the silk industry in the north was declining. Catherine had much experience as a district visitor: from 1852, she had been active in work among the poor in the newly-established Sunday School & District Visiting Society and had seen firsthand what real poverty was like. That experience is background to her translations of the *Life of Amelia Sieveking* (1863), which urged work with the poor and sick as a proper use of what women uniquely could do, and of the *Life of Pastor Fliedner* (1867), who had founded an order of Protestant deaconesses. Women's work became one of her causes, and in 1872 she was one of only three British delegates to a conference about it in Darmstadt presided over by Princess Alice, the Queen's third daughter, wife of the Grand Duke of Hesse. Higher education for women became important too, leading her in 1868 to join the Clifton Association for Higher Education for Women. She became its Secretary. The association organized lectures, classes for women preparing for the Cambridge Higher Local examination, and helped the establishment of Bristol University College, which from the start offered scholarships to both women and men. She was elected to the governing body of the Red Maid's School in Westbury-on-Trym – founded 1634, it is the oldest girls' school in England.[1] She was one of the people behind the foundation

---

[1] It amalgamated with another foundation, the Redlands School (1882) to form the Redmaids School in 2016.

of the Clifton High School for Girls (1877) – they named a school house after her – and from 1875 until she died was on the Council of Cheltenham Ladies' College.

In summer 1878 she travelled to Geneva to join her sister and an invalid nephew. She died suddenly of a heart attack at nearby Monnetier, just over the French border, and was buried there. Soon after, her old mentor Dr Martineau wrote in *The Inquirer*:

> The translations contained in these volumes are invariably faithful [which is not quite true, for she does sometimes edit], and for the most part both terse and delicate; and an admirable art is applied to the management of complex and difficult versification. They have not quite the fire of John Wesley's versions of Moravian hymns, or the wonderful fusion and reproduction of thought which may be found in Coleridge. But if less flowing they are more conscientious than either, and attain a result as poetical as severe exactitude admits, being only a little short of 'native music'.

It is a fair comment. Translation is a difficult art, as anyone who has tried it knows, especially when you try to match form to form, or the words in a new language to a tune written for the old. She has not the verbal flair of J. M. Neale, who sometimes went right away from his original and made something new, but she triumphantly kept the great virtue of the original: the singability of these hymns. And, most of all, she domesticated for us Anglophones the rich Lutheran congregational choral tradition. I'd miss not having *Vom Himmel hoch, da komm ich her*, (Martin Luther, 1534: 'From Heaven Above to Earth I Come', and *Wachet auf, ruft uns die Stimme*, (Philipp Nicolai, 1599: 'Awake, for Night Is Flying'); *Wie schön leuchtet der Morgenstern*, (Nicolai, 1597: 'How Brightly Beams the Morning Star!'; and the Christmas hymn that always brings a wetness to my eyes: *Es ist ein Ros entsprungen* (Anon., 1599: 'A Spotless Rose')

A JOYFUL NOISE

And finally: we owe to her one of the best, shrewdest, puns in the language. In 1843, many were shocked by General Napier's unauthorised and ruthless annexation of the province of Sindh. His despatch to the Governor General of India was simply, smugly, 'I have Sindh'. Hearing of this, she remarked that it ought to have been in Latin: 'Peccavi' – 'I have sinned.' She sent it to the new magazine *Punch*, which printed it in March 1844. Not bad for a sixteen-year-old.

XXIV
Robert Bridges
1844–1930

Who now reads Robert Bridges? Yet he sticks in my memory. In the top class at Beach Road County Primary School I can remember, one winter Friday afternoon, as the gas lights outside lit up the falling flakes of the snow that was so rare on that flat Lancashire coast, Miss Murphy reading us his 'London Snow'. I can't say I have ever read him seriously, extensively, in all the years since, but that poem stuck in my imagination as something – well, lovely. A ten-year-old me had never been to London, or seen a snowfall of full seven inches. And we do sing a number of his hymns, and owe him much as one of the people who influenced the compiling of the *English Hymnal*

Bridges was Poet Laureate for 17 years, till his death in 1930, and his last poem, *Testament of Beauty* (1929), was a runaway success. If you look up his bibliography, you find he published 12 volumes of poems between 1876 and 1929 (of which *Testament of Beauty* and *Eros and Psyche* (1885) are perhaps now the best known). Also, between 1885 and 1894 he wrote eight verse dramas, mostly on classical themes. He had a huge reputation in his later lifetime: Oxford University Press in 1912 brought out his *Poetical Works, Excluding the Eight Dramas* in the *Oxford Standard Poets* series, which considerable honour was based partly on the influence his theories of prosody had on younger writers, and partly on the fact that his *Shorter Poems* had been reprinted four times in five years. *Poetical Works* sold 27,000 copies in its first year, and such popularity led to the offer of the laureateship in 1913 when Rudyard Kipling refused it. Had he known what the Laureateship would require him to write in the next five years he too might have turned down the post and its small honorarium and its 720 bottles of sherry (far more convenient that the old-fashioned barrel John Dryden and his successors had got).

He was born in 1844 at Walmer, Kent, fourth son and eighth child of John Bridges and Harriett Affleck (1807–1897). (She was the daughter of Revd Sir Robert Affleck, who lived in (to my mind) the most covetable of all small country houses, Dalham Hall, near Newmarket.) The family was steeped in the ideas and practice of the Oxford Movement, and during Robert's time at Corpus Christi, Oxford (after Eton, where he began a lifelong friendship with Hubert Parry, the composer) he became close friends with William Sanday (later Lady Margaret Professor of Divinity) and Gerard Manley Hopkins. He had become an ardent follower of E. B. Pusey, and joined the ascetic, High Anglican, Brotherhood of the Holy Trinity.

But Oxford was an unsettling, unsettled, place too: the ferment of ideas about the authority of Scripture fuelled by the German Higher Criticism, and the explosive reactions to Darwin's *Origin of Species* (1859), could leave nobody untouched, and Bridges had to explore his faith anew in the face of this and his own personal griefs.

And he indeed had many. In 1853, his beloved father had died suddenly. The next year his mother married the Vicar of Rochdale, John Nassau Molesworth, to whom Robert found it hard to relate. His brother Edward died in 1866 and his cousin Digby Dolben, a precocious poet, was drowned, aged 19, the next year. After leaving Oxford, he travelled in the Holy Land (partly to test his own beliefs) for a year. He returned in June 1868 to find his elder sister, Harriet, dying. She had married Revd Antony Plow, vicar of Todmorden, and they had a new baby. The lover of a servant girl, whom they had sacked because of his illicit visits, went for the family with a hatchet. Plow and the baby died immediately; she died later of her wounds.

He chose medicine as a career, studying at St Bartholomew's. Here again everything was in ferment, with the explosion of scientific knowledge, and after qualifying he was vocally critical of some practices accepted as normal in clinical medicine. The strain on physicians in Casualty was immense, for they were expected each morning to diagnose the ailments of 150 patients in under two hours. Bridges, exceptionally conscientious, spent significantly more time on each patient, but even so in one year saw nearly 31,000 patients in Casualty. (Edward Thompson, a friend in Bridges' last years, later remarked that he had never known anyone as sensitive as Bridges to others' physical suffering.) His damning report on the Casualty Department of Bart's, criticising its organization for physicians and patients, probably explains why he was offered no further appointment there.

In 1881 he developed serious pneumonia, and after a year's slow convalescence decided he must give up medical practice and devote himself to writing, for which his reputation among his friends was growing. Since most of his siblings were dead he now had a greater share of the family money, and by combining incomes he and his mother (widowed again, 1877) could make a home together. He no longer needed a salary.

Bridges had long been friendly with Alfred Waterhouse the architect (in Cambridge think of the building that faces Little St Mary's across Trumpington Street, Caius College's first court, and the joyous former Foster's Bank, now Lloyds, on the corner of Hobson Street, and, in London, the Natural History Museum). In 1884 he married Waterhouse's daughter Monica (1863–1949). (One of their children was Edward Bridges, Cabinet Secretary during WW2.) It was an exceptionally happy marriage, with shared interests, especially in music. Through Monica, Bridges came to know her cousin Roger Fry, painter and critic, and through him a younger generation of poets and writers: W. B. Yeats, Ezra Pound, Henry Newbolt, Mary Coleridge, Robert Graves, Virginia Woolf, and E. M. Forster. (Yet, despite Bridges' friendliness, only Newbolt and Mary

Coleridge seem to have been at ease with him and few publicly acknowledged his help or any admiration for his poetry.)

The titles of Bridges' works – *Eros and Psyche, Prometheus the Firegiver, Nero, The Feast of Bacchus* (1889), *Achilles in Scyros* (1890), *The Return of Ulysses* (1890), for example – indicate how soaked he was in Greek and Latin literature. Indeed, his friend W. J. Stone, son of a former Eton master, persuaded him to try writing English verse in classical quantitative metres. (It had been tried before, without much success or lasting fashion, in the sixteenth century, and the method does not sit easily to the sounds of English.) In *Testament*, he successfully used another metre (unusual at any length in English), the 12-syllabled Alexandrine, which started life in the Renaissance as a weighty sort of domestication of the Latin and Greek hexameter. He translated parts of the *Aeneid* and wrote two long discursive epistles and, using some Classical forms, lyrics. Indeed, add music, and Sapphics, adapted from the Greek, can work very well, as in Bridges' plangent version (via the German) of an eleventh-century meditation, *NEH* 62 'Ah, holy Jesu, how hast thou offended?' Bridges was really interested in prosody, and his *Milton's Prosody* (1893; 1901; 1921) still repays thoughtful consideration if not always eliciting agreement. But we also owe a huge debt of gratitude for his editing, and publishing in 1918, the poems of another metrical virtuoso and a profound spiritual writer, his friend Gerard Manley Hopkins, who became a Jesuit. Born in the same year as Bridges, he had died in 1889 without publishing any poetry – yet Christopher Ricks called him the 'the most original poet of the Victorian age' and T. S. Eliot saw him as the 'founder of the modern movement' in poetry.

But there is another debt. Comb through the index of *NEH* and you find Bridges gave us as well as 62, 90, 'O sacred Head', adapted from Paul Gerhardt's (1607-76) version of a fourteenth-century hymn; 229, 'Joy and triumph everlasting', translated from Adam of St Victor, c. 1150; 247, 'O gladsome light', translated from a pre fourth-century Greek hymn – one of the oldest poems we still use; 253, 'The duteous day now closeth', translated from Paul Gerhardt, with a (much loved) late-fifteenth-century melody harmonised by Bach; the wonderful 333 (*A&M* 336), 'All my hope on God is founded', based on the German of J. Neander, for which the young Herbert Howells wrote a splendid tune; 369 (*A&M* 176), 'Happy are they, they that love God' (based on a Latin poem of the French seventeenth-century Huguenot, Charles Coffin); 409, 'Love of the father, Love of the Son' – a fourteenth-century Latin hymn; 411, 'My Lord, my Life, My Love' – adapting Isaac Watts; and 493 (*A&M* 296), 'Rejoice, O Land, in God thy might' – the only one wholly his.

For his interest in hymns and their place in liturgy was profound. After marrying Monica, they lived at Yattendon, Berkshire, where Waterhouse was squire and Lord of the Manor. The family and their friends, intensely musical, sang madrigals and part songs together, formed a local orchestra, which included some villagers who thus became proficient readers of music, and with the support of the Rector, Henry Beeching,[1] formed a church choir. Bridges, despite his diffidence about his 'gruff' voice, was soon Precentor and a fine trainer of the church choir. Robert Wyatt, as a very young boy once pressed into the choir, remembered him as pretty forceful, even intimidating, but later said, 'it wasn't hard work, it was just natural', and clearly enjoyed it. In services, the choir sang the psalms to chants composed by Monica Bridges. Bridges and his friend Harry Ellis Wooldridge put together between 1894 and 1899 the *Yattendon Hymnal*, which they printed privately – Bridges was, unsurprisingly, meticulous about typography and its aesthetics. Also in 1899, Bridges published *A Practical Discourse On Some Principles Of Hymn-Singing*. The *Hymnal* had only a small circulation but very great influence. Its appearance, with Bridges' forceful notes and prefaces, was certainly one of the stimuli that led to a new edition of *Hymns Ancient and Modern* in 1904; it was also a major influence on Dearmer and Vaughan Williams' *English Hymnal* of 1906. For he was very alert to the marriage of music and text – after all,

---

[1] Minor poet, widely respected critic and scholar, who later became Dean of Norwich.

he was friendly with John Stainer, Charles Villers Stanford, Hubert Parry and Gustav Holst, and RVW set several of Bridges' poems, as did Holst, and Gerald Finzi.

His despair at the state of English hymnody then might find an echo in what many of us think of the contemporary CofE's 'songs' (I think that is the word used now):

> We are content to have our hymn-manuals stuffed with the sort of music which, merging the distinction between sacred and profane, seems designed to make the worldly man feel at home, rather than to reveal to him something of the life beyond his knowledge, compositions full of cheap emotional effects and bad experiments made to be cast aside, the works of the purveyors of marketable fashion, always pleased with themselves, and always to be derided by the succeeding generation.

Well then … and the *Hymnal*'s music utterly rejects the banal: thirteen tunes are plainsong, sixteen Genevan psalm tunes, seven are by Tallis, eight by Gibbons, eight others from sixteenth-century psalm tunes, ten from the seventeenth, eleven German Chorales, nine by Jeremiah (Bridges calls him 'Jeremy') Clarke, and four by William Croft. There are three eighteenth-century tunes and one early Italian one.

In 1926 Bridges' daughter Margaret died – another grievous loss in a life marked by many. Urged by Monica, he spent the next three years writing what became *The Testament of Beauty*. This response to his loss, his longest poem, is discursive and anecdotal in method, and Oxford University Press published it just before his eighty-fifth birthday in 1929. It was a remarkable success: by 1946 it had sold over 70,000 copies. The reading done to put this short note together makes me feel I ought to – shall – go away and read the poem, this time properly: its author deserves it.

XXV

Percy Dearmer
1867–1936

New English Hymnal, Nos 31, 39, 46, 78, 102, 144, 149, 150, 153, 170, 183, 217, 290, 306, 372, 387 … Percy Dearmer's was one of those names always cropping up, yet hardly noticed at the bottom of the page, at Friday evening choir practice. A young, deplorably inattentive, slightly dyslexic, me read it as 'Dreamer'. (The only 'Percy' I knew was a dachshund, an unimpressive dog.) Any word less appropriate than 'dreamer', in the sense it was addressed to me in lessons or choir practice when I was looking out of the window, to this energetic and visionary man is hard to imagine. Hardly surprisingly, we sang him a lot, for he wrote or translated many hymns that kept on coming up: in *NEH*, his 17 hymns make him third only to Charles Wesley's 26 and J. M. Neale's 39.

But that is small beer. To his energy and vision we owe *The English Hymnal*, revolutionary in its time and in its revised *NEH* form still in use after over a century. To him we owe the inspired choice of drawing in Ralph Vaughan Williams as Music Editor. To him we owe much that we take for granted in the way the liturgy is celebrated.

Biographical outline first. His father, Thomas Dearmer, was an artist and teacher of drawing. The family were in circumstances comfortable enough, according to the 1881 census, to keep quite a number of servants in his large house in Kilburn. Kilburn then was a prosperous, growing suburb round a small chalybeate spring, which some people once hoped they could make into a spa. Percival, born in 1867, was sent to school first in Streatham, and in the early 1880s to Westminster. Then followed a spell at a Lutheran school, at Vevey in Switzerland, before going up to Christ Church, Oxford, in 1886, to read Modern History, in the last years of Henry Liddell's tenure as Dean. Liddell's friend Charles Lutwidge Dodgson ('Lewis Carroll') was still a Student of that House. By all accounts, as an undergraduate Dearmer, strikingly handsome, was something of a dandy, anticipating his interest in vestments and performance later. A stay at Pusey House, Oxford, introduced him to its remarkable Principal, Charles Gore – for whom he acted as secretary. Graduating BA in 1890, he was ordained deacon the next year and priested in 1892. Four London curacies in poor parishes followed, until he became Vicar of St Mary's, Primrose Hill, in 1901. It was while he was Vicar that he did most of his work with the *English Hymnal*, and in recognition of that Oxford made him a Doctor of Divinity in 1911. He stayed at Primrose Hill until he volunteered for war service in 1915: the first his wife Mabel (a talented playwright and novelist) knew of this was when he announced it from the pulpit. He went to Serbia as chaplain to the British Red Cross, with Mabel, who served with an ambulance unit. (She died of typhoid in 1915 while working as a hospital orderly: the same year their son Christopher was killed in action.) Afterwards he worked with the YMCA, lecturing in France and India, and in the last years of the war visited the USA. In 1918-9 he was visiting professor at Berkeley Divinity School in New Haven, Connecticut, and then, as an acknowledged authority on matters liturgical and iconographic because of his writing, in 1919 he became the first Professor of Ecclesiastical Art at King's College, London. For fifteen years, Dearmer had no official ecclesiastical posts, concentrating on writing and arguing for radical social change, until in 1931 he was made Canon Librarian of Westminster Abbey. This was an appointment that raised some of the more conservative eyebrows. He immediately ran a canteen for the unemployed from the Abbey. Heart disease killed him in 1936.

༜

Pusey House had, and has, a considerable influence. It had been founded, a few years before Dearmer went up to Oxford, as a memorial to Edward Bouverie Pusey, a leading early member of the Oxford Movement, and to house Pusey's enormous library – he had been Regius Professor of Hebrew for 50 years. Its Principal, Gore, was a powerful influence on many younger clergy and undergraduates, and it was largely through Gore that the Movement changed significantly. Pusey and his followers had been theologically and liturgically very conservative, relying on authority and tradition and rejecting any modern critical and liberalising ideas. But Gore found this refusal to engage with modern thought no help at all in his experience of dealing with the doubts and difficulties of intelligent young men in a University where intellectual inquiry was of its very lifeblood. Therefore, still regarding the Divine authority of the Catholic Church as a first principle, he set himself to reconcile authority in religion with authority in science, recognising their different discourses. He persuasively welcomed some aspects of biblical criticism and scientific discovery, while remaining Catholic in his view of faith and sacraments.[1]

Gore was also an early proponent of the importance of trade unions, and of Christian Socialism. For the High Churchmanship of Pusey House which Dearmer imbibed, was very much part of a vision of social justice, of the dignity of work, and of the moral importance of beauty, all ideas which F. D. Maurice, John Ruskin and William Morris shared. Work among the poor and marginalised was central to the Anglo-Catholic agenda, and bringing joy to lives often starved of beauty and drama and colour was important in that work. Dearmer

[1] Gore became Bishop in turn of Worcester, Birmingham and Oxford. He also founded the Community of the Resurrection at Mirfield in Yorkshire.

was one of the founding members of the Oxford branch of the new Alcuin Club which sought to preserve, or restore, church ceremony, arrangement, ornament, and practice in an orthodox manner. (Much later, in 1912, to foster in practical and visible ways the Alcuin Club's work, Dearmer helped found the Warham Guild[2] of craftsmen and artisans to make Church ornaments or vestments under fair working conditions, and with proper knowledge of function in liturgy and symbolism.) While an undergraduate, Dearmer had worked among the very poor in London's East End in the Christ Church Mission, Poplar, during the dock strike of 1889, and his first curacy was in South Lambeth. There he saw at first hand just what real poverty could be like. Not much, indeed, had changed since Henry Mayhew's shocking reportage in *London Labour and the London Poor* (1851). He was the London Secretary of the Christian Social Union from 1891–1912, and throughout his life was deeply, loudly, concerned with social justice.

He was passionate about so much. He was impassioned in the introduction to his first book,[3] *The Parson's Handbook* (1899). He says he wrote it to remedy 'the lamentable confusion, lawlessness, and vulgarity which are conspicuous in the Church at this time' – strong words! In great detail he explains how he thinks the Prayer Book liturgy can be conducted in a properly Catholic and English manner, stressing the importance of dignity, beauty and ceremony. Dearmer's argument was that the Prayer Book derived ultimately from the liturgical 'uses' of medieval England (e.g. Sarum, York, Hereford and Lincoln) and that it replaced them with a

---

[2] Named after Erasmus' friend William Warham, Archbishop of Canterbury in the run-up to the breach with Rome.

[3] There were many, including *Christian Socialism and Practical Christianity* (1897); *Highways and Byways in Normandy* (1900); *The Dragon of Wessex: A Story of the Days of Alfred* (1911); *Everyman's History of the Prayer Book* (1912); *The Art of Public Worship* (1919); *The Power of the Spirit* (1919); *The Legend of Hell: An Examination of the Idea of Everlasting Punishment* (1929).

uniform, Reformed, vernacular – an 'English Use', as he called it. Consequently the meagre ceremonial rubrics of the *Book of Common Prayer* could justifiably be elaborated by reference to Pre-Reformation service books. This would accord fully with canons governing the Prayer Book's use, and thus spike the guns of those Evangelicals opposed in principle to ritual and vestments. (There were many: my own very Evangelical great-grandfather, much loved in his parish, always officiated in a simple black gown. He would have been shocked to see me, in amice and alb, after my voice broke, serving a celebrating priest wearing a chasuble.) It was while Dearmer was the 'methodical and innovative' Vicar of St Mary's (as the parish website remembers him) that he 'introduc[ed] radical changes from day one … us[ing] the church as a sort of practical laboratory for the principles he had outlined, revising the book several times during his tenure.' Thirteen editions followed. Nothing teaches like experience.

Which brings us to *The English Hymnal,* Dearmer's most visible legacy even if most people are unaware of his role in its genesis. Oxford University Press published the first edition in 1906. It has been called a musical companion to *The Parson's Handbook,* as *A&M* is for the *Book of Common Prayer,* but that is rather a broad brush stroke. Like Bridges (see p. 214), Dearmer was fed up with the quality – words and music – of many of the hymns commonly sung, and Bridges' privately printed *Yattendon Hymnal* (1899) almost certainly spurred Dearmer's project for a collection of hymns of good quality with good music to enhance the beauty of holiness in the yearly liturgical round. Both men – and a lot of the Anglo-Catholic movement – might well have agreed (as I would) that beauty communicates in ways for which we do not always allow: the beauty of holiness may well be the holiness of beauty.[4] There is

---

[4] As George Herbert realised, 'a verse may find him who a sermon flies/ And turn delight into a sacrifice'. And consider the evidence for the neurological basis, and importance, of this discussed in Ian McGilchrist's *The Master and His Emissary: The Divided Brain and the Making of the Western World* (Yale, 2019).

a passage in Bridges' *Testament of Beauty* (ii, 842ff.) which puts this well:

> *What is Beauty? saith my sufferings then?.*[5]– I answer
> the lover and poet in my loose alexandrines:
> Beauty is the highest of all these occult influences,
> the quality of appearances that thru' the sense
> wakeneth spiritual emotion in the mind of man:
> And Art, as it createth new forms of beauty,
> awakeneth new ideas that advance the spirit
> in the life of Reason to the wisdom of God.

Dearmer, acting as Secretary, was helped by friends – W. J. Birkbeck, Athelstan Riley, T. A. Lacey, D. C. Lathbury, and A. Hanbury-Tracy. Like him they deplored the embarrassingly bad quality of what congregations were too often expected to sing. (Some things have a way of repeating themselves ...) Like W. Garret Horder, the Congregationalist minister whose *Worship Song* (1885) he knew, he argued that a hymn should be worth the attention of anybody sensitive to literature – or, at the least, appreciative of decent verse expressing sound moral teaching and genuine religious experience. His Preface, typically direct, announced 'a collection of the best hymns in the English language and [it] is offered as a humble companion to the *Book of Common Prayer* for use in the Church', with 'complete provision for the liturgical requirements of Churchmen'. It added 'many modern hymns of the first rank'. Some of them were mint new: G. K. Chesterton's passionate 'O God of earth and altar' (*NEH* 492) – which has a grand adaptation of a traditional English tune by Vaughan Williams, for example. Like the Prayer Book, it was suited 'for all sorts and conditions of men'. But what about the music, about which these men cared greatly?

Dearmer's choice was inspired. He did not approach the

---

[5] Christopher Marlowe's Tamburlaine the Great asks this when he first looks on the face of his captive, Zenocrate (V.i).

obvious people with reputations in church music, like Arthur Sullivan, Hubert Parry, Villiers Stanford, E. J. Hopkins (e.g. *NEH* 250), C. Steggall (56), Luard Selby (183) or Frederick Bridge. From Cecil Sharp, the pioneer folk song collector, he had got wind of a talented young man who had been organist at St Barnabas, South Lambeth – the area where Dearmer had served his first curacy. Ralph Vaughan Williams, like Sharp a member of the Folk Song Society, had held that uncongenial job[6] for four years, and told his friend Gustav Holst that at least he got an insight into good and bad church music. He was, formally and openly, an atheist – though that term can mean many things: he once said he heard even in an errand boy's cheerful whistling 'nothing else than an attempt to reach into the Infinite', which sounds not quite atheist to me. Just before he met Dearmer, he had published his first work, the delectable setting for voice and piano of William Barnes' poem *Linden Lea*, which preceded other notable settings of Christina Rossetti, D. G. Rossetti and Tennyson. Dearmer called on him:

> It must have been in 1904 that I was sitting in my study in Barton Street, Westminster, when a cab drove up to the door and 'Mr. Dearmer' was announced. I just knew his name vaguely as a parson who invited tramps to sleep in his drawing-room; but he had not come to see me about tramps. He went straight to the point and asked me to edit the music of a hymn book.

Dearmer, always optimistic, said the job would take two months. It was actually two years. After all, the 1906 edition had well over 600 hymns. RVW was exactly the practical musician needed as Music Editor. Just as Dearmer and his colleagues felt strongly about the quality of the words, so (Vaughan Williams wrote later), it 'ought no longer to be true anywhere that the most exalted moments of a church-goer's week are associated

---

[6] He called it 'this damned place' in a July 1897 letter to Holst – oddly enough, suggesting he might take on his job!

with music that would not be tolerated in any place of secular entertainment.'

The collaboration was a triumph: RVW cast his net very widely, drawing on plainsong, English folk song, Lutheran chorales, Bach, French and Swiss traditional melodies, the American gospel singer Ira D. Sankey's and D. W Moody's *Sacred Songs and Solos* (1873), seventeenth-century Scottish Psalters, Welsh hymn tunes, Italian, Spanish, Flemish, and Dutch church melodies. He also added new, or adapted, melodies of his own and commissioned others. (In the first edition these are 'anonymous'.) In later editions composers are named: for example, Gustav Holst's 'Cranham', for 28, Christina Rossetti's 'In the Bleak Midwinter'; RVW's own adaptation of a folk song, *The Ploughboy's Dream*, which becomes 'Forest Green', for 32; tunes from outside the Anglican tradition like 'York' from the Scottish Psalter (441), which Vaughan Williams also used again in his *Pilgrim's Progress* (1949); and several of his own including the wonderful, life-enhancing 'Sine nomine' for W.Walsham How's 197 ('For all the Saints'), and his 'Salve Festa Dies' (for Venantius Fortunatus' 'Hail Thee Festival Day' 109). It was a happy collaboration, and Dearmer again worked with RVW (and Martin Shaw, who like RVW and Gustav Holst, had studied under Charles Villiers Stanford) on *Songs of Praise* (1926) and *The Oxford Book of Carols* (1928).[7]

The book caused some stir. From a political point of view, the book does have a strong whiff of Christian Socialism:[8] not pleasing to all. Some bishops objected to hymns to the Virgin Mary, to other saints, and for the Faithful Departed being included. Many thought *The English Hymnal* undermined the uniformity of the CofE, for it challenged the (by then) common use of *Hymns Ancient and Modern* in High or Broad Church worship, or, in Evangelical parishes, the *Hymnal Companion to*

---

[7] In the 1931 enlarged edition of *Songs of Praise* Eleanor Farjeon's lovely 'Morning has broken', which Dearmer commissioned, first appeared: *NEH* 237

[8] E.g. *NEH* 492!

the Book of Common Prayer. Some disliked RVW's use of folk song as basis for hymn tunes, complaining of the 'atmosphere of secularity' such melodies suggested. The Diocese of Bristol banned the book; there was outrage in the papers ... and the naturally conciliatory Randall Davidson, Archbishop of Canterbury, felt he had to censure it. None of this did sales any harm. Dearmer refused to contemplate revision, and Oxford University Press became jittery about sales. But nothing makes a book better known than controversy, even if it is not any good, and quite soon this very good book took off and has never been out of print in one form or another since.

ے

This turbulent priest could not have been further from my juvenile misreading of his name as 'Dreamer'. Yet dreams he had aplenty and worked to make them real: social justice, and the honouring of work and craft – values stressed by his 'Litany of Labour' in his 1930 manual for communicants, *The Sanctuary* (1930*)*. He dreamed of a reformed, dynamic Anglicanism – not a return to Rome by any means, for he abhorred the modern Roman Church as a 'political machine'. He dreamed of an English church with a liturgy dignified, beautiful, choreographed, full of symbolism and memory of the church's tradition, in which people could take full part in joy before the Lord as David danced before the Ark of the Covenant. In many places he made that happen, and it still happens a hundred years later in his own parish. Radical in other ways too, as a Canon of Westminster he argued against the ban on contraception, and supported the public ministry of women – though not their ordination. He opposed all gambling, and was closely associated with Conrad Noel, the 'Red Vicar' of Thaxted, Essex – in whose parish Gustav Holst chose to live.

He had style. A certain extravagance of dress, as when an undergraduate, was characteristic. After all, clothes are statements. A priest in vestments says much about his office by what he wears. G. K. Chesterton, one of Dearmer's religious protégés, and himself not uncolourful in appearance or language, recalled Dearmer's custom, when out and about on pastoral calls, to walk in a cassock topped by a priest's gown. Wearing a voluminous scarf round his neck, and his square cap (velvet for a Doctor of his University, he insisted), he would accompany Chesterton on their loquacious walks together. Street urchins would completely mistake the strictly traditional, national character of his garb. Chesterton reported,

> Somebody would call out, 'No Popery', or 'To hell with the Pope', or some other sentiment of a larger or more liberal religion. [I am old enough to remember myself such sentiments being expressed, though I was not a street urchin.] Dearmer's response was sternly to confront them with concise historical and ecclesiological facts, concluding, 'Are you aware that this is the precise costume in which Latimer [the Protestant martyr] went to the stake?'

I wonder if those boys, surely astonished, were ever made curious to know their heritage.

XXVI
ELEANOR FARJEON
1881–1965

❦

IN 1972 MY YOUNG daughter came home singing, 'Morning has broken' because they had just sung it at school. They had listened to a recording made the previous year by the folk singer Cat Stevens – which went, as one might now say, 'viral', as much as the technology then allowed. As it happened, I had never heard it before though it had been around for some time; and I loved it even in a somewhat breathy off-key eight-year-old voice. By an extraordinary coincidence, at just that time daughter (who gobbled books) was reading Eleanor Farjeon's *Martin Pippin in the Daisy Field* (1937).

Benjamin Farjeon, Eleanor's father, was a prolific novelist, now largely forgotten. Her mother was the daughter of a celebrated American actor, Joseph Jefferson. Theatre bulked large in their children's education: writers, actors, musicians frequently visited the house in north London, and the four talented children grew up in an atmosphere where it was taken for granted the arts mattered. Eleanor was going to opera and theatre at 4, writing on her father's typewriter at 7. Her brother Harry eventually taught at the Royal Academy of Music – and indeed she first came to public attention at 16 as the librettist of Harry's opera, *Floretta*, produced by the Royal Academy of Music. Joe and Herbert Farjeon both became writers: Joe wrote thrillers, Herbert plays, and also edited the

A Joyful Noise

Nonesuch edition of Shakespeare's First Folio. Eleanor had no formal education, but (what was probably as good) the run of her father's 8000 books.

All this sounds enviable. But there were strains, and what an adult might see as mere irritation a child can see as frightening. Her father's impulsive nature could be dictatorial, and there could be family rows, which she could hear in her bedroom. When she wrote of her childhood in *A Nursery in the Nineties* (1935), she remembered lying in bed, listening 'to the tone of the talk in the dining room underneath'. If it continued as quiet murmur, she slept peacefully, but too often 'the strong voice grew excited, and the gentle voice silent. Then I did not sleep till nearly morning'. She was 'a dreamy, timid, sickly, lachrymose, painfully shy, sensitive, greedy, ill-regulated little girl ... intensely absorbed in my writing, my reading, my family and my imaginative life ... no wonder that many years later when I came to write books myself they were a muddle of fact, fiction, fantasy and truth'.

When Benjamin died (1903) he left nothing. Eleanor had to make her own living. Slowly, shyly, she began to make friends. One autumn day in 1912, her brother invited Edward Thomas to tea. Thus began a deep friendship between a painfully shy woman of 31 and a reserved writer already known for his prose works and literary criticism. Thomas[1] and his wife, Helen, became close to her, and Eleanor's encouragement of Thomas's development as a poet – and the shock of his death in the Battle of Arras in 1917 – helped her own writing to mature. She wrote a fine book on this great poet, *Edward Thomas: the Last Four Years* (1958), and published their correspondence. Other friends included D. H. Lawrence, Walter de la Mare and Robert Frost.

Soon after Thomas's death, Eleanor rented a cottage on her own in Sussex. Two years there produced her fantasy

---

[1] On 11 November 1985, Ted Hughes unveiled the memorial stone to 16 poets of WW1 at Poet's Corner in Westminster Abbey. Last on the list is Edward Thomas, whom Hughes declared that evening to be 'the father of us all'.

of the wandering troubadour *Martin Pippin in the Apple-Orchard* (1921). It was not written for children, but to amuse Victor Haslam, an officer serving in France to whom Thomas had introduced her. As she wrote each instalment, she sent them to Haslam. In fact, the six love stories show the influence of Charles Perrault's (1628-1703) *Histoires ou Contes du Temps Passé* (1697), which she had probably found among her father's books years earlier. Perrault laid the foundations for a new genre, fairy tale, derived from earlier folk tales.[2] In Eleanor's stories, the apparent loss of a loved one, betrayal, the yearning of a woman to whom it seems love will never come are regular themes. The influential Rebecca West[3] reviewed the book very favourably in the *New Statesman* in December 1921, which marked Eleanor's writing being taken seriously.

In 1920, she returned to London, to Hampstead. Books appeared. Her volume of poems, *Pan Worship*, had appeared in 1908, and in 1916 came *Nursery Rhymes of London Town*. But with *Martin Pippin* she had found her niche: verses and songs for children, stories, rhymed alphabets, retellings of traditional tales, appeared regularly.[4] There was also much journalism: as 'Tom Fool' she wrote a topical verse a day for thirteen years for left-wing *Reynolds News* and the *Daily Herald*; as 'Merry Andrew' for the *New Leader;* as 'Chimaera', a weekly poem throughout the twenties for *Time and Tide*.

---

[2] The best known are perhaps *Le Petit Chaperon Rouge* (Little Red Riding Hood), *Cendrillon* (Cinderella), *Le Maître Chat ou le Chat botté* (Puss in Boots), *La Belle au bois dormant* (Sleeping Beauty), and *Barbe Bleue* (Bluebeard).

[3] Not her 'real' name: Cicily Isabel Fairfield (1892-1983), feminist, novelist, socialist, critic, took the name provocatively from Ibsen's play *Rosmersholm* (1886). She had clout: in 1916 George Bernard Shaw said in 1916 that she 'could handle a pen as brilliantly as ever I could and much more savagely.' She was for a time H. G. Wells' lover.

[4] Stephen Fry, discussing how he himself came to poetry, cited her children's poems with those of A. A. Milne and Lewis Carroll as 'hardy annuals from the garden of English verse'. (*The Ode Less Travelled: Unlocking the Poet Within*, 2014.)

Her standpoint in these poems was firmly socialist. Her first fantasy novel, *The Soul of Kol Nikon* (1923)—which is misted with Celtic Twilight[5]— was a serial in the *Irish Review*. It was the first of several novels, inspired by fairy tales and legends, that she wrote between the wars. By 1930 she could find a publisher for whatever she wrote (lucky woman!). There were also some happy collaborations with her brother Herbert: a Victorian operetta, *The Two Bouquets*, in 1936, (recast as novel, 1948), and a children's play, *The Glass Slipper* (1944), (recast as a book, 1955). *The Silver Curlew* was also successful as both play (1949) and book (1953). Though she did write novels for adults, her most important books are those for children. She rightly made few concessions to a child's immaturity – as C. S. Lewis advised in his essay 'Three Ways of Writing for Children', never talk down to those who one day will be at least as clever as you are – and her work perfectly captures a child's sense of wonder. Her stories may be magical, but they are also unsentimental, often mocking how adults behave. The best were reissued—and in a few cases written—in her last fifteen years. *Silver-Sand and Snow* (1951) and *The Children's Bells* (1957) contain her best poetry; her finest short stories are in *The Little Bookroom* (1955), which in 1956 won both the Library Association's Carnegie medal and the international Hans Christian Andersen medal.

Many friends loved her, and her generous spirit. As always, generosity entails risk, and there were some who took advantage of hers. More than capable of astutely managing her affairs, even so she did make many impulsive, extravagant gestures. Clearly, she inspired affection, and gave good advice to the many who told their troubles. Talking was a delight as much as writing. She never lost her enthusiasm and sense of wonder at the world, and even in the daily round, the common task, provided excitement and drama. And people remembered her astonishing energy and sense of fun.

---

[5] Antony Powell characterised this in *At Lady Molly's* (1957) as 'a mournful haunt of the third-rate'.

Eleanor Farjeon

This woman who had so fine a gift for communicating with children had none of her own. She lived with George Chester Earle (1870–1949), a schoolmaster and scholar, to whom Edward Thomas had introduced her, from 1920 until his death, and after that became close to the actor Denys Blakelock (1901–1970).

※

Her upbringing, and life in the literary world of London in those years where religion, if considered at all, was 'ABC' – 'Anything But Christianity' – was not an obvious route to her being received into the Roman Catholic church. Her first publication, indeed, *Pan-Worship and Other Poems* (1908) shows the influence of the sort of thought that attracted, for example, the 'Grantchester Neo-Pagans': Rupert Brooke, Ludwig Wittgenstein, Bertrand Russell, Virginia Woolf, E. M. Forster, John Maynard Keynes, and Augustus John. She herself had contributed to *Orpheus: the Transactions of the Theosophical Art Circle*, produced in London between 1907 and 1914. But clearly the Christian narrative was drawing her: Percy Dearmer included her fine 'People, Look East' as an Advent carol in *The Oxford Book of Carols* (1928), and Martin Shaw could suggest she write a poem to accompany the Gaelic tune 'Bunessan' he had found in the British Museum for the enlarged *Songs of Praise* (1931) which he and Dearmer were editing. By 1951 she regarded becoming a Catholic as 'a progression toward which her spiritual life moved rather than a conversion experience', but to take the formal step is never simple and can be painful. She wrote a troubled letter to Father Richard Mangan, who was instructing her: 12 typed pages, forthrightly expressing her doubts on many aspects of Catholic teaching.

The result of Martin Shaw's invitation was 'Morning Has Broken'. Neither it nor 'People, look East' is a conventional hymn. 'People, look East' uses none of the usual seasonal imagery, but concentrates on the whole world preparing itself for the coming of Christ:

A Joyful Noise

> Furrows, be glad. Though earth is bare,
> One more seed is planted there:
> Give up your strength the seed to nourish,
> That in course the flower may flourish.

Some see 'Morning has broken', often now heard at funerals, as having little specifically Christian about it: which is true. Revd Robert Canham, of the Hymn Society of Great Britain and Ireland, for example, pointed out its Edenic vision said nothing about original sin, and notes that 'It's certainly not specifically Christian, echoing some sort of harmony with Judaism and Islam, I'd imagine.' But this lyrical, almost mystical, song of joy, glimpses a *redeemed* Creation that is a theophany, that reminds us of what we all long for, the joy of the unfallen angels in the being that is given them. The inclusion of this hymn, which I certainly regard as expressing profound religious joy, in *NEH* is a measure of how far the CofE has travelled from its cautious acceptance in 1820 of hymns as part of regular worship.

XXVII
Sydney Bertram Carter
1915–2004

ℰ

VAUGHAN WILLIAMS AND CECIL SHARP were not by any means the only people interested in popular traditions of melody and song. Right back in the early 1800s Walter Scott had collected the sometimes very ancient ballads, some still current, in *The Minstrelsy of the Scottish Border* (1802; later expanded). He was not the first. Interest in 'popular' or 'folk' song (i.e. not 'polite') was growing throughout Europe, as it was in folk and fairy tale. Often these songs are subversive, even anarchic, genuinely 'popular', voicing the trials and sorrows as well as the rare joys of the poor. Theorists like the Brothers Grimm, or collectors like F. J. Child (1825–96) who published his *The English and Scottish Popular Ballads* in 8 volumes (1882–92) fuelled this. England saw several 'folk song' revivals. The first, led by collectors like Revd Sabine Baring-Gould (1834–1924), Frank Kidson (1855–1926), Lucy Broadwood (1858–1939), and Anne Gilchrist (1863–1954), came to centre on the Folk Song Society (founded 1911). It influenced what performers sang, and the indefatigable Cecil Sharp (1859–1924), who founded the English Folk Dance Society, was probably the most important figure in the collecting and understanding of this important part of British musical heritage. This revival, and others later in the twentieth century, when technology and distribution could make a big difference to form, performance and reception, are essential to understanding Sydney Carter's stature as poet and singer. He changed the map.

His father earned his living selling jeweller's sundries. He and his wife Ada were living in north London, in Canonbury, when their son was born. The boy was sent to the school in Montem Street, Islington, built in 1886 after the 1870 Education Act – which Christopher Wordsworth had opposed – made universal primary education compulsory. The curriculum had not changed much when I went to a similar sort of school three decades later in Lancashire: it included weekly class singing of 'traditional' English, Welsh, Irish and Scottish songs – 'Early One Morning,' 'Land of my Fathers', 'I dreamt I dwelt in marble halls', 'Afton Water' and so on – and I loved, as Carter did, singing together even if I had little idea of what the words were about. (What *could* 'dashing away with the smoothing iron' *mean*?) Carter won a scholarship to Christ's Hospital in Horsham, where singing hymns happened every day in Chapel and twice on Sundays, and he apparently loved it. But when at home he also went with his father to the demotic delights of Music Hall at the Finsbury Park Empire (demolished 1965: like so many theatres that catered for that community culture, it fell victim to the separating spread of television).

Carter read Modern History at Balliol College, Oxford, graduating in 1936. For four years he taught English and History at Frensham Heights in Farnham, Surrey. One colleague was the poet and translator Rex Warner, who taught Classics, and whose *Men and Gods* (1950) – he wrote much else besides – awoke for so many of us a passion for Classical myth.

But after 1936, despite the momentary optimism after Munich, most people knew war was coming. P. Daniel's *Frensham Heights, 1925–49: a study in progressive education* (1986) recalls Carter as 'gentle, shy and sensitive, much troubled by the wartime dilemma of conscience'. Like Donald Swann (1923-1994), his later collaborator, Carter was pacifist, and in 1940 he joined the Friends' Ambulance Unit, serving in

Sydney Bertram Carter

North Africa and the Mediterranean theatres of war. In Greece in 1944, with Swann, he was fascinated by *Rebetiko*, the usually modal popular song of urban Greeks, especially the poorest, and its rhythms (9/8 *zeïbekik*, 2/4 *hasapiko* and 4/4 *tsifteteli*); he was captivated by Greek dance patterns and rhythm, and (in an article much later, 'Folk and the Songwriter') he observed. 'The aim of rhythm, rhyme and repetition is to enchant: to put a part of you to sleep in order to liberate another part.' Thirty years later he said, 'Nearly everything that I am doing now goes back in one way or another to the time I spent in Greece'.

In 1945, he returned to teaching. His earlier hopes of becoming a painter or film producer were abandoned in his passionate involvement in the postwar folk revival. He started singing in pubs and clubs in the 1950s, and was soon singing beside stars like Martin Carthy, Ewan MacColl, Pete Seeger and Judy Collins. Folk music had indeed taken him over. He studied its many forms, and later became a leading commentator on its increasingly rich public scene. Something of an iconoclast – it goes with the territory – he also got involved in the 1960s in the 'satire boom', and contributed material to the radical TV programme *That Was the Week That Was*.

There were several literary/musical partnerships, most importantly with Donald Swann, who called him 'a shining light of the original folk poet-composers'. In 1952, he began writing lyrics for Swann, who always needed material for his next review, and his were the words for Swann's *The Youth of The Heart*, the libretto for Swann's dream-musical *Lucy and the Hunter*, and the lyrics for the EP record *Songs of Faith and Doubt* (1964). He also wrote the libretto for Peter Albery and William Fry's *Brother Francis* (1976).[1]

Though now remembered best for his songs, his coverage of the 'folk scene' in the mainstream press was important too. On television, he played a major part in popularizing

---

[1] In 1955 he married Natalia Beckendorff, an *emigrée* from Leningrad. She died in a climbing accident on honeymoon in Minorca. He married again in 1964: Leela Nair was an English teacher originally from Malaya, and they had one son.

folk and *engagé* song, in series such as ABC's *Hallelujah* and Harlech TV's *The Sweat of your Brow*. He became editor of the English Folk Dance and Song Society's *English Dance and Song* (1960–63) and of *Books*, the National Book League's monthly magazine. These positions gave him enough clout to place material in publications as different as *Melody Maker* and the Catholic *Tablet*. During the 1960s, folk's boom years, he was writing *The Gramophone's* folk column. Writing in the mainstream press, he was read not simply by the converted—whether speaking musically or politically, for urban folksong, including modern folk, is often on the subversive side—who might read the Marxist, folk or music press like *Melody Maker, Sing* or *The Daily Worker*. The typical reader of *The Tatler and Bystander*[2] in 1958, for example, was hardly the natural enthusiast for an article on 'Folk-songsters Find Themselves in Vogue' – and Carter did not mean the magazine. Presumably, most *Tatler* readers had, if any, only a fleeting interest in folk. But he recommended that

> To experience the new kind of folk-singing at its liveliest, go to the King & Queen, a pub at Paddington Green, on a Sunday night. The queue of able-bodied young men on the pavement will be lining up, not for mild-and-bitter, but for folksong.

(I wonder how many took the advice …) Some measure of how mainstream folk had become by the 1960s, and of

---

[2] In 1940, *The Tatler* (named when founded in 1901 after Richard Steele's 1709 periodical of society gossip and comment) absorbed *The Bystander*. In 1961, Illustrated Newspapers bought it. It carried news and pictures of high society balls, charity events, race meetings, shooting parties, fashion and gossip, with horsey cartoons by 'The Tout' (Peter Ronald Griffiths-Buchanan) and by H. M. 'The Man who…' Bateman. It continues to focus on fashion and lifestyle, covering high society and politics, and, as it always has been, is aimed at the British upper-middle class and upper class. Tina Brown (editor 1979–83), referred to it as an upper-class comic.

Sydney Bertram Carter

Carter's important place within it, was the regular slot given to Kenneth Williams in the hugely popular BBC Radio 4 comedy show, *Round the Horne*. Williams, speaking the expected Mummerset, was introduced as Rambling Syd (note the 'y'!) Rumpo, the folk singer. The sketch would begin with Horne inquiring, as if deeply scholarly, about the nature and origin of the song. Rambling Syd's songs were full of smutty innuendo, but, of course, the 'dialect' words that did the work were all nonsense words. To engender parody might be seen as an artist's ultimate accolade of having arrived.

❧

The recognition of folk as a distinct genre, its capturing space in the media, is roughly contemporary with the craze for rock 'n' roll in the post-Elvis years – in fact the two genres are two sides of a musical, indeed cultural, revolution which could not have happened without the rapid development of an electronic technology to support it. Folk was ideological, very often seen as the expression of 'common folk' asserting an 'old' tradition, often shading into political or social protest. Initially, it abhorred the heavy, technology dependent, amplification associated with rock. When Bob Dylan, the leading singer/songwriter of the American revival, at the 1965 Newport Folk Festival played an electric guitar, many people booed, and things got even bitterer in his subsequent British tour. Audiences jeered, and in a Manchester concert someone shouted 'Judas!'.

Carter's songs became regulars in magazines like *Sing*, founded by the songwriter Eric Winter and based first in Cambridge and later in London. It published several of his most original pieces, in particular 'Lord of the Dance' (1964; written 1963). Stainer and Bell published several books of *In the Present Tense* for voice and guitar. Though he made fewer records than his output of song might have led people to expect, they were important in getting his work known – pre-eminently the EP *Songs of Faith and Doubt*, the first track of which was 'Lord of the Dance'. In the sleeve note, there was a health warning about the religious content, in case people expected yet more songs like 'Down Below' (about the London sewers) and the bittersweet 'My Last Cigarette' – about failing to give up smoking. After all, his popularity had been made by songs which guyed lazy reading habits ('Waiting for the Film to Come' and 'Plato in a Paperback'), or the commercial exploitation of folk-song ('Man with a Microphone'), or censorship ('Last Exit to Brooklyn'), or, very topically, the Bomb and disarmament ('I Want to Have a Little Bomb' and 'Marching to Aldermaston'). And there are those poignant songs about ageing ('Run the Film Backwards' and 'Silver in the Stubble') ...

'Lord of the Dance' was written for a Shaker[3] melody, 'Simple Gifts'. (Aaron Copland makes brilliant use of it in *Appalachian Spring*, 1944.) This was pretty well known already – Judy Collins the American folk-singer had recorded it, for example. But Carter's words were something else: he said he saw Christ as

> ... the incarnation of the piper who is calling us. He dances that shape and pattern which is at the heart of our reality. By Christ, I mean not only Jesus; in other times and places, other planets, there may be other lords of the dance. But Jesus is the one I know of first and best. I sing of the dancing pattern in the life and words of Jesus.

He drew the idea of the cosmos as dance from Shiva, Hinduism's cosmic dancer, whose dance, 'Ananda tandava' (Dance of Bliss)

---

[3] Associated now by most people with styles of architecture and furniture, the Shakers (properly, the United Society of Believers in Christ's Second Appearing), established communal settlements in the US in the eighteenth century. They were led by Mother Ann Lee, a millworker from Manchester, who had a vision commanding her to establish a community in America. Shaker teaching emphasized simplicity, celibacy, and honest work. They originated as a branch of the Quakers (in the seventeenth century a really radical group respectable people regarded with some horror) and their practices included shaking, shouting, dancing, whirling, and glossalalia – as indeed is common in many religions.

expresses the cosmic cycles of creation and destruction, as well as the daily rhythms of birth and death. 'Lord of the Dance' was included in the revised *Hymns Ancient and Modern* and *NEH*, and became one of the ten most popular hymns of the period. You heard it everywhere: on radio, whistled in the street, in the school playground. Quite possibly that catchy tune, and hearing it so often in so many contexts, dulled many to the levels on which the lyric could be interpreted. Carter once said that when he sang he liked sometimes to change the words into the present tense: to make people think.

Making people think ... The EP *Songs of Faith and Doubt* had other songs, including 'Friday Morning' and 'The Devil Wore a Crucifix'. 'Friday Morning'[4] is in the voice of the *un*repentant thief crucified with the Lord, and its daring irony shocked many:

'It's God they ought to crucify instead of you and me'
I said to the carpenter, a-hanging on the tree ...

Carter was brought up Christian. But he admitted he could not believe half the things he was told. He also wrote, *à propos* of 'Lord of the Dance', that 'Scriptures and creeds may come to seem incredible, but faith will still go dancing on' (*Green Print for Song*, 1974). The undogmatic Society of Friends, relying on personal experience and social activism and asserting God's presence in every human being is perhaps the church with which he would have been most comfortable. Jesus was central to his experience, but not, (as he put it), the 'official Jesus' – 'but the Jesus who is calling you to liberty, to the breaking of all idols including the idol which he himself has become'. To be without doubt he saw as the height of godless pride. *The Rock of Doubt* (1978), not quite an autobiography, powerfully endorses the value of honest religious enquiry, unfettered by

4 Revd Paul Oestreicher, Carter's friend and obituarist, wrote, 'I had to fight the BBC management to get that song on the air. A brave, liberal head of religious broadcasting was my ally. Today, the fear of a backlash would be far greater.'

A Joyful Noise

rigid doctrine. Paul Oestreicher said, 'his life was a musical journey in search of an unconventional God'. His friend Rabbi Lionel Blue compared his songs to 'psalms for today', the fruit of a free-thinking spirit always questioning and doubting – as indeed are the Hebrew Psalms! – in ways that reflected broader twentieth-century approaches to belief and faith. Carter himself said his songs 'can be sung in a Christian context, but they all had to mean something to me because I was often on the edge of not believing'. A perceptive review by Michael Grosvenor Myer of his 1972 collection of poems, *Love More or Less*, called him 'an impressive spokesman for the believer in an age of general unbelief'.

He was good at aphorisms: 'Bibles, legends, history are signposts: they are pointing to the future, not the past. Do not embrace the past or it will turn into an idol.' Or again, 'Give me the good news in the present tense ... So shut your Bibles up and show me how/ The Christ you talk about is living now.' Aphorisms: he wrote his own epitaph 30 years before he died:

> Coming and going by the dance, I see
> That what I am not is a part of me.
> Dancing is all that I can ever trust,
> The dance is all I am, the rest is dust.
> I will believe my bones and live by what
> Will go on dancing when my bones are not.